D1433869

~~d on or before t

`   ~~quested ~~ ~~

`~~ or by

ERNEST BLYTHE IN ULSTER
THE MAKING OF A DOUBLE AGENT?

Ernest Blythe in Ulster
The Making of a Double Agent?

DAVID FITZPATRICK

CORK **CUP** UNIVERSITY PRESS

First published in 2018 by
Cork University Press
Youngline Industrial Estate
Pouladuff Road, Togher
Cork
T12 HT6V
Ireland

British Library Cataloguing in Publication Data
A CIP record for this book is available from the British Library.

ISBN: 978-1-78205-278-4

Printed in Poland by HussarBooks.
Print origination & design by Carrigboy Typesetting Services, www.carrigboy.com

www.corkuniversitypress.com

Contents

TABLES

Preface

Ernest Blythe (1889–1975) was a central figure in the Irish revolution and the first decade of the Irish Free State, enjoying an unexpected renascence as managing director of the Abbey Theatre (1941–67) after his premature departure from parliamentary politics in 1936. Brought up in the Church of Ireland parish of Magheragall near Lisburn in County Antrim, he developed an active interest in the Irish language and nationalism only after moving to Dublin, aged fifteen, as a boy clerk in the civil service. His great mentor in Dublin was Seán O'Casey, who introduced him to the Gaelic League and the IRB and long remained a friend. Infatuated with drama, he performed and sometimes depicted his life as a theatrical production.

Before the Great War, Blythe became a close associate of influential Ulster republicans such as Denis McCullough, Bulmer Hobson, and Seán Lester, and a powerful propagandist and Irish-language advocate in the republican press. He was a leading organiser of the Gaelic League, IRB, and Irish Volunteers before 1916, an inveterate 'exile' and inmate of prisons, a member of the Dáil Ministry from 1919, and a prominent and controversial minister in W. T. Cosgrave's Executive Council, of which he became vice-president after the murder of Kevin O'Higgins in 1927. Though unfairly remembered mainly for docking a shilling from the old age pension in 1923, he was an effective if conservative minister for finance who, with Churchill, signed the settlement in 1926 which made the Free State financially viable and cemented partition. His seminal role in the Blueshirt movement and Irish fascism continues to bemuse historians.

After losing his North Monaghan seat in the Dáil in 1933 and leaving representative politics when the Free State Senate expired in 1936, Blythe was indefatigable in declaring his views, especially on the Irish language and partition, through newspapers, journals, radio, and correspondence with politicians. In all of these roles he was widely regarded with interest and sometimes suspicion because of his Protestant and unionist background. His cantankerous personality and expostulatory manner ensured that he never became widely popular. Yet his judgements and opinions were typically intelligent and well-informed, as well as unorthodox.

Blythe was not only an able and influential activist and politician but an accomplished writer, often in Irish, which he learned in Kerry while working for Thomas Ashe's family in 1913–14. For much of his life he was, above all, a proficient journalist, writing under many pseudonyms that test the historian's detective skills. He wrote three detailed and engrossing autobiographical volumes on his life up to 1919, published in Irish between 1957 and 1973, which have never appeared in English translation. Together with his compendious statement for the Bureau of Military History (1954), these provide considerable insight into Blythe's upbringing, revolutionary education, and interaction with other activists and society at large.

Yet that insight is partial, as one would expect of any former politician seeking to justify and explain his career without giving away potentially damaging information. Though his specific recollections typically had some basis in fact, careful examination often reveals telling inaccuracies and omissions in cases where relevant documentary evidence can be found. To Blythe's credit, some of that evidence is preserved in his personal papers, held in the UCD Archives. According to a fellow journalist in Ulster, he was 'essentially honest'. Though Blythe richly deserves a full biography, this book has the more modest aim of deploying fresh documentation to challenge and subvert Blythe's own version of his revolutionary education up to 1913. In doing so, it ranges freely over relevant writings and episodes from his later career, which is outlined in the Chronology. Any future assessment of his subsequent career must take account of the astonishing duplicity, even multiplicity, of his conduct as a young republican.

The origin of this project was my discovery, some years ago, that the young Blythe, when already a member of the IRB, joined an organisation profoundly at odds with Irish republicanism. This occurred during his four-year stint as a journalist for the unionist *North Down Herald* in Bangor and Newtownards. Had that fact become widely known, Blythe's revolutionary and political ambitions would have been immediately and permanently dashed. Nowhere in his writings did he allude to this episode, though he indicated clearly his need to lead 'a double life' while working in north Down and simultaneously organising republican bodies in nearby Belfast. By this he meant that he concealed his republican sympathies from all but a few comrades in north Down, while reassuring his Belfast brethren that his work on a unionist newspaper was a matter of money rather than conviction.

Though partly true, Blythe's account of his 'double life' is utterly inadequate. The purpose of my book is to unveil the reality of his double life as a young activist, to explore its probable origins and significance, and to relate this episode to his subsequent views on partition, Ulster unionism, and fascism. More broadly, it challenges the assumption that militant republicanism and unionism were polar opposites. Ernest Blythe was not alone in discerning the pre-war revolutionary potential of militant loyalism – yet what other republican dared to pursue that perception to its logical conclusion?

II

Blythe's life up to 1919 is covered by his three volumes of autobiography in Irish: *Trasna na Bóinne* or *Across the Boyne* (1957), *Slán le hUltaigh* or *Farewell to Ulster* (1970), and *Gaeil á Múscailt* or *Awakening of the Gael* (1973), all published in Dublin by Sáirséal agus Dill. The first volume offers a detailed, revealing, but tantalising account of Blythe's early revolutionary education in Dublin and County Down up to 1913. His 200-page typed statement for the Bureau of Military History (1954) covers the civil war as well as his political activity between 1905 and 1921. Other witness statements for the Bureau (now digitally searchable) contain references to Blythe and his associates. In addition, Blythe wrote various accounts in Irish and English of his experiences, which form part of the extensive Blythe collection in the UCD Archives. Though mainly relating to events after 1914, it contains many documents and writings relevant to this book.

Since Blythe was a tireless journalist, the newspapers to which he contributed are invaluable for comparing his contemporary and retrospective ideas and opinions. Though hampered by his preference for anonymous or pseudonymous contributions, I have drawn extensively on the files of pre-war propagandist papers such as the *Irish Nation and the Peasant, Irish Freedom*, and the *Ulster Guardian*. Much use is made of the *North Down Herald*, for which he worked in Bangor and Newtownards from 1909 to 1913, as well as its rivals the *Newtownards Chronicle* and the *Newtownards Spectator*. For the epilogue on 'Fascist Echoes', the *Star*, the *United Irishman*, and *United Ireland* (organs of Cumann na nGaedheal and Fine Gael between 1930 and 1936) were particularly useful. These journals have all been read in microform in the National Library of Ireland or the Central Newspaper Library in Belfast. Particular events and individual careers have been documented from a wide range of other newspapers, many of which are digitally searchable through Irish Newspaper Archives, the British Newspaper Archive, and digital editions of the *Irish Times* and the *Times* of London.

This book incorporates extensive nominal and genealogical research, especially in Part One. This has been greatly assisted by the ever-expanding range of digitalised sources and indexes accessible through ancestry.com and other websites for family historians. The largest collection of Ulster church registers remains the undigitalised microform collection at PRONI. All key players have been matched, where possible, with family returns of the Census of Ireland for 1901 and 1911, as well as probate records, civil registers, valuation lists, and kindred sources. Birth dates inferred from records of age at marriage or death are given in italics. Addresses, occupations, and holders of public offices have been traced through annual issues of *Thom's Official Directory* and the *Belfast and Province of Ulster Directory*. Basic biographical information has also been taken, sometimes without specific citations, from indispensable compendia such as the *Dictionary of Irish Biography* (DIB) and *Oxford Dictionary of National Biography* (ODNB). In pursuing fraternal involvements, systematic use has been made of the registers of the Grand Lodge of Freemasons of Ireland (now digitally searchable), and printed and manuscript records of the Grand Orange Lodge of Ireland.

Though no full biography of Blythe has been published, the late Patrick Buckley's article for the *DIB* offers a judicious survey of his life and work. Michael McInerney's five-part 'political profile' in the *Irish Times* (30 December 1974 to 4 January 1975) remains useful, drawing on interviews conducted just before Blythe's death. I am much indebted to the rapidly expanding corpus of studies of the Irish revolution and its aftermath, many of which document Blythe's significant but often controversial contributions. These debts are acknowledged in endnotes, which also indicate points on which I differ from other students of the period. This applies particularly to the Epilogue, which concerns the contentious issue of Irish fascism and its debt to revolutionary nationalism. I have also benefited from the renewed interest of other scholars in that not-so-rare bird, the 'Protestant nationalist', recently illuminated by R. F. Foster in *Vivid Faces: The Revolutionary Generation in Ireland, 1890–1923* (2014), Conor Morrissey in 'Protestant Nationalism in Ireland, 1900–1923' (PhD thesis, TCD, 2015), and the late Valerie Jones in *Rebel Prods: The Forgotten Story of Protestant Nationalists and the 1916 Rising* (2016).

I wish now that, when myself interviewing Ernest Blythe on 19 June 1972, I had asked quite different questions. But I retain sharp impressions of his helpful manner, incisive memory, and vivid, even slanderous anecdotes about various contemporaries. He had not discarded the 'sharp dialect' and 'homely metaphors' which Frank Gallagher witnessed in 1918. I could not have completed this book without access to Blythe's relevant writings in the Irish language, which have been painstakingly translated by Colm Mac Gearailt, a doctoral student at Trinity College Dublin, who (like Blythe) learned much of his Irish in Lispole, County Kerry.

I am grateful to the TCD Association and Trust and the School of Histories and Humanities for generously providing grants to cover the cost of translation. I am equally indebted to the helpful and courteous staff of Irish libraries and archives, especially the National Library of Ireland, the Gilbert Library, the National Archives of

Ireland, the UCD Archives, and the Grand Lodge of Freemasons in Dublin; and, in Belfast, the Public Record Office of Northern Ireland, the Central Newspaper Library, the Ormeau Road Public Library, and the Grand Orange Lodge of Ireland (whose senior archivist, the late David Cargo of Newtownards, was particularly helpful). William Roulston, director of the Ulster Historical Foundation, generously tackled various genealogical puzzles. Lizzy Shannon and Ben Greer were kind enough to clarify aspects of Blythe's family and background. The illuminating reports of two anonymous assessors persuaded me to broaden the scope of this study.

I am particularly grateful to Professors Eunan O'Halpin, Eugenio Biagini, and Ian McBride for inviting me to explore the Blythe conundrum in lively discussions at their Irish history seminars in Dublin, Cambridge, and Oxford. For her invaluable counsel and involvement over many years, I am profoundly indebted to Jane Leonard.

This book is dedicated to our daughters, Julia and Hannah, with all my love.

DAVID FITZPATRICK
August 2018

Initiations

I

On 26 September 1910, the Newtownards District Orange Lodge confirmed the admission of a 21-year-old recruit into 'Volunteers' lodge 1501. He was returned as Ernest Blythe of East Street, where the *North Down Herald*'s town correspondent had recently taken lodgings with the family of William Laird Doggart of the *Newtownards Chronicle*. Twelve days earlier, Blythe had been introduced to the mysteries of the Loyal Orange Institution in the town's Orange hall.[1] This plain two-storey building in Mary Street had been erected three decades before on a site donated by the Marquess of Londonderry, opposite the Second Presbyterian church. Having fallen into disrepair, it was reopened after refurbishment, with much ceremony and many speeches, in the following month.[2]

Like all candidates for the Order's first (Orange) degree, Blythe participated in a simple ritual of initiation, in marked contrast to the arcane Masonesque ceremonies for those graduating into higher orders such as the Royal Arch Purple and Royal Black. Before admitting him, the lodge was required to satisfy itself that Blythe fulfilled the 'particular qualifications' for an Orangeman, notably 'that he is not, and never was, and will not become a member of any Society or body of men who are enemies to the lawful Sovereign, or the glorious Constitution of the Realm, as established in 1688; and that he never took, and never will take any oath of secrecy, or any other oath of obedience, to any treasonable Society'.[3]

Blythe's presence at the door was announced by the tyler (James Robinson, a 60-year-old labourer), the proceedings being recorded by his son Frank.[4] After Blythe had been ushered in to the lodge room, the worshipful master (a draper named James Wright) first asked his sponsors to 'answer for this Friend, that he is of good report, a true

1

and faithful Protestant and a loyal subject'. He then addressed some
pertinent questions to the candidate himself:

> Do you promise, God being your helper, that you will continue
> to be faithful, and to bear true allegiance to His Majesty the King;
> that you will support and maintain, to the utmost of your power,
> the Laws and Constitutions of these Realms . . . ; and that you
> will be always ready and willing to aid and assist the Magistrates
> and Civil Authorities, when called upon, in the lawful execution
> of their duties? . . . Do you promise to avoid and discountenance
> all societies and associations composed of persons who seek to
> subvert the just prerogatives of the Crown, the independence of
> each branch of the Legislature, the established rights of property,
> and the union which connects these Kingdoms; and will you to
> the utmost of your power make your public acts and exertions
> harmonize with the principles of the Orange Institution? . . . Do
> you promise that you will not communicate or reveal any of the
> proceedings of your Brother Orangemen, in Lodge assembled,
> nor any matter or thing therein communicated to you, unless to
> a Brother Orangeman, well knowing him to be such? . . . And
> do you also solemnly promise never to marry a Papist?

To each question, the young republican idealist responded with
exclamations such as 'I do promise, the Lord being my helper'.[5]

II

Three and a half years earlier, Blythe had been sworn in to the Irish
Republican Brotherhood, an emphatically secret society devoted to
repudiation of the Union, the sovereign, and the Constitution, and to
'the establishment of a free and independent republican government
in Ireland'. Since 1873, in view of the embarrassing collapse of
Fenian attempts to secure the republic through 'physical force', the
organisation had adopted the more pragmatic strategy of infiltrating
and influencing the broader nationalist movement. As its revised
constitution proclaimed:

The I.R.B., whilst labouring to prepare Ireland for the task of recovering her independence by force of arms, shall confine itself in time of peace to the exercise of moral influences – the cultivation of union and brotherly love amongst Irishmen, the propagation of republican principles and the spreading of a knowledge of the national rights of Ireland. The I.R.B. shall await the decision of the Irish nation, as expressed by a majority of the Irish people, as to the fit hour of inaugurating a war against England, and shall, pending such an emergency, lend its support to every movement calculated to advance the cause of Irish independence, consistently with the preservation of its own integrity.[6]

Despite the new pragmatism, each initiate was bound to 'contribute according to his means for the production of war materials', as Blythe did when his Belfast circle set up a pistol fund.[7]

The IRB, like the Orange Order, had adopted a much plainer ceremony of initiation than sister organisations such as the American Clan na Gael. When Blythe was sworn into the euphemistic 'Bartholomew Teeling Literary and Debating Society' in a back room off Parnell Square, his mentor was not expected to lead him blindfolded into the circle, or to submit him to terrifying physical and mental ordeals before admission.[8] Yet, as recollected in *Trasna na Bóinne*, the ceremony was solemn enough:

He brought me into the back room by myself. Then, in the semi-darkness, and according to the tradition, with no witnesses present, he asked me to raise my right hand and to repeat the words of the oath after him. Within a minute I had sworn on the book to be faithful to the Irish republic, to be loyal to the Supreme Council, to be obedient to my officers, and to keep all of the organisation's secrets. After I had repeated the formula after him, Micheál Mac Amhlaidh shook my hand and, without any further ado, I was a member of the Republican Brotherhood.

Blythe and other recent recruits were then led into the front room, where the roll was called in Irish and the four or five recruits were introduced in person to the 120 members of the circle.[9]

The oath, more imposing as set out in the IRB's constitution, matched his undertakings as an Orangeman in its invocation of divine power, affirmation of allegiance, and insistence on secrecy:

> In the presence of God, I . . . do solemnly swear that I will do my utmost to establish the national independence of Ireland, and that I will bear true allegiance to the Supreme Council of the Irish Republican Brotherhood and Government of the Irish Republic and implicitly obey the Constitution of the Irish Republican Brotherhood and all my superior officers, and that I will preserve inviolable the secrets of the Organisation.[10]

Blythe remained unfamiliar with the full constitution until it was read out at a later meeting, at first thinking 'that it was dangerous to have such a document in print'.[11] It required each recruit to be one 'whose character for sobriety, truth, valour and obedience to authority' would bear scrutiny, and to swear an 'oath of allegiance to its government', a Supreme Council which was also 'declared in fact as well as by right the sole government of the Irish Republic'. Any member breaching his 'oath of fidelity and inviolable secrecy' in peacetime was guilty of a 'grave misdemeanour'; but, 'in time of war, every such act or attempted act shall be treason and punishable with death'.[12] As in all fraternities with elaborate paper hierarchies and ferocious but unenforceable penalties, these solemn injunctions were routinely abused by members of the IRB – most conspicuously by the clique that launched the Dublin rebellion of 1916 without direction or consent from the supposed 'Government of the Irish Republic', let alone sanction by 'a majority of the Irish people'.

The problem of multiple and conflicting secret allegiances so troubled the organisation that its constitution was further revised a decade after Blythe's initiation. Each new candidate was required to 'affirm on oath that he does not belong to any other oath-bound society', as well as taking the existing oath with the exclamatory coda 'So help me God!' The new prohibition extended to current members:

> Should any man, while a member of the Irish Republican Brotherhood, be asked to join any other oath-bound society,

he shall immediately inform his superior officer in the Irish Republican Brotherhood . . . No man who is a member of any other such society shall be admitted to, or allowed to retain membership of, the Irish Republican Brotherhood without the express permission of the Supreme Council.[13]

Though technically inapplicable to the Orange Order, whose obligations were no longer formulated as an oath for fear of its suppression as an illegal organisation, the ban on dual allegiance served as a rebuke to those, like Blythe, who had dabbled in several fraternities with radically conflicting objectives. It is no wonder that Blythe remained silent about his Orange interlude throughout his recorded life, apart from the off-hand observation that, when a journalist in north Down, 'I would get invitations to join with the Orangemen and with the Masons'.[14]

PART ONE

The Man from Magheraliskmisk

CHAPTER ONE

Origins

I

Ernest Blythe was born on 13 April 1889 in Magheraliskmisk, a tongue-twisting townland in the fertile parish of Magheragall in south-west Antrim, midway between Lisburn and Ballinderry.[1] He was eldest among the four children of James Blythe and Agnes Thompson, a farmer's daughter from Deneight (officially Duneight) in County Down, on the south-eastern fringe of Lisburn.[2] The Thompsons were Presbyterians, and James and Agnes were married in Lisburn's second Presbyterian church on Railway Street, a by-product of the 'Great Revival' of 1859. Yet all four children were baptised in the Magheragall parish church, and the entire family belonged to the Church of Ireland according to the census schedules of 1901 and 1911. Members of both families were active in their congregations: in 1892, when James Blythe was serving on the select vestry in Magheragall, Agnes' brother John Thompson was elected to the congregational committee in Legacurry.[3]

Within Protestantism, movement across denominational boundaries (usually prompted by marriage) was commonplace. James Blythe's sister Mary became a Methodist after marrying Francis Brady, a power-loom 'tenter' or machinist, in the Magheragall parish church.[4] Once or twice each year, undeterred by her conversion, James and his Episcopalian family would take the train to Belfast to visit the Brady home in Grosvenor Street, which also provided shelter for James' mother in her old age.[5] Ecumenical tolerance of religious conversion and 'mixed marriages' did not extend to Roman Catholics, who in any case were vastly outnumbered by Protestants in both Deneight and Magheraliskmisk.[6] About one-fifth of the population of Magheraliskmisk in 1901 were Catholics, including three servants (one employed by James Blythe) and two boarders.[7] The eight Catholic households were headed by a carpenter, two weavers, a seamstress, a farm labourer, a road labourer, a labourer's mother, and just one farmer. Deneight had only three Catholics, all women: a solitary housekeeper, the wife of an Episcopalian mill carter, and the servant of a Presbyterian farmer and rate collector.[8]

James Blythe took over grandfather Robert's farm of eighty-three acres after his death in 1895, remaining in possession until about 1921. The farm was held in fee, having formerly belonged to the Hertford estate. Apart from the Halls (Magheraliskmisk was also called Hallstown), the Blythes were the largest farmers in the townland and sometimes referred to their home as Hallstown House.[9] The local press regularly listed prizes awarded for Robert Blythe's cattle, butter, and horses at agricultural shows.[10] Though the Thompsons were likewise among the largest farmers in Deneight, their holding was much smaller, the townland being dominated by small farmers and sub-tenants.[11] Agnes's father Thomas Thompson rented thirty-one acres from William Mussenden, which passed on his death in 1899 to his son John. Though the farm was only of moderate size, the Thompsons had a decent second-class house with four rooms, seven front windows, and seven out-offices in 1901. The Blythes' farmhouse was more impressive: a first-class house with seven rooms, seven windows, and no less than eighteen out-offices. Though much deteriorated and long unoccupied, its solid frame and massive garden walls still testify to the substantial asset that Ernest might have inherited. Apart from their farms, neither family accumulated much personal estate (at least as valued for probate), but the Blythes were somewhat better endowed. The declared effects of Thomas Thompson's sister and brother amounted to only £145 and £91 respectively, while those left behind by Robert and his widow Chelley Blythe were valued at £512 and £368.[12] The Blythes presumably looked down on the Thompsons, whose inferior social status was evident in the modest size of the home farm and the menial occupations of those who moved elsewhere.[13]

Ernest's father James was the second of ten children of Robert Blythe and Chelley Gawley, who had married in 1850.[14] Chelley, a farmer's daughter from the neighbouring parish of Aghalee, accumulated property in her own right, bequeathing almost a dozen houses in

Belfast to her married daughters Helena and Mary, including six in
Blythe Street off Sandy Row.[15] As an only child, Chelley also inherited
her father's farm when he died at Christmas 1873, while resident
with the Blythes.[16] Robert thereupon took possession of her 'dowry',
twenty-six acres of good land about six miles from Magheraliskmisk,
which soon passed successively to James' two elder brothers.[17] In
Trasna na Bóinne, Blythe wrote contemptuously of the relatively
humble origins and domineering character of grandmother Chelley,
and her success in thwarting James' desire to take over Aghalee rather
than remain as a dependant in Magheraliskmisk: 'This resulted in
my mother having to spend nearly seven years under the control of
an old woman who was cranky, quarrelsome, and unsatisfiable.'[18] So
great was little Ernest's resentment for 'the old witch' that he picked
up a rusty butcher's knife and hid it under his pillow with a view to
'killing the old woman', only to be caught out and gently admonished
by his mother for 'the sinfulness of the thought'.[19] Blythe's mature
predilection for 'ruthless warfare' and 'the doctrine of the sword' was
already developing nicely.

Ernest Blythe, as the elder son of a 'strong' farmer, seemed poised
to take over his father's property in due course (his father was forty-
three when he finally secured rateable occupancy upon Robert's
death). The fact that he left home at fifteen to work in the Department
of Agriculture and Technical Instruction suggests an interest in
agricultural production but not necessarily a desire to farm. When
he left Newtownards in 1913 to work as a labourer on the Ashe
family farm in Kerry, Blythe seemed oddly unready for hard physical
labour, despite helping out on the farm as a child on Saturdays and
holidays: 'Although I was brought up on a farm, I had not done any
manual work for some years and found it exceedingly hard at first.'[20]
Perhaps, even as a youth, Blythe would have identified himself with
Uncle Dan in *The Drone*, whose part he acted with such panache in
Newtownards, letting his relatives do the work and pay the bills while
he played the fool and pursued grandiose intellectual schemes.

Blythe's lifelong rejection of alcohol and tobacco (though not
gambling) suggests the enduring influence of his mother's Presbyterian
forebears in Deneight, a rural townland best known for its motte,

about three miles south-east of Lisburn. The absence of key registers unfortunately precludes full reconstitution of Agnes Thompson's antecedents.[21] Thomas Thompson of Deneight, presumably her grandfather, was registered as a forty-shilling freeholder in 1813 and a tithepayer in 1834.[22] Her father, likewise Thomas, was admitted to communion in the recently established Legacurry congregation in October 1847.[23] Contemporary session minutes made no reference to the Famine or destitution, being preoccupied with the problem of fornication. Between 1847 and 1850, at least six members of the congregation were readmitted, though 'guilty of the sin of Fornication', having demonstrated 'Repentance' and undergone 'instruction, exhortation and prayer'. The most emphatic proof of repentance was marriage, however belated.[24]

Thomas' son and successor, John Thompson, was sufficiently devout to secure election to the Legacurry congregational committee in 1892, though he attended only one meeting during his nine years in office.[25] Other Thompsons of Deneight belonged to different Presbyterian congregations. Agnes herself was married in the Railway Street (Second Lisburn) church, while ten progeny of John and William Thompson of Deneight (doubtless her uncles or grand-uncles) were baptised in the First Lisburn church between 1824 and 1842. The fluidity of Ulster Protestantism was evident in the fact that John Thompson the elder, though married in a Presbyterian church in 1826, had his first three children baptised as Episcopalians in Lisburn.[26]

Though far less precise in identifying his mother's relatives by comparison with the paternal line, Blythe's autobiography indicates that as a child he would make Sunday visits to relatives in four locations around Lisburn including Deneight. When about twelve years old, he and the family would also spend at least a week each year in the home of his mother's brother. His unnamed uncle was evidently Thomas Thompson, a carter in Sandy Row, a paving-stone's throw from the battle-scarred 'Boyne Bridge' and the Great Victoria Street railway terminus. Once a heavy drinker without steady employment or a long-term home, Uncle Thomas had recently settled down in a drapery shop, where his twenty-year-old daughter Maud was returned as the occupier. The shop in Sandy Row provided a convenient base for visits to Ben Madigan, the Botanic Gardens, the Belfast Museum in College Square North, and Custom House Square, where Blythe witnessed the soap-box oratory of politicians such as Thomas Sloan, founder of the Independent Orange Order.[27] Another uncle, a bricklayer's labourer named Hugh, lived in the Shankill district until his death in 1907.[28] As a young man returning home from Dublin or Kerry on holiday, Blythe would also visit another Thompson family, of 'distant relatives' living in the Woodvale district of north Belfast.[29] Samuel Thompson, a Presbyterian carpenter and builder from Dromore, County Down, kept a close eye on vacant nearby properties, moving into the opulent surroundings of Edenderry House shortly before his death in 1917.[30] Blythe never lost contact with Samuel's son, Samuel Ernest Thompson, an actor in the early Ulster Literary Theatre who became a prosperous estate agent.

Blythe wrote warmly of his mother's stories about the United Irish heritage of her Presbyterian forebears, while noting that she had no truck with modern nationalism. She also confided a 'shameful secret' which was clearly 'nothing for us to be proud of':

> The secret that my grandfather [Thomas Thompson] let slip, as he was approaching the end of his days, was that his great-grandfather was a Roman Catholic (from County Cavan, he said), until he received a farm in County Down, as compensation for converting to Catholicism.

The shame was compounded by the fact that Thomas Thompson was estranged from the Blythes, so that the first time Ernest saw his grandfather was in his coffin.[31] Thomas may well have resented his daughter's 'mixed marriage', consecrated in Lisburn rather than Legacurry and unwitnessed by any of the Thompsons. Blythe did not attribute his Irish-Ireland inclinations to his mother or her unverified Catholic ancestor, but rather to the influence of one of the serving-girls picked up by his grandfather or father at the Newry hiring fair, an Irish-speaking Catholic.[32]

Though the interplay of Orange and Green is a major theme in Blythe's autobiographies, no specific information is given about his own family's fraternal proclivities. Both the Blythes and the Thompsons had close neighbours who were prominent Orangemen. In the late nineteenth century, the Magheragall Orange district included six lodges drawing members from the immediate vicinity of Magheraliskmisk, though the townland had no Orange hall. Thomas Clarke, district master of Magheragall from 1872 to 1901, lived in the same townland. A future grand master of Ireland (William Henry Holmes Lyons) resided at Brookhill, a mile or so to the north. James Blythe had connections with both men outside the Order. He served with Lyons on the Magheragall select vestry, and in December 1892 he attended a unionist meeting at Mullaghcarton schoolhouse along with Clarke and two other Orange district officers.[33] James, apparently alone in the immediate family, was a signatory of the Ulster Covenant in September 1912.[34] Grandfather Robert was passionately attached to the Crown and its defenders:

> It was a source of pride to him that his uncle or granduncle was in the Yeomanry[35] and he would boast that the old rusty sword that was hanging on the kitchen wall had been carried by a yeoman. He would often talk of Queen Victoria, and used the title 'the Queen's team' for soldiers and armed police.[36]

Yet Blythe's family apparently had little sympathy with the Orangemen, looking down on them as social inferiors:

> Neither of my parents had any respect for the Orange Order, nor were any of my close relatives in it. First of all, though the 'nobility' – the only family of that type that was in the parish – were in the Orange Order,[37] in general only the labourers and the very small farmers would join it, apart from the publicans, grocers, and the odd person who intended to run as a candidate for the county council or for the local district council.[38]

Outwardly respectable families like the Blythes despised Orangemen for their former habit of holding lodge meetings in public houses, and for the widespread belief that most attended church only on the Sunday preceding the Twelfth, when they assembled 'with their sashes over their shoulders' to hear an 'Orange sermon' on the Spanish Inquisition, the St Bartholomew's Day massacre, or those martyred by 'Bloody Mary' Tudor.[39]

Neighbours would ridicule the Orangemen for having 'to ride a goat as part of their initiation ceremony'.[40] On one Eleventh night, 'a bunch of Protestant boys', including Blythe's prankster brother James Alexander, put a green flag over the house of John Clarke, master of a dormant local lodge, of which he was unaware 'until his neighbours started making fun of him. He got a ladder in order to take the flag down, but he was so angry and in such a hurry that he dropped the heavy stone, that was keeping the rod standing upright, down the chimney and broke the grate below, a thing which added to the enjoyment that the boys received from the event.'[41] John Clarke, identified by Blythe as a shopkeeper, occupied a small farm in Magheraliskmisk.[42] He had taken over from his late father as master of lodge 1180 in 1902, Thomas Clarke having led the lodge for half a century including his three decades as district master.[43]

Blythe was scathing about Robert Walsh ('Roibeard Breathnach'), the only man working for his father 'who would speak in a bigoted manner'. Walsh boasted that he had denounced one of their servant boys named James Johnston ('Séamus Mac Eoin') for marrying a Catholic, leading to his expulsion from both the Orange and the Black.[44] Though Blythe states that Johnston converted to Catholicism, his census return indicates that both spouses belonged to the 'Irish Church'. This would not have saved him from expulsion, except through a special dispensation from the Grand Orange Lodge of Ireland.[45] Since Walsh was allegedly unable to read, 'he was mocked behind his back for the verbose speech that he made', supposedly beginning: 'O pre-eminent Master, O Noble Knights and Brethren.' This parody was close to the mark: the late Unionist Party leader and Most Worshipful Sovereign Grand Master of the Imperial Grand Black Chapter of the British Commonwealth, James Molyneaux, would greet the brethren gathered for the sham fight on Scarva each 13 July as 'distinguished Sir Knights, Sir Knights all'. Walsh's bigotry was illustrated by his refusal to eat one of his customary dishes when Blythe's mother provided herring for Friday breakfast to avoid offending two Catholic harvesters. When challenged by James Blythe, Walsh replied: 'I never ate it on a Friday . . . and I won't eat it: death is better than shame'.[46]

Yet Blythe was careful to emphasise that most Orangemen were not 'miserable humourless bigots without humanity like Robert Walsh'. A counter-example arose from another 'mixed marriage', in which a Catholic servant girl gave birth to three illegitimate children, who were placed in orphanages, before finding an elderly widowed farmer who was willing to husband her. According to Blythe's typically unsympathetic account, she broke her promise to convert to Protestantism, resulting in a confrontation with her husband and a shouting match at the garden gate. Matthew Beckett, described as master of the local Orange lodge, offered a perfectly poised judgement at their request. 'If I were in your place I would not allow her to go to Mass,' he told the husband; but the wife was advised that 'if I were in your place, I would go to Mass in spite of him'. The source of this Solomonic wisdom was a general labourer with a wife but no children to cloud his judgement. Blythe gloatingly remarked that she 'surrendered to force and truly converted to Protestantism', after which 'she and her husband progressed in life' and her earlier indiscretions were 'forgotten, for the most part'.[47]

Blythe's youthful ambivalence concerning the Orange Order was matched by his attitude towards the few Catholics he knew in Magheragall. From early childhood he had 'daily contact' with Catholic servants, especially girls, as well as extra workers hired in peak seasons: 'When we thought of Catholics, it was of labourers and of people who were not well off in life generally'. Since there was no risk that they 'would get the upper hand . . . no one held any ill-will towards them as Catholics, nor were they excluded nor would any adults insult them, beyond putting a bit of extra energy into the drumming, when they were going by a Catholic's house during the march on the Twelfth of July'.[48]

He also believed that Catholics were more likely than Protestants to have children out of wedlock, because of their greater poverty and 'the extra difficulties and temptations which the young Catholic women had to overcome' (presumably referring to advances from lecherous Protestant masters). 'Fornication' was commonplace in Magheragall: 'I must say that it was not something rare or surprising for an illegitimate child to be born in our area, and no religious community could insult the other religions regarding the same.'[49]

Blythe was particularly perceptive in dissecting the origins of his parents' aversion to sectarian talk and conduct. His mother Agnes would urge a Catholic servant girl to 'do her duty' by going to Mass, believing that even Catholic religious observance was better than none as a defence against immorality: 'She would say that she would not keep any girl in the house who would not go to the church every Sunday.' James Blythe was a model of discretion with the Catholic servant boys: 'If he ever heard any of us children talking about priests, Mass, church, or the Pope, he would put an end to the talk, in case any of the Catholic workers might hear us and take it as an insult.' Yet tact did not imply ecumenical tolerance, but deeply entrenched prejudice against the Church of Rome. Though 'incredibly mannerly' towards Catholics, James attributed their acute sensitivity to the fact 'that their religion was based on superstitions and idolatry, of which they were half ashamed.'[50]

His mother purported to be suspicious of Catholic plots, warning Ernest not to drive about with William Fleming, the son of a Catholic grazier who kept 'old worn-out cows that were bought up the country' on several nearby farms. With a straight face, she warned him not to go near the drain on a farm they had visited: 'Don't you know . . . that Fleming is a Papist? If he got the chance to push you into the drain and to drown you, and do it in such a way that nothing could be proved against him, that he would do without fail, as every Catholic believes that it is a good deed to kill a Protestant.' Blythe never again 'went on a trip with William Fleming' (even though he had once had a meal with the family after helping them to drive cattle home from the Hillsborough fair). His account suggests that, while his mother 'did not believe a word of that talk', she was determined to prevent fraternisation with a social inferior who happened to be Catholic.[51]

No member of Ernest Blythe's immediate family has been identified as either an Orangeman or a Freemason, apart from his schoolmaster-uncle Alfred Ernest. When Ernest was five years old, Alfred was initiated as a Freemason in Caledon, County Tyrone, becoming master of Phoenix lodge 210 in 1906.[52] The only Blythe known to have held office in the Orange Order was Thomas Blythe from Reilly's Trench near Hillsborough, County Down, who was James' first cousin. According to *Trasna na Bóinne*, grandfather Robert had left the Hillsborough district as a young man to replace an evicted tenant in Magheraliskmisk, Robert 'being the last man in the family' and therefore without prospect of succession to the home farm.[53] Several generations of Blythes have been traced in and about Lisadian, Thomas' branch having moved on to Reilly's Trench in about 1830.[54] Thomas Blythe (1856–1928) was an Episcopalian farmer who became a weighmaster in Belfast, but remained secretary of Lord Arthur Hill's lodge 1090 in Hillsborough. Apart from a four-year break in the 1890s, he served as district secretary from 1883 to 1920.[55] Thomas Blythe was also initiated as a Freemason in 1882, though he was struck off the register in 1895.[56] At least three of his relations also joined Masonic lodges in Maze or Hillsborough.[57] His father Thomas had been a churchwarden, evincing a family of impeccable respectability. Yet, as so often in ostensibly devout nineteenth-century Ulster, the parish registers suggest otherwise. Three years after his election as churchwarden, Thomas the elder had fathered a child out of wedlock (yet another Thomas, who presumably died young), emulating his uncles Mark and William, both publicans in Hillsborough, who had each fathered an illegitimate child.[58] As we shall show, the Blythe tradition of promiscuity was maintained in Ernest's branch of the family.

Deneight, where Ernest's mother Agnes Thompson was born, had supported its own Orange lodge ever since the renewal of the Institution in 1848. Forty years later, lodge 756 was redesignated as 'The Rising Sons of William', and in 1904 the townland acquired its own Orange hall. For nearly half a century, John McAnally and Hercules Leathem presided over the lodge, and the printed annual reports up to the 1920s record no worshipful master named Thompson.[59] But a kinsman, named Stanley Wellington Thompson, was remembered on his death in 1964 as a Freemason and British Legion advocate who was also 'closely identified with the Orange and Black Institutions'.[60] During his four years as a boy clerk in Dublin, Blythe had made regular holiday visits to the Woodvale Road home of his 'distant relatives' the Thompsons, being particularly interested in Stanley's elder brother Ernest, of the Ulster Literary Theatre.[61] Stanley spent half a century as a Presbyterian minister in Dungannon's 'Church of the Volunteers', apart from two years in wartime France as a YMCA chaplain. For most of his ministry he also served as a deputy grand chaplain for County Tyrone, being first elected in 1920.[62] His father and brother Ernest were also longstanding Freemasons, joining the same lodge in Ballymacarrett.[63] But the family name was brought into Orange disrepute in 1864, when Joseph Thompson of lodge 756 was expelled for 'marrying a papist', the most serious offence among those deemed to endanger 'the honour and dignity of the Institution'.[64] Joseph was almost certainly another kinsman of Agnes Thompson, though again the precise affinity cannot be determined.[65] If Ernest Blythe had remained an Orangeman in 1919, when he married Annie McHugh, he would have incurred expulsion for the same offence.

The documentary record, though fragmentary, confirms Blythe's accounts of his immediate family's dissociation from Orangeism. While sharing the Institution's basic political and religious precepts, the Blythes and perhaps the Thompsons regarded most brethren with condescension as members of an inferior social caste. Though equally hostile to popery, they deplored open expression of this sentiment because of its divisive consequences in the workplace and the neighbourhood. Blythe emerged from Magheragall with considerable knowledge of Orangeism, acquired through critical observation rather than close association. Few of his people had 'worn the sash', and his family and neighbours would not have expected him to embrace Orangeism after returning from Dublin. Indeed, Blythe's conversion to Orangeism may well have shocked them almost as much as his conversion to republicanism.

CHAPTER TWO

Family Secrets

I

In his autobiographies, Blythe was discreet to a fault when mentioning his family, with the exception of his detested grandmother Chelley and his uncle Thomas William, who was to have inherited the farm at Magheraliskmisk but 'turned out to be lazy and wasteful' and was therefore 'banished to America'.[1] These negative background figures are balanced by his adored grandfather Robert, Chelley's hen-pecked husband, and friendly references to his uncle Robert Blythe of Aghalee. Historical fossicking reveals rakish aspects of both Roberts, leading us into a chamber of family horrors of which Ernest must have become somewhat aware.

Grandfather Robert's first two children were born out of wedlock during the Famine (in 1847 and 1850), and both probably died young. The second birth would have been particularly galling for Chelley, as Robert's child was baptised in Hillsborough (rather than Magheragall) six months after their wedding in May 1850.[2] Robert evidently gained a reputation for promiscuity, as indicated by proceedings at Belfast Quarter Sessions in 1860.[3] Catherine Smith, a servant to John Connor of Magheragall, had taken an action for seduction against Thomas Lavery, who had 'said when I would have a child he would make me all right – he meant he would marry me'. Under cross-examination, she portrayed herself as a woman of independent inclination but no libertine:

> I have left my father three or four years. I left him because I thought when I would be with the strangers I would be my own mistress and have more money for myself. Many a man has slept in the same loft with me, but not in the same bed. There was a wall between the room I slept in and the room the men slept in. I had to go through their bed-room to mine. I swear the defendant is the father of the child.

At this point, the defendant's solicitor slyly interjected 'Robert Blythe? A Voice – I know nothing about the case. What do you want? (Laughter.)' After the defendant's brother had 'made several statements with regard to the plaintiff's moral conduct which cannot be published', the presiding barrister sealed Catherine Smith's public humiliation: 'You ask a decree for 30*l.* – take a decree for 3*l.*' By contrast, the chortling response to Robert Blythe's incrimination by innuendo implied that boys would be boys. It is noteworthy that John Connor was almost certainly Blythe's immediate neighbour, and a member of the family evicted for non-payment of rent from the farm acquired by Robert Blythe in Magheraliskmisk during the Famine.[4]

Forty years later, when Ernest was eleven years old, the family name was again besmirched when uncle Robert of Aghalee was sued for £50 damages by Israel Moorecroft, who alleged that Blythe had seduced Moorecroft's sister while in his service.[5] Though the action was dismissed, it must have been a severe blow for his wife Minnie (Mary Simpson Harrison), whom Robert had wed in Holywood, ten years earlier, in a 'shot-gun' marriage. Ida Violet, their only known child, had died as a toddler in 1892. Uncle Robert remained farming in Aghalee, adding three further holdings between 1886 and 1898 to the farm he had taken over from his brother in 1884. Though still listed as occupier in 1928, neither he nor his wife was in Aghalee when the census was taken in 1911.[6]

Thomas William Blythe, who had briefly farmed Aghalee before surrendering possession to his younger brother Robert, had a long but troubled life. According to *Trasna na Bóinne*, he 'only wrote home a few times' after being 'banished' to America at his mother's urging (so Ernest surmised), never responding to advertisements in American newspapers arising from the legacy of 'a few hundred pounds' (in fact, £100) specified in Robert's will. Writing in 1957, Ernest Blythe added that 'a few years ago, news came from New Zealand that he had died there, and he nearly one hundred years old, without a word being received previously by anyone in Ireland about him in well over seventy years'.[7]

Typically, every claim in Blythe's account is slightly wrong, yet with some basis in fact. In July 1899, a notice appeared in the *Thames Star*, a newspaper catering for a mining district south-east of Auckland. This demonstrates that the family had heard of his presence in New Zealand: 'WANTED, – THOMAS WILLIAM BLYTHE, last heard of at Parawai, to Communicate with Joseph Blythe, Rangiuru, near Tauranga. Will hear something to his advantage.' Joseph Robinson Blythe (1855–1944), brother of the Orange district secretary from Reilly's Trench, had landed at Tauranga in January 1881, successively working as a butcher in Tauranga, a farmer of virgin ground at Rangiuru, and then a carrier between the two settlements.[8] Though no record has been found of Thomas Blythe's voyage to New Zealand or his presence in America, he had apparently already troubled the Auckland police in 1890, when Thomas William Blythe was convicted of discharging a revolver in Western Park 'without reasonable cause'. Blythe failed to attend court, but the park caretaker 'deposed to hearing the shots and finding the man' and a sergeant 'deposed that the man stated he had just bought the revolver and went to the Park to try it. He fired three shots and two bullets were extracted from the tree. Behind the tree was a path.' Though it was not alleged that he had fired at or injured any passerby, Thomas was fined £1 with costs.[9]

Thomas William Blythe's later career in the Thames (Waikato) district may be traced through directories and electoral rolls ranging from 1896 to 1939, which record that he was successively a gardener, a farmer, a labourer, and finally a retired labourer before dying in November 1939, aged eighty-eight, intestate, and apparently without wife or children. Though the burial register identified him as an Anglican born in Scotland, there is little doubt that the press report of his death referred to Ernest's long-lost uncle: 'An inmate of the old men's home at Tararu, Thomas William Blythe, was discovered dead this morning, hanging from a tree in the grounds. Deceased had been an inmate of the institution for about four years.'[10] Such was the long-delayed and miserable outcome of uncle Thomas' banishment from Aghalee and Magheragall.

Meanwhile, the death of Ernest's grandparents had belatedly given James and Agnes Blythe full control over the home and farm at Magheraliskmisk. Though James inherited the land, stock, crops, implements, and household furniture, the estate was charged with payment of Thomas' legacy of £100 and a rather miserly annuity of £40 for Chelley, who was also allowed lifetime use of the 'parlour and best bedroom above said parlour with their furniture'.[11] According to Ernest's autobiography, Chelley also received an annuity of £10 charged on uncle Robert's farm at Aghalee. He remarked that after her husband's death, 'until she left us, complaining and grumbling often occurred', perhaps because 'my mother was not as submissive to her, once my father owned the farm, as she had no need to be, when all the power and the upper hand had been relinquished by the old woman'. She was finally driven out of her parlour and best bedroom following a child revolt led by Ernest, whom she had hit when he refused to eat his afternoon meal. All four children 'gathered around the door calling her by her baptismal name and mocking her', 'shouting scornfully', and throwing 'sods at her'. Chelley objected to the fact that only Ernest was beaten by his father for insulting her, and 'went to live with my aunt Mary in Belfast', after which 'the house was comfortable and we had peace'.[12] Ernest's zestful recollection of this nauseating episode highlights not only his shameless misogyny, but also his pride in having led a successful guerrilla campaign.

II

By contrast, Blythe's reminiscences completely ignore the lurid career of his younger brother James Alexander, whose physical prowess and practical jokery he clearly admired and envied as a boy. When James Alexander Blythe married Harriett Christiana Hill in the Broomhedge Methodist chapel in January 1919, he seemed headed for a secure future.[13] With Ernest otherwise occupied, he could expect to take over the family farm in Magheraliskmisk, whose value had been enhanced by four wartime years of spiralling prices for Irish agricultural products. Being the eldest of ten children of a 'strong' farmer in nearby Magheramesk, Harriett probably contributed a substantial dowry.[14] Yet, within three years, he faced disgrace and ruin. We cannot tell whether his financial losses during a period of sharp deflation and global recession were the result of recklessness or bad luck. By July 1922, James Alexander was bankrupt, eventually agreeing to pay two shillings in the pound to his unsecured creditors. Though resident in Lisburn, he was described as a 'cattle and sheep grazer'.[15]

While his bankruptcy case meandered through the civil courts, James Alexander was also charged for the first time with a criminal offence, having been accused of forging and uttering a cheque for £80 with intent to defraud an auctioneer (an old acquaintance), who sold sheep for him, in January 1922. At this stage, he retained support from family and friends: two sureties of £100 were lodged by his father and father-in-law to keep him out of custody after the initial court hearings,[16] and the auctioneer decided to drop the forgery case as 'he could not swear that prisoner forged his name'. Though cleared of the major charge at the Antrim Assizes in February 1923, Blythe was sentenced to six months' imprisonment with hard labour for uttering the cheque. Lord Justice [James] Andrews expressed 'a very great deal of pain' in judging someone who 'was not a man who should have ever been in the dock', noting 'especially' that his father had 'tendered £80, the amount of the cheque' after delivery of the verdict.[17] Yet, a couple of months after his sentence had expired, James Alexander was back in the dock before Lord Justice Andrews, charged with receiving stolen sheep. On that occasion, he was discharged when the prosecuting counsel stated 'that he had read the depositions carefully and could find no evidence whatever against Blythe'.[18]

Over the next few years, he reappeared as a notorious but careless fraudster in various parts of England, receiving no less than four sentences between 1926 and 1935 for terms rising from six months to five years. Harriett evidently accompanied him to England, for their third child was born in Lancashire in 1925.[19] A detective testified that he had 'travelled about England with a woman accomplice now in prison. They went about in a motor car, carrying out fraud.' In Peebles (September 1926), he was imprisoned for six months. In Leeds (March 1927), he received a sentence of eighteen months' hard labour for forgery (by altering the value of a money order and using it to induce a bank official to cash a dud cheque). The Judge of Assize considered imposing penal servitude, stating that he was 'a very clever forger and a menace and a danger to the public'. 'A man of many aliases', he had posed on that occasion as John Brown, a motor driver. The court heard that Blythe's wife and family were currently living in Moira, County Down, while he roamed England in search of illicit wealth and excitement. When reporting the case, the *Belfast News-Letter* identified him as a native of County Antrim with a previous conviction in Belfast, but refrained (as always) from embarrassing the Irish Free State's squeaky-clean minister for finance by revealing that the fraudster and bankrupt was his brother.[20]

By 1929, James Alexander Blythe (now a butcher) had been reunited with Harriett, with an address in Upper Parliament Street, Liverpool. Both were brought before the Manchester Assizes, charged with possession of tools for making coins and with counterfeiting three-shilling pieces. As a serial offender, James Alexander was sentenced to five years' penal servitude, but 'his wife, who pleaded guilty to uttering counterfeit coins, was bound over'.[21] He was scarcely out of prison before being hauled before the Old Bailey (June 1934) 'on a charge of possessing a mould for coining purposes', but the 'blacksmith' was acquitted after pleading 'not guilty'.[22] Less than eighteen months later, he received his last known conviction, also at the Old Bailey (November 1935). Now a 'dealer', he was condemned to five further years of penal servitude for possession of a tool and for making and possessing counterfeit coins, being jointly charged with another female accomplice (Margaret Sandford, a widow previously imprisoned in Oldham for uttering). When the police arrived at his accomplice's house in London, Blythe managed to put some coins down the drain, but the police dredged up 45 half-crowns, one of which was inspected by the jury through a microscope. Blythe showed some gallantry when pleading on behalf of his accomplice:

> Mrs Sandford is a type easily imposed upon. I did not make the coins in her house. You [the Common Serjeant] are a shrewd man, and know I could not have made them with the tools found in the house. Whatever you do to me be merciful to the woman.[23]

The impact of these events on Harriett Blythe and her children must have been catastrophic, not least because Harriett herself was among his female accomplices in crime. The family (evidently without James Alexander) had returned to Ulster by 1948, living in a flat on the Malone Road, just up the hill from Methodist College, Belfast.[24] Annie Elizabeth (Betty), born in Lisburn in March 1922, married Benjamin William Hezlett (a 37-year-old clerk) at the University Road Methodist church in 1952, and they settled in Coleraine, where his father was a local government officer.[25] Ernest preserved two letters from Betty, an enthusiastic member of the Coleraine Drama Club, the first asking his advice about putting on an 'Irish play' for the club's spring production. Betty's second letter, clearly in response to Ernest's condolences on her mother's death in 1968, gave only a hint of past tribulations: 'She was a very happy and fulfilled person in spite of her early troubles and sorrows, or was it, perhaps, because of them?'[26] Harriett (known as 'Harena') was remembered in a Methodist journal for having 'lived a truly Christian life' despite her 'many trials'.[27] I have not ascertained when, where, or under what name James Alexander Blythe died.[28]

III

How do these family misfortunes illuminate the outlook and career of Ernest Blythe? First, the succession of sexual improprieties involving his father's family suggests a continuing tussle between conspicuous piety and personal recklessness in an outwardly respectable lineage of snug farmers. When the young Blythe sought Holy Communion in an 'Orange' church before seeking admission to the IRB, he revealed a similar internal tussle.[29] Second, the tragic life and death of his errant uncle exemplifies the bitter consequences, especially for farming families, of conflicts over inheritance and control of property. Thomas William's career provided Ernest with an object lesson in the importance of sustaining family solidarity, even when disruptive factors such as dispossession, migration, or political cleavage threatened to destroy it. Third, his brother's record as a fraudster exhibits not just avarice but personal charm, foolhardy adventurism, delight in deception, and theatrical deployment of multiple identities. Like Ernest, James Alexander sheltered behind a multitude of aliases, using his considerable powers of persuasion to recruit and manipulate accomplices. Ernest Blythe's fascination with the techniques of deception, and his lifelong love of drama, were surely fostered by observation of his own close family, even if some family secrets eluded him while others were discreetly reshaped or ignored in his autobiographies.

The remainder of Ernest Blythe's immediate family stayed in Ulster, though not in the vicinity of Magheragall. Mary Helen, James' younger daughter, was the only sibling to find a spouse within the church of her upbringing, marrying William Nassau Gibson, a Belfast teacher, in 1930.[30] Jo (Josephine Chelley) became a nurse and served in Malta during the Second World War.[31] She never married, living for most of her long life with her father and other relatives in Holywood and Marino, County Down.[32] By 1922, James Blythe had sold the farm at Magheraliskmisk to William Greer and retired to Holywood. Upon his death in neighbouring Marino in 1941, his effects were valued at only £397, considerably less than his father's assessment forty-five years earlier. We cannot tell to what extent the family's withdrawal from Magheragall was precipitated by shame arising from James Alexander's disgrace.

The family had suffered another setback in November 1919 when Ernest flouted tradition by marrying Annie McHugh, a Roman Catholic (albeit a police officer's daughter), in the University church on St Stephen's Green, Dublin.[33] Their first child was born ten months later at a house in Harold's Cross, but sadly died of heart failure only five hours after delivery. 'Baby Blythe' was registered rather evasively as 'daughter of company director' (unnamed), possibly alluding to Ernest's membership of the suppressed Dáil ministry.[34] Their only surviving child, Earnán Pádraig de Blaghd, was born in Ranelagh in March 1925.[35] In many respects, Earnán was emphatically his father's son, becoming a bilingual journalist and drama critic as well as a barrister.[36] He was also an accomplished amateur historian, celebrating the memory of the Dublin Metropolitan Police with 'pride and affection', and exhibiting particular insight into the devious *modus operandi* of the IRB.[37] He never married and long remained in the parental home in Rathgar.[38]

Though his father died within the Church of Ireland, Earnán Pádraig, like his mother, was reared and buried as a Catholic.[39] Annie cherished a lingering but forlorn hope that Earnán's example would expedite her husband's salvation. When Blythe's private secretary as minister for finance, Leon Ó Broin was asked by Annie if he 'might be able to lead her husband towards the Catholic Church, and said so to me when we happened to meet on Stephen's Green one day'. The pious Ó Broin kept quiet until he noticed a 'Maynooth Catechism' on his minister's desk, eliciting the explanation 'that young Earnán had started to ask questions about religion and, rather than that Annie and he should confuse the boy with different answers', Blythe had bought the catechism so that 'he might understand what the Catholics taught on these difficult subjects'.[40] Unlike so many Protestant converts to nationalism, Blythe declined to celebrate his acceptance by undertaking a dual conversion. Apart from compromising deep-rooted convictions, this would have negated the authority and gratification he derived from being the only Ulster Protestant in the Dáil ministry and the political élite.

Blythe's political conversion must have sorely strained relations with his parents and siblings, yet his autobiographies reveal intimate contact long after his departure from Newtownards for Dublin and the Kerry Gaeltacht. During a brief stay at Magheraliskmisk, 'before I went south' in April 1913, he was still apprehensive about his father's reaction:

> I did not make it abundantly clear to my father what I was about to do, but I did not hide anything from the rest of my family. My sister Helen asked me if I had everything that I needed. I said that I did. She then asked me how many shirts I had. I said that I had two shirts, the one that was on me, and one in my trunk. This made her slightly angry and she said that I had no right to be so childish and senseless. She went with me directly to Lisburn and she bought me two more shirts.[41]

In spring 1914, he spent a few more days 'at home' before cycling to Aghagallon to visit two old Fenians, in the vain hope of reviving the IRB in south Antrim:

> I intuitively felt that they were suspicious of me. It occurred to me that I was working in a place that was too close to my family's lands and altogether too close to Aghalee where my uncle Robert lived. The two would know him as a protestant and as a unionist – they were middle-aged men. My father might recognise them. And they could think that I was not trustworthy.[42]

It is unclear whether Blythe was more fearful of his father's disapproval or of nationalist distrust. On his next visit at the end of the year, he 'spent a week or two in Magheragall doing nothing but becoming a little reluctant to start the research and futile canvassing again'.[43] And when Blythe, Denis McCullough, and Herbert Moore Pim were released from Crumlin gaol in October 1915, having been imprisoned upon ignoring an order under the Defence of the Realm regulations to leave Ireland, the welcoming party at Ina Connolly's home included one of Blythe's sisters.[44]

Just before the 1916 rebellion, he sent each sister an uninformative postcard (presumably retrieved after their deaths) from his place of 'exile' in Abingdon, Berkshire.[45] Having missed the rebellion and its aftermath while detained in Abingdon, Oxford, and Reading, Blythe acquiesced in spending the first half of 1917 within a triangle centred on Mullaghcarton (inaccurately named as his home place), as an alternative to renewed imprisonment or the life of a fugitive.[46] He returned to Magheraliskmisk to help out on the farm:

> One thing that made my time in the north less tiresome than I feared, was that the government issued a tillage order around that time. My father, who had fully retired from tillage a short time previously, had to buy another horse and plough a few fields. I did my share of the work and was again surprised that the people of Kerry were happy to continue with the old swing plough, when it was far easier to handle the wheel plough.

Though I was willing to do every sort of work, I was not made
do much. My father was still able and willing to do light work
and that meant that my brother James was not left with much to
do, even if I were not there.[47]

Despite his notoriety as a serial offender under the Defence of the
Realm Act and as one of the most effective republican organisers,
Blythe was clearly still being cosseted by his ever-protective family.
When he invited Thomas Ashe's sister Margaret (then teaching in
Belfast) to visit him, she arrived with Henry Shiels, 'a volunteer
whose arm was maimed in the Rising' and his old comrade in the
Belfast IRB:[48]

My whole family and even my father gave her a warm welcome
and she was well liked by them, even though she was a Papist
from the extreme opposite side of Ireland. They were so taken
with her that my mother, after I had gone south again, invited
her to come out to Magheragall to spend a weekend in the
house and to accompany my brother and my sisters to the Maze
races – the boycott by the respectable farmers of horse racing
had been relaxed a short time previously. When I received word
of Margaret's second visit, I took it as proof that my family did
not feel, even secretly, that I had shamed them in the eyes of
the neighbours. To tell the truth, during my half year at home,
I did not feel any of my Orange neighbours held any ill-feelings
towards me.[49]

Blythe's papers demonstrate that he never lost amicable contact
with his sisters. In March 1932, Helen congratulated him on his final
electoral success in Monaghan,[50] quoting a local newspaper report
that 'in difficult circumstances he did excellent work, & established
a reputation that should stand him in good stead now'. They had
'listened in every night during the counting of the votes'. With
Cumann na nGaedheal out of office, 'naturally we are a bit anxious
at the moment, but you will be all right, won't you Ernest?'[51] Blythe
survived the change of power, but was ousted almost a year later by

Alexander Haslett, a prominent Orangeman favoured by Fianna Fáil preferences following a bizarre clerical and Hibernian campaign to outflank and oust the 'Blueshirt'.[52] During the campaign, Blythe had gloomily observed 'that they had been told there would be a renewal of armed revolutionary activity if Fianna Fáil were not returned to power', a prediction that was not put to the test.[53] Eleven years later, as Helen was dying from cancer, she bid her 'dear Ernest' an emotional farewell: 'I never forget how good you were to me when I was a child. I don't really know what I would have done without you then.'[54] Nor did he neglect his surviving sister, Josephine. After admission to Towell House, an old people's home in Knock (east Belfast), 'Jo' sent several amiable if slightly catty letters thanking him for presents (usually stoles chosen by Earnán the younger) and referring to forthcoming visits.[55]

A less predictable token of family solidarity was unveiled in 1928, when Blythe was vice-president of the Executive Council. On 3 February, County Inspector John McNally of the Royal Ulster Constabulary (a Galwegian transferred from the RIC) signed a firearm certificate for 'Ernest Blythe, Esq., 4 Moffetts Ter, Demesne Rd', his father's address in Holywood, County Down. This allowed him to retain his .38 Webley revolver and ammunition, the certificate being renewed annually up to 1932–3. Any senior officer would surely have known that Blythe had long since ceased to reside in Northern Ireland, implying that he retained friends in high places as well as a supportive family in Moffett's Terrace.[56] The Free State authorities proved less indulgent after de Valera took power and set about disarming O'Duffy's National Guard in 1933.[57]

PART TWO

Disguises

CHAPTER THREE

'Earnán de Blaghd'

I

The key to Ernest Blythe's sense of nationality was his romantic attachment to the Irish language, which he struggled patriotically to master throughout his political apprenticeship in Dublin and north Down. It was only in 1913, when he moved to Lispole in west Kerry to learn the language from native speakers, that he began to overcome his admitted linguistic ineptitude and eventually to write in Irish. Yet, like so many Irish Irelanders, he already rejoiced in belonging to the esoteric elite of language enthusiasts, separated from their neighbours by the adoption of Irish names, attendance at language classes, and occasional utterance of an exotic phrase serving as a password.

According to his statement for the Bureau of Military History, Blythe began studying O'Growney's *Easy Lessons* on his first night in Dublin in March 1905, soon joining the central branch of the Gaelic League and submitting himself to the bewitching tutelage of Jenny Flanagan (later Sinéad de Valera). The Gaelic League, though officially 'non-political', was mainly patronised by 'advanced' nationalists who soon provided introductions to other organisations. Protestants were attracted by the League's ecumenical ethos (its founder-president Douglas Hyde was a rector's son), though by 1905 sectarian tensions were apparent within its leadership. Blythe was initially fearful that his Protestantism would make him unwelcome in the League, and regretted having given his lodgings as 16 Upper Sackville (O'Connell) Street, otherwise Presbyterian Church House.[1] He was reassured to note that his classmate George Irvine failed to remove his hat as they passed the Catholic pro-cathedral, and soon discovered that the class was teeming with fellow Protestants.[2]

Over the next two years, Blythe thoroughly explored the alternative Dublin scene, befriending Seán O'Casey in the hurling club associated with central branch, developing an interest in Griffith's Sinn Féin and his newspaper *United Ireland* on the advice of George Irvine, and finally joining the Irish Republican Brotherhood, at O'Casey's invitation, in spring 1907.[3] Before accepting O'Casey's suggestion, he spent the evening 'thinking and praying' before taking communion at the 'Black Church' (St Mary's Chapel of Ease, then a mission church). The body of Christ would have been given to him by the Revd John Dougherty, a long-serving Orange chaplain who later became master of the Trinity College district lodge.[4]

While still a teenager, Blythe became acquainted with Dublin's leading republicans and Irish Irelanders, especially his fellow Protestants, establishing friendships and contacts that served him well throughout the revolutionary period and beyond. An early notebook gave the names and addresses of future celebrities such as Henry Dixon, Jenny Flanagan, Bulmer Hobson, and Kathleen Lynn as well as Irvine; while other names in a retrospective list of his brethren in the Dublin IRB included Seán T. O'Kelly, George Nicholls, George Sarsfield Lyons, Seán McDermott, and Con Collins.[5] With O'Casey, Irvine, and Séamus Deakin, he joined a Committee of Protestant Gaelic Leaguers to lobby the Church of Ireland for services in the Irish language, the use of parochial halls, and the inclusion of Irish language and history in the school curriculum.[6] 'Earnán de Blaghd' was already a familiar figure in the charmed circles of Irish Ireland when he completed his four-year stint in the Department of Agriculture and Technical Instruction for Ireland.

When Blythe moved from Dublin in March 1909 to work as a journalist in Bangor and then Newtownards, he was almost as much a stranger in north Down as he had been in Dublin four years earlier. Though Magheraliskmisk was scarcely three miles from Lisburn and relatives lived or owned property in Belfast, his knowledge of urban Ulster was that of a country visitor who had lived on the home farm until his appointment as a fifteen-year-old boy clerk in 'the Department' in 1905. In *Trasna na Bóinne*, Blythe portrayed himself as more experienced than a regular country lad, yet by no means a city lad. His knowledge of the world beyond Magheragall was derived from Sunday and holiday visits to relatives, summer school excursions, and attendance at cattle fairs.[7] Between 1909 and 1913, Blythe became intimately acquainted with Belfast as well as Bangor and Newtownards, which were only a few miles from the city with railway connections. Blythe, by his own grandiloquent account, had turned his back on the 'English civil service . . . in order to be free to work for the cause of Ireland', though his more pressing motive was to find a job once his contract as a boy clerk terminated on his twentieth birthday.[8] As for 'the cause of Ireland', Blythe found many ways of working for it under various disguises.

Instead of relying primarily on family contacts, Blythe was introduced to Belfast by his fellow 'Organisation men' in Dublin, who recommended him to Denis McCullough.[9] His social life when visiting the city was grounded in republican organisations associated with the Irish Republican Brotherhood, especially the Dungannon clubs and Fianna Éireann, part of an intricate network of small but ultimately influential coteries instigated by McCullough and Bulmer Hobson. 'Due to a lack of time and opportunity', he did not attend Gaelic League meetings in Ulster, though in 1912 he attended fortnightly Irish classes at Coláiste Chomhghaill on the Falls Road.[10] Before long, Blythe had replaced McCullough as 'centre' of a circle that never exceeded a dozen members at once. McCullough subsequently reclaimed the Belfast command, in order, so Blythe understood, to qualify himself for higher office in the IRB.[11]

Little was achieved at its monthly meetings beyond collecting a shilling from each attender to buy pistols, five or six of which were eventually acquired and assigned by raffle. Though Blythe never won the raffle, he used his privilege as 'centre' to practise shooting during the month between acquiring and assigning each pistol. He trained 'in an old ring fort on my father's land, far from any house. My aim did not improve much. Instead of placing any of the blame on my own eyes, I was inclined instead to think that the small pistols were useless.'[12] The Belfast circle used the front organisations under its control to recruit and test potential brethren, and also to spice the spirit of brotherhood by enticing girls (often sisters of brethren) into Irish classes and even Fianna drills – albeit in a separate sluagh named after Betsy Gray.

Table 3.1. Members of Belfast IRB, 1911

Name	Occupation	Age	Religion
Ernest Blythe	journalist	21	Episcopalian
David Culbert Boyd	reporter	16	Presbyterian
Albert Wesley Wellington (Alf) Cotton	medical student	20	Brethren
John Mitchel(l) Darby	teacher of navigation	28	Catholic
William R. Gilmore	commercial clerk	22	Catholic
Archibald Osborne Heron	engineer	23	ex-Presbyterian
John Bulmer Hobson	journalist	28	Quaker
Arthur Lavery	iron salesman	22	Catholic
John Ernest (Seán) Lester	journalist	22	Methodist
Denis McCullough	musical instrument dealer	28	Catholic
Joseph McCullough (brother)	pianoforte tuner apprentice	20	Catholic
Robert G. (Gordon) McKinstry	pharmacy apprentice	19	Episcopalian
James Patrick O'Donnell	joiner in shipyard	21	Catholic
Charles Francis Shannon (Cathal O'Shannon)	shipping clerk	20	Catholic
John Sullivan (Seán O'Sullivan)	harness maker	28	Catholic
John N. Peyton (S. Paden)	sculptor	23	Catholic
Joseph Robinson	ship painter	24	Catholic
Henry Shiels	drier	26	Catholic
Michael Shiels (brother)	upholsterer	20	Catholic
Daniel Turley	bottler of mineral water	22	Catholic
Francis Wilson	lamplighter	30	ex-Brethren
Thomas Wilson	flesher	19	Catholic

Apart from McCullough, Hobson, and Blythe himself, the Belfast circle included future revolutionaries such as Alf Cotton and Archie Heron (key organisers in MacNeill's Irish Volunteers), the Labour organiser Cathal O'Shannon (who greatly impressed Blythe with his well-informed volubility), and the journalist and diplomat Seán Lester.[13] Lester, as a fellow 'Protestant Nationalist', became a close friend immediately after their introduction in the Dungannon club, and accompanied Blythe when he was assigned to cover the Twelfth demonstration in 1909.[14] Before long he too became a journalist, working for the *Portadown Express*, the *Armagh Guardian*, and then the *County Down Spectator* in Bangor.[15] John Mitchel (or Mitchell) Darby achieved note as an Antrim footballer and official before succumbing to tuberculosis and asthma at the age of thirty in 1912.[16] Another IRB member who became prominent in the Belfast IRA, Dan Turley, was murdered as an 'informer' in 1936.[17]

Using lists provided by Blythe and Cotton and Blythe's invaluable address book, a collective profile of all twenty-two reported members may be compiled from family census returns.[18] The list in Table 3.1 reveals a medley of young men from diverse backgrounds, whose median age in 1911 was twenty-two years; only one (Frank Wilson) was married. In each census year, over two-thirds were resident in Belfast, about two-fifths of these being in the Falls ward. The majority (twelve) were natives of Belfast, and only two (Seán O'Sullivan from Cork and John Darby from Liverpool) were born outside Ulster. By contrast, 86 per cent (nineteen) of their fathers came from outside Belfast, the most exotic being a native of France (James, father of Joe Robinson). Though two-thirds of the group (fifteen) were Catholics, the minority spanned the Protestant spectrum, with members of the Church of Ireland, the Presbyterian and Methodist churches, the Society of Friends (Bulmer Hobson), and the 'Brethren' (Alf Cotton). Between 1901 and 1911, a Presbyterian (Archie Heron) became Catholic, and a second member of the Brethren in 1901 (Frank Wilson) decided to refuse information about his religion.[19]

Upbringing in an evangelical sect, far from precluding future nationalism, provided converts with an armoury of readily adaptable moral zeal and missionary rhetoric. As Denis McCullough, a Catholic, wrote of Cotton:

> I had one especially sincere man in my command in Belfast named Alf Cotton. Alf was reared in the sect of the Plymouth Brethern [*sic*] and I cannot say what influence brought him into contact with our movement. But having come in, there was no more sincere or loyal man in the movement.[20]

As shown below, Frank Wilson was notably persuasive in forging republican zealots out of unpromising material, ranging from the Hibernian Seán McDermott to the Moravian Ulster Volunteer and Orangeman, Rory Haskin.[21] David Boyd was reared by the family of his grandfather, a Presbyterian colporteur in Omagh, and George Irvine of the Dublin IRB and the Church of Ireland Gaelic Society was the son of an evangelical bookseller in Enniskillen.[22]

The Belfast IRB included seven skilled workers and nine men with some professional training (four journalists, a teacher, a medical student, an engineer, a sculptor, and a pharmacy apprentice), along with three dealers or salesmen, two clerks, and a lamplighter. Their fathers were more socially diverse, with only one professional man (Peter Darby, a teacher of navigation like his son), one manager (Archie Heron's father), and one official (John, father of Seán Peyton, was a police pensioner). In addition to nine fathers in skilled occupations, there were three farmers and three labourers, two dealers, and two clerks. Though neither wealthy nor of high social status, the families of brethren had adequate accommodation. Four fathers inhabited 'first-class' houses compared with seventeen in 'second-class' dwellings. The median house featured five rooms and three front windows. A statistical comparison between the brethren and their fathers is presented in Table 3.2.[23]

All members of the circle could read and write, and between 1901 and 1911 the number of declared Irish-speakers rose from six to seventeen (30 per cent to 77 per cent). The only 'native' speaker was Seán O'Sullivan from Kealkil in west Cork, though three other brethren had fathers who had already acquired the language by 1901.[24] This startling increase doubtless reflected some genuine advance in linguistic skill through school or Gaelic League classes, as well as the campaign to make fools of the police enumerators in 1911 by inscribing the census forms in Irish. Others might have done so but for fathers who, as the responsible heads of household, preferred to use English. Eight brethren gave Irish versions of their names in 1911,[25] though the Mac Con Ulodh (McCullough) family's collective proficiency in Irish was not sufficient to dispense with English when giving information about occupation, literacy, and religion. Frank

Table 3.2. Profile of Belfast IRB

Characteristic	Brethren	%	Fathers	%
Census Matches	22		22	
Religious Denomination				
Roman Catholic	14	64	13	59
Episcopalian	2	9	3	14
Presbyterian	2	9	3	14
Brethren	2	9	1	5
Other	2	9	2	9
Birthplace				
Belfast	12	55	3	14
Antrim	3	14	8	36
Down	2	9	1	5
Other Ulster	3	14	6	27
Other	2	9	4	18
House Class				
First			4	19
Second			17	81
Median Figures				
Rooms in House			5	
Front Windows			3	
Age in 1911 (Years)	22		59	

Wilson was honest enough to erase his original claim to speak Irish and English. Such was the innermost circle within which Ernest Blythe moved and plotted while working in north Down.

A notable feature of Blythe's republicanism between 1909 and 1913 was its irrelevance to his social and political activities in Bangor and Newtownards. Though ostensibly eager to seek out sympathisers and potential recruits in this unfamiliar terrain, he was well aware of the perilous local consequences of acquiring a republican reputation. Blythe was frustrated to discover that even those with an interest in Irish language and culture were not inclined to translate their sentiments into politics. In Newtownards, he was disappointed upon discovering that the Unitarian minister respected the United

Irishmen but cared nothing for modern nationalism, and repelled by 'Fenian Geordie' McKibbin who turned out to be a disagreeable drunkard.[26] Having dismissed the latter as unworthy to be cultivated, Blythe was unable to confirm stories about a 'Green Lodge of Grey'ba' (Greyabbey in Ulster-Scots dialect) consisting of Orangemen such as McKibbin who had all defected to Fenianism.[27]

Blythe later heard from John Daly of Limerick and Bulmer Hobson that Protestant-dominated Fenian circles had indeed existed in both Greyabbey and Newtownards.[28] According to Frank Roney, who organised north Down with John Nolan in the early 1860s, they formed Fenian circles or groups in Newtownards, Greyabbey, Donaghadee, Bangor, and Comber. Viewing the small Catholic minority as 'utterly worthless' potential informers, they concentrated on reawakening the Presbyterian United Irish tradition. Among their most notable supporters were the 'Greenboys of Greba' ('Grey'ba'), who allegedly embodied a continuous tradition of separatism dating from 1798. Neither Roney nor Blythe's informants suggested that the Greenboys had previously belonged to an Orange lodge, though Jeremiah O'Donovan Rossa claimed to have met Fenian ex-Orangemen in Newtownards in 1885.[29] Though it is possible that the Unitarian minister was indeed immovably apolitical, McKibbin irretrievably sloshed, and Hobson's Fenian Protestants dormant or dead, prudence was surely a factor in dissuading Blythe from pursuit of the fading republican scent.

Blythe's memoir mentions only one potential radical ally in Newtownards, a long-standing contributor to *Sinn Féin* who became prominent in the Irish Women's Franchise League and Cumann na mBan: Elizabeth Bloxham.[30] As a Protestant, according to Blythe, she succeeded in defeating the only other qualified candidate (a Catholic from Tralee) for appointment as a 'cookery teacher' at a meeting of the technical instruction committee that he attended, neither the committee nor himself being aware that 'she was also a nationalist and a Sinn Féiner'. As so often, Blythe twisted or misremembered the facts to make a political point, claiming that the defeated candidate 'was called Nóra Ní Shúilleabháin, or a name like that', and that the appointment of a Protestant 'disappointed me that night'.[31] The loser, though indeed currently posted in Tralee, was in fact a Presbyterian named Lewis from Tyrone.[32]

Blythe noted that 'Elizabeth' subsequently 'angered a few people' by walking ostentatiously out of the parish church when the rector (William Twist-Whatham of lodge 1501) made disparaging remarks about nationalism and 'the cause of Ireland'. She 'suffered as a result, but I say that there were just as many people who felt no animosity towards her for what she did. The account of the event was spread by the populace as a funny story.'[33] Bloxham's signed letters of protest to the *Newtownards Chronicle* created a minor uproar in early 1912, when spirited women with independent political views were still a novelty in Newtownards. The *Chronicle* juxtaposed her first letter with a report that the 'school-girl cookery classes' had 'proved a huge success', and that her annual salary as domestic economy instructress had just been raised to £35. Bloxham was careful to avoid any overt political declaration: 'It is not my intention to enter into or to provoke political discussion. I hold that every man has a right to his political convictions, and that men can disagree strenuously and honourably as to whether any political measure may or may not benefit our country.' The provocative element of this letter was its fearless accusation that the rector had used his sermon as 'an appeal to party prejudice', having claimed 'that his political opponents were actuated solely by a desire to crush the Protestant religion and to take from Protestants their means of livelihood'.[34]

Several pseudonymous correspondents in the *Chronicle* came to Twist-Whatham's defence, sometimes in verse, but others deplored the continuing battle of the muses:

> 'Tis now the topic of the hour –
>   Miss Bloxham's letter;
> The godly say they'll make her cower,
>   Her tongue they'll fetter.[35]

The controversy was picked up by 'Town Tattle' in the *Newtownards Spectator*, which gleefully reproduced some particularly inept doggerel by 'Puritan' in the *Irish News*:

Miss Elizabeth Bloxham, I thank thee!
And your letter I wish to recall,
For I'm glad that even in 'Newtown,'
There is one who has not bowed to Baal.

Twist-Whatham's sermons were denounced in the nationalist press as 'sickening diatribes' expressing 'fear-ridden appeal to bigotry and religious prejudice'.[36] Blythe seems to have avoided the issue in the *North Down Herald*, which carried a positive and respectful report of a subsequent sermon by Twist-Whatham that 'continued his remarks in regard to the importance and gravity of the present political situation'.[37]

Bloxham's own account of her protest revealed diverse local responses to her attacks on the rector's perpetration of 'politics in the pulpit' and his subsequent allegations about 'the terror in which Protestants lived in the West'. Though cold-shouldered by the Twist-Whathams and deserted by some of her students, she was loyally supported by a Technical Instruction Committee consisting of 'Orangemen and Freemasons', and remained in Newtownards until her dismissal after the 1916 rebellion.[38] Oddly, there is no indication in either account that Blythe was closely acquainted with his only potential soulmate resident in the town. She might have been a useful ally, being a lively and curious person who formed 'sparring' relationships with an Ulster Volunteer whose sister she taught, and with an Orange bread-server who 'wondered how I would dare to face my God if I died holding such opinions' on Home Rule.[39] Unlike the cagey Blythe, however, she relished teasing her unionist quarries by flaunting her heresies in public.[40]

Two others factors may have discouraged Blythe from cultivating her. As a 'southern' Protestant with no prior Ulster connections apart from in-laws, she was even more an outsider in Newtownards than himself, and therefore of limited value as either an informant or a proselyte. And, if not aspiring to the 'ascendancy' so much despised by Blythe, her family was bound to attract republican suspicion because of the vocation of her father and brothers.

Like so many republican veterans when recording their contribution to 'military history', Elizabeth Bloxham was notably reticent
about her background:

> I was one of the younger members of a large family living in
> the West of Ireland. Being Protestants, we were, as a matter
> of course, Unionists. I have no recollection of any political
> discussion in the family. . . . It wasn't as if we were ascendancy
> Protestants of the class in whose power it then was to use their
> influence for or against the common people. We had neither
> influence nor power and as little of this world's goods as had the
> people amongst whom we lived.[41]

In 1901, 23-year-old Bessie was living with her elderly parents and a
young nephew in the Westport Demesne in Mayo, as tenants of the
Marquess of Sligo. Her father was a police pensioner aged seventy-
four, who had enrolled in the Irish Constabulary in 1844 and retired
as a sub-constable, before Bessie's birth, on an annual pension of
£59. Three brothers, one younger than Bessie, had followed family
tradition by joining the RIC, though one was repeatedly fined for
breaches of discipline and another was immediately discharged as
unfit in 1888. Her younger brother, Henry Joseph, had an exemplary
record throughout twenty-two years of service, becoming a full
sergeant in 1908 and receiving a £5 reward for good conduct in July
1920.[42] Though it was common for sons to follow fathers into the
force, the Episcopalian and unionist Bloxhams were part of a small
minority within the overwhelmingly Catholic RIC.[43] As a Protestant
police family, they were doubly damned in republican eyes.

On 21 January 1921, Sergeant Bloxham's career ended abruptly
near Waterfall, four miles from Cork, when he was ambushed by
four members of the 3rd battalion, Cork brigade, and shot dead.
He and Head Constable Larkin had been cycling from Ballincollig
to investigate a raid on a train carrying mail. Larkin fired back and
escaped, but the ambushers made off with Bloxham's bicycle and
revolver.[44] His young widow and their two boys (John was born
seven months after the ambush) received an even smaller pension

than that awarded to his father in 1875.[45] It was probably Henry who had come to Elizabeth's defence after 1906, when a friend 'expressed disapproving surprise that I should be "mixed up" with "Sinn Féin". My brother's reply was, "Hasn't she as good a right to her own opinions as we have".'[46] If Blythe knew about Elizabeth's intimate associations with the RIC, he would have been all the more inclined to keep her at arm's length. Both had embarrassing secrets that they needed to preserve from fellow nationalists, and from each other.

II

While still in County Down, Blythe became a notable figure in republicanism beyond Ulster, exhibiting his developing journalistic skills in the propagandist monthly *Irish Freedom: Saoirseacht na h-Éireann*, first published in Dublin in November 1910. This organ of the 'Central Executive of the Wolfe Tone Clubs', a front for the supreme council of the IRB, was dominated by Blythe's comrades McCullough and Hobson. Over the four years until its suppression in December 1914, *Irish Freedom* published sixteen articles, leaders, and verses signed by 'Earnán' or 'Earnán de Blaghd'.[47] All of these appeared after Blythe's resignation from the Orange Order in February 1912, but it is likely that he had already contributed anonymously or under another pen-name, as he did to the *Irish Nation and the Peasant* in Dublin and the liberal *Ulster Guardian* in Belfast. All of his contributions to nationalist journals were unpaid until 1917, when he unexpectedly received a small cheque from *An Claidheamh Soluis*, the organ of the Gaelic League.[48]

Just before the general election of December 1910, and soon after Blythe's Orange initiation, *Irish Freedom* published an anonymous leading article on Ulster which matches Blythe's prose style and knowing tone. Though ridiculing the military pretensions of the Ulster Unionist Council and its threat that 'Ulster will Fight', it made an important point about the revolutionary potential of the resistance movement:

> The decision, whether serious or not, is tantamount to an admission of the whole Irish case for self-government. If it means

anything it means that Ireland north as well as south of the Boyne refuses to recognise any inherent right of the electors of Great Britain to decide how it shall be governed. The Orangemen say, in effect: – 'As long as your rule falls in with our wishes we obey it, but if you attempt to impose any system to which we object we claim the right to resist it by force of arms.' This, of course, is the Nationalist position much more strongly put than a good number of Home Rulers would phrase it. From that it is only a step to a recognition of the fact that the Irish question must be settled by an arrangement between the Irish parties at home, not by appeals to the English people, whose decisions both sides hold themselves free to repudiate.[49]

The onus was on nationalists to win over their Ulster adversaries, who would not always submit to manipulation by the UUC and their British allies: 'The party of the future must make the conversion of Ulster the first plank in their platform, and recognise that a national settlement from which Ulster dissented would not be worth winning.'

Blythe may also have been the 'Protestant Nationalist' who addressed an exhortatory letter 'to an Ulster Lad' in July 1911, describing himself as 'of the "Black North," the son of a "staunch Unionist," and nephew of an Orange District Master'. This letter gave a romantic account of his conversion:

In a second-class railway carriage, on the six p.m. train from Dublin to Belfast early in December, 1906, a young man spoke earnestly to a boy of 17 years, telling him in fervent tones of Ireland's martyred dead, "the men who loved the cause that never dies." The answers the boy gave must have been very disappointing, for of these things he knew nothing; yet to that conversation I can trace the opening of my heart to Ireland.[50]

Blythe was indeed seventeen in December 1906, though his initial conversation with Seán O'Casey about the IRB had reportedly occurred a few months earlier. While the Orange officer in his family was not an uncle but a first cousin once removed (and a district secretary rather than master), Blythe's father was indeed a staunch unionist, and the word 'earnestly' may have been a coded identification.

In mid 1912, 'Earnán' exposed his limited talent as a versifier in his first signed pieces, 'The Piper' and 'The Constitutionalists'. 'The Piper' extolled each new generation of martyrs, for 'when they fall for Ireland they shall join the piper's men'. The dead would continue to inspire emulation and hold the Sassenach at bay:

> For she may slay her living foes but not the Piper's men
> Who straightway raise new armies to confront her hosts again.

'The Constitutionalists' lampooned the 'coward hearts' who venerated the martyrs in Cave Hill while standing 'aghast' if called upon to fight themselves:

> With tender hearts they praise the dead
> And bless the cause for which they bled.
> They kneel upon the grave of Tone
> And pray that England be o'erthrown. . . .
> So shall the children they beget
> Applaud our stubborn effort yet.[51]

These verses show how thoroughly Blythe had already immersed himself in the trope of bloody sacrifice.

His articles were not confined to that lofty theme, with three pieces advocating a co-operative commonwealth and four mainly concerned with language issues and the Gaelic League.[52] These were inseparable in Blythe's mind from nationality. In 'The Cause', he pronounced that 'every Nationalist must stand for three things – the winning of complete political freedom, the preservation of the national tongue, and the maintenance of the virility of the race, which latter involves the predominance of agriculture'.[53] As a farmer's son, Blythe did not hanker for 'by-gone things but the adaptation of their lessons and designs to new circumstances'. Though the 'wonderfully self-sufficient' agriculture of the past could not be restored, 'the old-time farm shall be re-formed in the new co-operative parish'. Even if country towns would suffer and shrivel as a result of co-operation, 'the country will gain much more than the towns will lose', and we might 'yet be glad that England suppressed our manufactures'.[54] Such passages suggest that, even as a young zealot, Blythe had a mischievously perverse streak that defied nationalist shibboleths.

In October 1913, he declared that 'as in the national language is all sanity and intellectual strength, so in the fresh blood of the martyrs is all hope and pride and courage'. While 'a mere intention to fight is not a sufficient service', neither was the bravery of the simple fighting man:

> In every insurrection the majority of those who fall are not heroes or martyrs but common men who go out with brave hearts, truly, but willing to risk death only because they believe themselves more likely to taste of the fruits of victory.

Yet more valuable was the martyr prepared 'to die for the people', since 'by suffering and sacrifice alone shall Ireland be freed'. Anticipating the logic of those who instigated the rebellion of 1916, Blythe placed heroic sacrifice above potential success:

> It is necessary that we should organise and plan and prepare that our rising may be successful, but it is more needful for each of us to gather in his heart the courage to go out though he should know failure and death to be inevitable.[55]

Like so many of the romantic revolutionaries of 1913, particularly those in the Belfast circle, Blythe was to miss the 'rising' in 1916 and never to offer his own life for the sake of the people. For Blythe, as for Denis McCullough, this fact raised lingering questions about his sincerity and courage, even if excellent alibis for 'not being out' with Pearse and the boys could be offered in each case.

Blythe's central preoccupations in *Irish Freedom* were death, violence, and virility. In July 1912, while still based in Newtownards, he had linked militarism with virility:

> But there can be no military spirit worth anything if the men of the country are not virile and hardy, if their arms are flabby and their palates crave delicate food, if they are but talkers and artists, crafty merchants and cunning artificers.

Military training was less important than 'stout limbs and resolute hearts', which could be cultivated through 'running and leaping and hurling' as well as shooting (though Blythe himself was a confessedly inept hurler and marksman). He voiced the schoolboy bluster of the GAA:

> If, in future, Irishmen, with mighty lungs and muscled frames, can soar higher than any of the enemy, we shall have an advantage . . . Let us therefore train our bodies to be strong and hardy, and our minds to the thought of war, that we may not shrink from slaughter.[56]

The same issue of *Irish Freedom* reported his bombastic address at a meeting in the Fianna hall, Victoria Street, to establish Belfast's first 'Freedom club'. Denis McCullough chaired the meeting with 'Earnan de Blaghd' as secretary. He said that the club should 'rehabilitate the doctrine of the sword, because no National movement could ever be successful if it could not rely on the ultimate backing of the sword'. Blythe's journalist friend Seaghan Mac An Leastair (Lester) playfully responded 'that "the sword" was of course a symbolical term. It really meant, amongst other things, modern rifles and automatic pistols.' It was agreed that a club should be established 'to justify and prepare for the use of any and every means, passive and aggressive, to attain that end' – the 'establishment of an independent Irish republic'.[57]

Though praising sacrifice above practical military action, Blythe became increasingly interested in the political benefits of armed displays after the formation of the Irish Volunteers in November 1913. In December, he snarled that 'he that enjoys the rights of manhood, but has not the courage or ability to guard them, asks to be spat upon. He is a cheat and a traitor. . . . Freedom is to be won only by the bloody toil of war.' The 'military spirit' could be deployed to intimidate the hereditary enemy even in the absence of war, as the example of the Ulster Volunteers had shown:

> How valuable to a people or a section of a people are the most trumpery war preparations is shown by the present importance of Orange Ulster . . . Eighty thousand men with wooden guns and

vaguest threats are of as much account as five times the number with resolutions of passionate aspiration. The lesson, however, is not that we should start rival battalions of bluff but that we consider whether, when one wooden gun will perturb a minister of the English Crown, five Mausers would not persuade him to keep to his own bounds. I know the Ulster Volunteers, and I am sorry that they are of no account. Nevertheless, advantage might be taken of the embarrassment which their existence causes the enemy, for Nationalists publicly to organise and drill.

Half impressed by the Ulster Volunteers that he had observed in Newtownards, half contemptuous, Blythe seemed oddly regretful that they were not (yet) a true army. He concluded that 'to become soldiers it is needful for each of us to do three things: first, to get guns; second, to learn to shoot with them; and third, to learn to act together and to obey and trust our officers'.[58]

The emergence of two rival Volunteer forces raised the possibility of a collision and perhaps a civil war. The Irish Volunteers had only two possible opponents: 'the "volunteers" of Ulster and the armed forces of England'. Once again wavering over the military potential of the Ulster Volunteers, Blythe mused that 'suppose the Orangemen were to come out, it would not serve Ireland for you to go against them'. The Home Rule issue was not worthy to precipitate 'fratricidal slaughter', which 'would leave us with darker prejudices and fiercer feuds than those which we desire to be rid of'. Indeed:

> If the Ulstermen cannot be broken they will have put us to shame, and there will be no honourable course left to us but to make submission to them and to ask them to hold this country against all alien powers. This they will gladly do; for there is no man or people but will prefer lordship to subjection.[59]

Blythe thus detected revolutionary potential in the Ulster movement, while affirming that there was 'no possibility' of the Irish Volunteers being called on 'to fight against your fellow-countrymen in Ulster'. He advised them to concentrate on 'fighting spirit' and discipline rather than the arts of war, in which 'the enemy are mostly killed because some of the thousands of bullets MUST hit somebody. In drilling it will, I think, be best for you to stick much to the variations of the goose-step and not to bother too much about the science of ducking behind bushes.'[60] An equally blasé approach was to be adopted by O'Duffy's Blueshirts, which Blythe enthusiastically promoted two decades later.

In spring 1914, after a year in Kerry, Blythe returned for a few months to Ulster, under instructions from Seán McDermott to initiate an IRB anti-partition campaign on the Falls Road.[61] At an outdoor meeting in Albert Street on 12 May, the speeches did not directly challenge the authority of Redmond or Devlin, instead calling for a lobbying campaign within the Home Rule movement:

> Mr. Denis McCullough drew attention to Mr. Asquith's latest speech as showing a willingness on the part of the Government to respond to the Ulster 'bullying methods' by granting still further concessions; and Mr. Ernest Blythe declared that the Orangemen, if granted exclusion, would look upon it as a victory, while Mr. Heron urged the necessity for some definite action being taken by the Nationalist organisations to have pressure brought to bear upon their public representatives.[62]

Blythe was also active in organising local Volunteer companies, ranging from his home district to Castlewellan, County Down, and beyond.[63]

It was presumably during this visit that he addressed the Belfast Fianna at Mac Art's Fort on Cave Hill, where Wolfe Tone and his fellow 'Pikemen' had sworn in June 1795 'never to desist from their efforts until they had subverted the authority of England and asserted the independence of their country'.[64] Taking this declaration as his gospel, Blythe explained that 'the work of the sword is not to persuade our enemies or to profit ourselves but to kill as many of them as possible and terrorise the remainder'. Ascending a metaphorical pulpit, he pronounced that 'a time will come we are told when men shall beat their swords into ploughshares and not suffer for it but that time has not come'.[65] In keeping with his early distaste for the Invincibles' assassination campaign and in later years for the killing of policemen, Blythe advised against the 'slaughter of those who cannot put up a fight'. Addressing himself to 'idealists' and 'hot-headed young men', he concluded anti-climactically that 'there is at present going on in Ireland the drilling and training of men'. Though no specific reference was made in the text to either the Irish or Ulster Volunteers, this passage was perhaps so well rehearsed that it required no full transcription. Blythe's fiery rhetoric jarred somewhat with the childishly neat hand that had inscribed these phrases in a purple national-school notebook ('Sapphire' series), decorated with a doodled profile of 'A.E.B.' featuring a moustache and an impressively aquiline nose. This presumably represented his uncle Alfred, the Freemason and teacher in Tynan.

By summer 1914, strokes such as the 'Curragh mutiny' and the UVF gun-running had made it absurd to dismiss Ulster's resistance as mere bluff. In April, as an eye-witness of the current campaign, Blythe admitted that 'Ulster has done one thing which commands the respect and admiration of all genuine Nationalists – she has stood up for what she believes to be right. . . . Her attitude in this affair is that of the O'Neills and O'Donnells.' Though 'we are willing to fight Ulster, or to negotiate with her', another possibility was rapidly emerging: 'The day that the Union Jack . . . fires upon the most rampant Orangeman in Ireland, that day the Irish Volunteers should range themselves with Carson and not against him.' Should this eventuate, of course, Blythe's dual obligations to the IRB and the Orange Order would be neatly reconciled.

Having finally accepted that the Ulstermen meant business, Blythe argued that the only acceptable course for nationalists was to resist the imposition of partition, even if ostensibly 'temporary', by force if required:

> Six years of Home Rule with East Ulster out, would merely increase the alienation and apprehension of the bulk of Irish Protestants. I am of the flesh and bone of those who are objecting to Home Rule. There is no blood in my veins but the blood of the Planters. I know the prejudices and fears which cause the Orangeman to stand against the majority of his

fellow-countrymen . . . if there were partition at all it would be permanent partition.[66]

In his last signed contribution to *Irish Freedom* in May 1914, Blythe outlined a way out of this impasse. If only Home Rule could be applied to the entire island, much though he despised this nod towards autonomy, the Ulstermen might be won over: 'We who know the Ulster Orangeman and know the inside of his mind, are well aware that nothing will alter his opinion about Home Rule save actual experience of it.'[67]

In the same month, Blythe developed this theme for a wider public in letters to the press. Writing to the *Kilkenny People* from his family home, he called for 'a National Convention representing all the Nationalist opinion of Ireland' to determine the issue of exclusion, so anticipating the Belfast convention that narrowly endorsed Redmond's qualified acceptance of temporary exclusion in June 1916. Blythe warned southern nationalists against imagining that 'Orange Ulster' could be 'wooed and won' during six years of temporary exclusion, as proposed: 'We in Ulster are certain that there is not a chance of it.'[68] A few days later, he addressed the *Irish Independent* from Belfast, stating that any purportedly temporary exclusion of six counties from Home Rule would 'be looked upon as a Unionist triumph, and the triumph will almost certainly be celebrated by the rowdiest Orange element with an anti-Catholic outburst in the factories and workshops'. He deemed it advisable, if required, to use force of arms to introduce Orangemen to the benefits of inhabiting a republic:

> If we cannot have Home Rule for an undivided Ireland, it will be a hundred-fold better for us to turn from the Liberal door-step and see what efficacy may be found in the arms of the Irish Volunteers.

He reaffirmed that 'if the Orangeman were given actual personal experience of the rule of an Irish Government, I (who am of his race and creed) am well assured that he would soon become the proudest and most patriotic of Irish citizens'.[69]

CHAPTER FOUR

'Purple Star'

I

'**E**arnán de Blaghd' was but one of many personae adopted by Blythe during his sojourn in Ulster between 1909 and 1913. Blythe the republican ideologue became adept at composing fierce manifestos on manliness and martyrdom for *Irish Freedom*, and advocating 'the doctrine of the sword' among friends in various Belfast societies, all tiny and ineffectual. But Blythe the pragmatist soon noticed that political debate, especially in Ulster, was becoming more strongly polarised on sectarian lines, sidelining those with radical or unorthodox views. By 1911, Asquith's government seemed to have the political will as well as the parliamentary means to enact Home Rule, rendering republican and Sinn Féin quibbles superfluous. Unionist threats to resist Home Rule by active or passive resistance, initially viewed as bluster, became more menacing as all shades of Protestant opinion were drawn into the struggle. It followed that many republicans, as in Parnell's time, threw their diminished weight behind the Home Rule movement that they had so long ridiculed, in order to present a common front against the unionist monolith.

This realisation and logic, according to Blythe's recollections, was responsible for the eruption of 'Purple Star' in the columns of Captain W. H. Davey's *The Ulster Guardian: Organ of the Liberal Party in Ireland, Printed in Belfast by Trade Union Labour*.[1] This idiosyncratic Belfast weekly catered primarily for a well-heeled minority among northern Protestants, with limited coverage of either mainstream or radical nationalism. It had previously been edited by the maverick Robert Lindsay Crawford, first imperial grand master of the Independent Orange Institution.[2] The name 'Purple Star' sent various signals to Protestant readers, being an emblem of the armies of William of Orange and a popular title for Orange lodges.[3] This strongly suggested that the writer was a Protestant insider, if not a former Orangeman, with an intimate insight into the psychology of loyalism.

In retrospect, Blythe offered a tactical explanation for his pseudo-nymous emergence as a liberal spokesman:

> I noticed, as it became more likely that a Home Rule Bill would be implemented, that the feeling of being under threat was growing stronger among Protestants, and that people who had at first refused to be involved with unionist clubs were joining them. I felt, therefore, that I should make an effort, through the *Ulster Guardian*, to reinforce those liberals around Belfast so that they would not abandon liberalism when the Home Rule Bill was being put through. As such, I wrote articles and verses under the pen-name 'Purple Star' making fun of unionist club activities, as well as a continuous sequence of reasoned essays, where I set out arguments that occurred to me that would influence Protestants in favour of Home Rule.[4]

Davey accepted Blythe's views at face value, attesting in April 1913 that he was 'a widely read and cultured gentleman', possessing 'a clear and original mind' with 'a profound grasp of the history of his own country & of other lands'. Davey added that 'he is & has always been a consistent & staunch supporter of the national demands of Ireland both in regard to the recovery of self-government and the preservation of the native language'.[5] Blythe recalled that 'the reference which he wrote for me was sweet, flowery and flattering', but less likely to secure him future employment than a more pedestrian testimonial from Harry Gaw of the *North Down Herald*.[6]

An early unsigned article headed 'The Unionist Club Farce' unmistakably exhibited Blythe's talent as a satirist, giving pride of place to a heckler who had caused mayhem at Cliftonville by raising the delicate issue of physical force: 'I want to talk about this revolver question. Our minister next door tells us to "make our swords into ploughshares and our spears into reaping hooks." Now, to-night the policy is "sell your sash and buy your gun." I say this is a shame. It is disgraceful.'[7] Blythe already knew how to raise a chuckle at the expense of dim-witted unionists, even though his own preference within lodge 1501 might well have been to trade in his sash or collarette for a revolver.

Satire soon gave way to evangelism. In a series of ten weekly 'Letters to Young Liberals' published between August and October 1911, 22-year-old Purple Star assumed the part of a seasoned but indulgent teacher addressing a younger generation: 'They alone have the ardour to be willing to enter whole-heartedly into the approaching struggle', which would be 'prolonged and exciting'. Many of their elders were merely 'negative Liberals . . . who allowed themselves to be scared by the Home Rule bogey, but who retained sufficient commonsense or sense of humour to prevent them from falling into hysterical convulsions of the Orange Unionist type'.[8] Suggesting that the majority of his intended audience had not made up their minds on the issue of Home Rule, Purple Star assured them that 'Home Rule is coming' and that 'all the talk of fighting is puerile bluff, . . . though it may awaken a stronger spirit of violence and disorder amongst the hooligan partisans of Orangeism'. Since the outcome was inevitable, liberals should intervene to help determine 'the exact provisions of the Home Rule Bill', confident of being 'on the winning side'.[9]

In subsequent letters, Purple Star refuted various common objections to self-government. Far from being 'completely subservient to their priests in all things', Irish Catholics had often defied their pastors in politics, as shown by the past popularity of Fenianism and the IRB in the teeth of clerical condemnation. Young liberals, with their democratic and progressive instincts, 'must never allow the religious persecution bogey to pass unchallenged'.[10] As for the belief that Home Rule would prompt the disintegration of the Empire, Purple Star pronounced that the Empire could only prosper if it secured 'the good-will of all the peoples with whom it has to do'. Home Rule was not a doctrinaire demand for a particular constitutional settlement, but an expression of 'social need and national sentiment. Any measure, therefore, which enables the Irish people to work for social and economic progress and intellectual and political development will meet the demand'.[11]

There was admittedly a 'possibility, however remote, . . . that Irish Nationalism is irreconcilable' and 'that under Home Rule the hostility and desire for Separation will continue'. Adroitly distancing himself from the irreconcilables, he observed that 'the promise of Home Rule checked the progress of the Sinn Fein movement, which was as radically and professedly hostile to the Empire as any that has ever existed in Ireland'. Yet, if the separatist spirit should re-emerge, 'your duty, both as Liberals and Imperialists, is to support Home Rule, even though its effect may be that prognosticated by our Orange brethren'. Having momentarily allowed his republican inclinations to surface, he hastily retreated: 'I think, however, I have sufficiently indicated above the improbability of Irish Nationalism proving irreconcilable – there will be no trouble, because the Imperialism of the future will not be opposed to Nationality, but will be based upon it.'[12] Already in 1911, Blythe was rehearsing his future endorsement of practising independence as a dominion within an evolving British Commonwealth of Nations.

Blythe went on to deny the existence of any racial or temperamental division between Protestant and Catholic or between northern and southern communities:

> You need have no fear that in accepting Home Rule you are entering into partnership with people who are idle, lawless, un-thrifty, reactionary, generally worthless, and aliens to boot. Your Nationalist fellow-countrymen are very like yourselves, but with a somewhat different outlook arising from a different corporate experience. They will not plunge the country into anarchy.[13]

Warming to his Home Rule brief, Purple Star gave a penetrating analysis of 'Home Rule finance', denying the prospect of insolvency and assuring his 'young' readers that 'the acquirement of self-government will never mean the stoppage of the old-age pensions'.[14] He did not contemplate the possibility of having to reduce the pension, the most infamous element of his first budget after the civil war.

At this stage, both Blythe and his readers must have been growing weary after so many refutations and negations, the pedagogue having 'said enough to convince any person who will allow himself to be guided by reason that all the Unionist ideas of Home Rule are misconceptions'. Before passing on to 'the probable benefits of Home Rule', Purple Star paused for a brief pep-talk to young liberals, urging them to take a positive view of the future in order 'to retain the allegiance of your weaker, and in many cases elder, brethren'. Otherwise, 'they will tend to be swept away by the mere numbers and vehemence of their Orange neighbours', even though 'all Orange opinion depends solely on ignorance and prejudice'.[15]

The first 'positive' implication of Home Rule was that 'within a decade and with the general consent of all creeds and classes the powers of the Irish Parliament will be extended almost to equal those exercised by legislatures of the self-governing dominions', though 'the three Kingdoms shall continue to be a unit for military and naval purposes'. A 'native government' would work far more efficiently and sympathetically than the current administration: 'A despot, however enlightened, however just, cannot help his people as they can help themselves.'[16] Native efficiency would entail thrift: 'Members of the Legislature having no longer a patriotic duty to wring as much money as possible from an alien treasury would not continue to be indifferent to public extravagance.' Though taxes would 'likely' remain stable, government retrenchment would allow the amount saved to 'be applied to useful public purposes'. Control of customs and excise should be devolved, and Purple Star (anticipating the tentative approach of Cosgrave's ministers) believed 'that as a temporary stimulus in an industrially undeveloped country like Ireland a moderate degree of Protection would not only be unobjectionable, but actually desirable'. Yet even within the restrictions imposed by 'Gladstonian Home Rule her economic condition will vastly improve'.[17]

In his final letter, Purple Star predicted that the experience of Home Rule would engender a cultural revolution:

> Ideas will at last begin to be prized, and Ireland will no longer stand completely outside the movements of European thought. As ideas come into favour literature and art will receive encouragement and support. . . . In short, an adequate measure of Home Rule will restore to Ireland healthy national life.

Despite his eloquent advocacy of Home Rule, Blythe reverted to the more menacing tone of a potential separatist when contemplating the consequences of not granting self-government:

> Like almost every other Protestant Irishman who has examined his political conscience and has fearlessly scrapped any inherited opinions which he found to be baseless, I am anxious, firstly and almost exclusively, for the welfare of Ireland. I believe that intellectual and material prosperity are attainable only through national freedom, and if the British Empire finally decides that Irish national rights are not to be recognised, I for one, as a Democrat and a descendant of the Planters, shall repudiate all allegiance to it. Let it be remembered that Irish nationality only ceased to be insurrectionary and menacing to Great Britain with the dawn of a reasonable hope of Home Rule. No one who knew anything of the abortive Sinn Fein movement a few years ago can doubt that the national instinct is as vigorous as ever, or can believe that the Irish people are any less willing to suffer for their country than they were at other periods of its history.

Such expressions of sentimental separatism were commonplace in Home Rule rhetoric, which routinely aroused enthusiasm for 'constitutional' methods by celebrating past violence and irreconcilability. Blythe's peroration was worthy of a priest presiding over an assembly of young Hibernians:

> Therefore, my young Liberal friends, if you wish to live in a progressive, prosperous, and cultured community, if you wish to avoid a recrudescence of turmoil and rancour, you must give all your energy in the near future to securing the grant of Home Rule to Ireland.[18]

Blythe's column-consuming if unpaid letters inspired 'great respect' from the editor, Captain Davey,[19] eventually provoking some rejoinders in a paper chronically short of correspondents. 'A Protestant Home Ruler', who considered the letters to be 'representative of the opinions of a large and increasing number of Ulster Protestants', was surely prodded to write by Blythe. Apart from celebrating the non-sectarian work of the Gaelic League, the writer cagily inserted an advertisement for *Irish Freedom*: 'P.S. – As to the proposed Ulster Republic, I would like to refer our Orange friends to a Republican organ issued in Dublin every month (*Irish Freedom*); they may be able to get some hints for their fiery anti-English speeches.'[20] The first negative respondent, in fact a retired fireman in his seventies, wrote ostensibly on behalf of 'young men like myself, who are believers in the Liberal programme' yet against Home Rule. James Cummings believed that, under 'Rome Rule', 'the reform and progress will be on the side of the publican and the brewer, the Sabbath-breaker, and the drunkard'. He clearly suspected that Purple Star was no more a 'young liberal' than himself: '"Purple Star," keep it up, old man.'[21]

Purple Star returned the compliment under the headline 'A Queer "Young Liberal"': 'Mr. Cummings professes to be a young Liberal (though I should not have thought it myself).' His letter was 'in all respects typical of the products of the Ulster Tory mind', failing to acknowledge that liberalism implied 'a profound confidence in the good instincts of the people and a readiness to trust them. ... He who will not trust the people with the exercise of new rights and the discharge of new duties is no Liberal.'[22] This provoked the potentially damaging insinuation that 'to follow our friend "Purple Star" wheresoever he leadeth' would entail associating with some truly '"queer Liberals," Liberals, for example, who pose as Unionists when in reality they are Home Rulers'.[23] Though the jibe was scarcely merited on the basis of Blythe's contributions to the *Ulster Guardian*, Blythe took it as a personal slur 'that I am in the habit of posing as a Unionist, when I am in reality a Nationalist'. Doubtless conscious of its relevance to his articles in the unionist *North Down Herald*, he performed a neat logical slide: 'I should like to assure him that it is no part of Liberal policy to gain votes or support by false pretences.'[24]

Blythe having fallen into his trap, Cummings gleefully retorted that 'he jumps to the conclusion that I accuse him of double dealing. Anyone with a spark of humour in their veins will at once see the absurdity of such a thing, as I haven't even the honour of knowing the gentleman by name. Nevertheless if the shoe pinches I am not to blame.' He explained that his intended reference was to those posing as 'Independent Unionist' electoral candidates in 1906 and 1910, 'when in reality they were Home Rulers'.[25] Purple Star professed satisfaction that his adversary had repudiated his apparent insinuation 'that I was myself amongst the deceivers': 'It is a sign of grace, and there are other like signs in his latest epistle.' At this point, the debate had become too polite to merit further press coverage, apart from an emollient letter from 'Fabius' chiding Purple Star for understating church power, while urging Cummings that only political freedom would confer the 'sense of responsibility' required to rescue citizens from clericalism.[26]

Blythe's scuffle of words in the *Ulster Guardian* reflected the prevalence of mistrust and duplicity in pre-war Irish politics. Faced with an ever-hardening sectarian division over Home Rule, protagonists with various agendas used disguise and trickery to solicit defectors from the opposite camp, while vilifying opponents for likewise resorting to disguise and trickery. Successful enticement depended on convincing the intended victim that the seducer came from the same stock. Blythe, as Purple Star, gave authority to his advice to wavering Protestants by emphasising his own 'Planter' lineage and intimate knowledge of Protestant Ulster. His letters may have encouraged another correspondent, in July 1912, to call for an Ulster branch of the National League of Young Liberals to cater for 'enlightened young people, of both sexes' who were disposed to compare notes on 'the great problems which are so full of interest to all progressive minds'.[27] An exciting prospect, indeed!

Blythe's own republican experience in both Dublin and Belfast taught him that the typical trajectory towards Protestant nationalism began with interest in the Irish language and the Gaelic League. Despite his confessedly poor Irish, he contributed articles to the *Ulster Guardian* 'in favour of the Irish language' which, astonishingly, were read by Desmond and Mabel FitzGerald in France. FitzGerald later jested 'that whoever wrote them did not have much Irish'.[28] He was right: Purple Star's six lengthy homilies on 'The Irish Language Movement', published in April and May 1912, contained not a word in that tongue. The only linguistic points referred to word order, 'roughly the reverse of that which is adopted in English', and the alleged absence of any 'proper equivalents for the titles Mr. and Miss', a 'simple fact which gives its tone to the whole social life of the Gaelic League'.[29]

The purpose of the series, an 'expression of independent opinion' from which Davey gently dissociated himself, was to show why 'the Irish Liberal' should endorse the language revival (any 'Irish Nationalist' failing to do so was 'of a very contemptible type'). Blythe offered several arguments for 'retaining the smaller languages', claiming that linguistic inheritance was the defining discriminant between Irish and English culture, and that only through 'the revival of her native language' would Ireland 'get into the current of European thought' and so develop 'an intellectual life of her own'.[30] He inveighed against 'bi-lingualism' except as a 'transitional expedient', though he grudgingly conceded that it might be tolerated for one-quarter of the population, including 'the official and commercial classes' and 'the Protestants of East Ulster'. To those who feared that Irish monoglots would fare badly in the Empire, he objected that French Canadians and 'Dutch' South Africans enjoyed full rights: 'In the British Empire, there are many tongues and kindreds, and its strength arises largely from the fact that it does not strive to mould all its peoples to one pattern.' As in his 'Letters to Young Liberals', he professed to be positive about the Empire's pluralist future: 'every indication seems to show that the experiment will be successful and bring another stage nearer the Parliament of Man, the Federation of the World.'[31] Citing the linguistic genealogy of the 'Scotch Planters of Ulster', Blythe argued that 'at most, the Ulster Protestant is but a few generations further from Gaelic-speaking forefathers than is the Leinster Catholic'. Adopting the histrionic tone of a preacher who has managed to convince himself, if not the congregation, he pronounced that 'the racial excuse for contemning the Irish language is verily an exceedingly lame one'.[32]

Blythe's later articles were devoted to the organisation and ecumenical character of the Gaelic League, praised in startlingly modern terminology:

> The Gaelic League is non-political and non-sectarian. Its members include men of all creeds and of none. In its ranks are to be found exceptional Orangemen, broad-minded Unionists, Liberals of all shades, moderate Nationalists, and old Fenians.

Blythe himself had feared he 'might get the cold shoulder and be made uncomfortable' when he joined a beginners' class, only to find that three of the other half-dozen students were Protestants.[33] He believed that thousands of Ulster liberals 'would find it both possible and profitable to become members of the Gaelic League', so promoting 'the welfare of the community much more forcibly than could ever be done by tea-table or tram-car disputations, or even by quinquennial outbursts of electioneering activity'.[34]

Though Blythe showed some ingenuity in explaining why Ulster liberals should feel obliged to learn Irish, many of his arguments must have seemed immaterial to readers caught up in the potentially revolutionary crisis over Home Rule. The series was welcomed by 'Cu Uladh' (P. T. McGinley), in his regular column of 'Gaelic League Notes'. The Hound of Ulster described Purple Star as 'a new and powerful colleague . . . whose identity is unknown to me. It is interesting to know that his point of view is that of a Liberal Home Ruler' (rather than a nationalist like 'Cu Uladh').[35] Otherwise, the only correspondent to respond was 'Seaghan', who confirmed that the Gaelic League offered a warm welcome to Protestants like himself: 'if anything, Protestants receive more privileges and kindnesses than they are entitled to.' Like 'Cu Uladh', he purported to have been taken in by Purple Star's disguise: 'I am glad to see that the Irish renaissance is receiving support and appreciation from Belfast Liberals.'[36] It is quite credible that both responses were planted by Blythe to conceal his true identity.

II

Blythe's dalliance with liberalism, as with Orangeism, demands closer interpretation. Blythe later maintained that, in his 'Letters to Young Liberals', he adopted the posture of a Home Ruler in order to gain the confidence of uncommitted readers, in the hope of strengthening nationalism and depleting unionism. His primary motives were presumably to diffuse nationalist ideas among 'progressive' waverers, and to identify potential recruits for the IRB and its front organisations. Yet the conviction with which he expounded the benefits of Home Rule, and analysed the practicalities of administration, suggest that his advocacy in 1911 was more than a tactical posture. His 'Letters' strongly suggest that he had little hope of a separatist revival and regarded Home Rule as defining the future nationalist agenda.

Frustrated by Sinn Féin's collapse and painfully aware of the unpopularity of the IRB and its front organisations in Belfast, he began to explore alternatives:

> I went to Belfast to attend some meetings of the Liberal Association. These meetings drove home for me that it was hopeless to depend on the Belfast liberals to run or operate Home Rule. Most of them were middle-aged or very old indeed.[37]

Among the meetings that he attended was the 'huge liberal demonstration' to welcome Winston Churchill (then First Lord of the Admiralty) in Celtic Park on 8 February 1912. Blythe preserved his complimentary press ticket for the grandstand, normally costing half a crown, with directions for the penny journey by the Falls Road tram.[38] The *Ulster Guardian* reported that the crowd of 8,000 listened with 'rapt attention' to Churchill's 'magnificent speech' and supporting acts by Viscount Pirrie (as chairman) and Home Rule leaders such as Redmond and Devlin. 'Bar a few suffragette interruptions', the 'greatest harmony' prevailed.[39]

The *North Down Herald*'s report, presumably contributed by Blythe, was dismissive about the visit of this 'Radical politician, obeying the dictates of his party managers and their Nationalist taskmasters'. Gloating over the Ulster Liberal Association's failure to secure the Ulster Hall for the demonstration, the reporter professed to deplore the presence of only one Union flag and one naval ensign amidst 'the bunting and flags of all nationalities', noting that Churchill was greeted by 'The Wearing of the Green' rather than 'Rule Britannia' or the National Anthem. Most of the crowd were accommodated in a 'huge tent imported from Scotland' and erected near the grandstand, the intervening space being 'taken up by a small army of Press men and photographers' less privileged than Blythe. The crowd, though mainly 'out-and-out Nationalists' (at least in 'the unreserved area'), included 'many hundred Unionists drawn to the scene out of curiosity and a desire to hear a speech from a Cabinet minister'.[40] He was most cutting about the party that had organised the meeting: 'There were, no doubt, many Ulster Liberals, whether convinced Home Rulers or not is another matter.' Blythe himself could have qualified under all three descriptions.

Fed up with the continuing absence of young Ulster liberals, despite his eloquent appeals, he continued to reject the Devlinite option and flirted with socialism, to which he had been attracted through reading Alfred Richard Orage's *New Age*. His experience of a Belfast Socialist Party meeting was dispiriting:

> The meeting was very small, and it was not questions on politics or the economy that were being discussed, but a lecture on the poet Burns. Though I had always thoroughly enjoyed Burns's work, the meeting did not increase my respect for the Belfast Socialists as a revolutionary or reforming force.

By his own later account, his brief sally into socialism was a last resort:

> There was one other thing that may have been partly to blame for my going there. That was the decline of Sinn Féin and the success of the MPs. Much as I wished for us to get Home Rule, I was unable to join with the UIL [United Irish League] and it was not worth my while dealing with the liberals.[41]

By summer 1912, Blythe's political trajectory was shifting. Purple Star became an infrequent contributor to the *Ulster Guardian*. His last detected contribution was a letter published in February 1913 on 'The Railway Nationalisation Folly', an innocuous polemic against public investment in an obsolescent industry that would soon be supplanted by 'motor cars and char-a-bancs for travelling and motor lorries for transport', served by 'special motor roads'.[42] As his interest in liberalism and socialism faded, he reverted to trying to revive republicanism, especially through the formation of the Belfast Freedom Club in June 1912 and through his contributions to *Irish Freedom*. During his last months in Newtownards, he became more outspoken 'about Home Rule and about political matters in general', despite the risk that 'people would turn against me'. Yet 'my talk had no effect: people's minds were hardening'. Even as he loosened his Ulster unionist mask, Blythe's animosity towards southern Protestants intensified. He blamed their hypocritical attacks on Catholics, with whom they had long coexisted in relative harmony, for deluding and inflaming northern unionists who lacked practical experience of living and working with their Catholic neighbours. He began to succumb to fatalism:

> Towards the end of my four years in Newtownards, even though I was busier writing and arguing about politics than I had been previously, . . . I felt as if the die had been cast and that what would happen would happen regardless of what I did. Therefore, from a political point of view, I was not reluctant to move out of Newtownards when the opportunity arose.[43]

Yet the potentially revolutionary and fraternal elements in unionism continued to fascinate Blythe, and he clearly found it less alien than Hibernianism, despite the sectarian mentality of both movements. And, so long as he remained on the payroll of the *North Down Herald*, he maintained his public persona as a conventional unionist, even if his reports were increasingly modulated by irony. Let us look more closely at his performance as a unionist and an Orangeman, disguises which became increasingly difficult to reconcile with his professed republicanism.

CHAPTER FIVE

'Reporter, Junior (Protestant)'

I

W hile Blythe the republican busied himself with sending fiery articles to Dublin and organising tiny groups of zealots and fellow-travellers in Belfast, and while Blythe the Home Ruler struggled to energise those elusive young liberals, Blythe the cub reporter was mastering his trade in Bangor and Newtownards. Though strongly unionist in editorial policy and tone, the local newspapers occasionally reported meetings and entertainments associated with Catholic parishes, periodically commending the few Catholics in public life for their impeccable conduct, and their Protestant colleagues for treating them with all due respect. Since less than one-tenth of either town's population were Catholics, they were largely exempt from the fear and distrust that fanned sectarian hostility in Belfast.[1]

Many of Blythe's closest companions were fellow journalists on the *Newtownards Chronicle* and *Newtownards Spectator*, as well as the *North Down Herald*.[2] Their names figure prominently in his autobiography: Bob Montgomery, Harry Gaw, and George Craig of the *Herald*, the three Henry brothers who owned and edited the *Chronicle*, and David Alexander of the *Spectator*.[3] Almost all were Freemasons, belonging to Friendship lodge 447 in Newtownards or Union lodge 746 in Bangor.[4] All were signatories of the Ulster Covenant except Craig, who had left for Scotland to edit the *Buteman*. Craig was also the only non-Presbyterian and non-Freemason among them. In Blythe's time, however, the only prominent Orangeman in the 'chapter' was Captain James Henry, for whom the Orange Institution embodied 'Protestantism in the best sense of the term' and offered the best defence against 'the subtle aggressiveness of Romanism'.[5]

Yet not all was as it seemed in north Down journalism. Bob Montgomery, the *Herald*'s proprietor, had no compunction in sacrificing political consistency for sales, as Blythe recalled when writing to the Labour politician Thomas Johnson in 1949:

> When I went there [Bangor] the proprietor was trying to work up a circulation in Belfast City for the paper, as a sort of Sloanite semi-official organ. He sent a reporter regularly to Sloan's public meetings and committee meetings and printed the reports in a special Belfast edition, while he kept the Bangor edition on strictly conventional Unionist lines. Of course Bangor readers occasionally bought copies in Belfast and compared them with the paper as sold in Bangor. The proprietor gradually found out that he was falling between two stools and shortly after I joined the staff he decided to drop the Sloanite stunt.[6]

Alas, it is no longer possible to consult and compare the two editions.[7] But Montgomery's dalliance with Thomas Henry Sloan's Independent Loyal Orange Institution should have provided Blythe with a useful lesson. It was no easy matter for a journalist to pursue a double political life as if Belfast and north Down were in separate countries.

Blythe had secured his job by responding to an advertisement under 'Situations Vacant' in the *Irish Times*, having failed to interest the editors of southern nationalist newspapers. This advertisement was remarkably precise in its requirements:

> REPORTER, Junior (Protestant), for Provincial Weekly; good shorthand writer and paragraphist; cyclist; state salary. Apply "North Down Herald," Bangor, Down.[8]

Blythe seems to have had no relatives or acquaintances in Bangor when he took up lodgings on 22 March 1909, only twelve days after publication of the advertisement. But he came equipped with a new bicycle, essential for both work and play, which his father had bought him in Lisburn that morning.[9] He lived in a boarding house in Abbey Street, kept by a Presbyterian widow. Another of her boarders was a cub reporter for the *Spectator* named David Boyd, one of Blythe's comrades in the Belfast IRB.[10] According to Blythe, 'Davy was a young lad from County Tyrone' who had been converted to Sinn

Féin by Seán Lester.[11] By going home at weekends, Blythe was able to save a florin out of the weekly rent of fourteen shillings, releasing valuable spending money. Indeed, once he had attained his peak weekly salary of £1 2s. 6d., he was seldom short of cash: 'As I did not spend a penny on drink or tobacco, I had an abundance of money to buy books or periodicals, to visit the theatre in Belfast, and to pay for small political subscriptions.'[12]

Some of Blythe's newspaper colleagues soon became friends, helping him to negotiate the invisible social barriers that confront every newcomer to an Ulster town. In *Trasna na Bóinne*, he portrays the *Herald*'s proprietor Montgomery as a niggardly employer, who was only induced to pay him an adequate salary after Blythe received a better offer from Alexander of the *Spectator*. Alexander, a 'genial and kind-hearted Scot' who had previously edited the *Herald*, had introduced linotype to Bangor when establishing the *Spectator* in 1904, placing his machine and its operator in a window for public exhibition.[13] Craig of the *Herald* was a demanding but conscientious editor, whose practical advice helped Blythe to master the essentials of old-fashioned journalism (accurate shorthand, facility in gathering exact personal details, rapid composition).[14] In his first week, Blythe's versatility was put to the test. He recalled writing a laboured 500-word piece on the beauties of Craigavad and a concert review (having 'no understanding of music'), but neither seems to have survived the cutting room.[15]

Even more useful as mentors were Harry Gaw, the *Spectator*'s reporter in Newtownards until he succeeded Craig as editor of the *Herald*, and Bob Henry of the *Chronicle*. Blythe was fascinated by Bob Henry's exotic appearance: a small man with a large belly ensconced in a silk belt in place of braces, 'a gold ring on his little finger and a flower in the breast of his jacket'. Blythe cheerfully observed that 'he would have had the appearance of a Jew were it not for his colour. His hair and moustache were blond, and he had blue eyes.'[16] Instead of being cut-throat competitors, they pooled resources when reporting court cases, and found common cause when treated with condescension by colleagues in Belfast. A test of journalistic solidarity arose when Belfast reporters were prevented from attending a meeting in Newtownards of the North Down Unionist Association, which had offended local proprietors by failing to advertise the meeting in their papers. Henry, Gaw, and Blythe refused to take notes, despite the secretary's attempt to win over Henry as a fellow Mason and Orangeman, and then to shame the others into rebelling against acting as Henry's 'lapdogs'. The outcome of the boycott was that 'the Unionist Association never failed to give the local newspapers notice after that'.[17]

Though the work of a provincial reporter could be tedious, it also provided diversion. Gaw and Blythe took particular delight in humiliating a pompous Bangor auctioneer who complained that they were failing to report his interminable and 'nonsensical' speeches to local boards. They responded by publishing a verbatim report of his next speech, having compared each other's shorthand notes:

> He rarely finished properly half of the sentences that he started. He was discussing figures, and it was clear that he had not added them correctly. His main argument was stupid and he made many grammatical mistakes. We heard that the conceited auctioneer was widely made fun of all over the town because of the stupidity of the speech.

As with the North Down Unionist Association, the effect of collective defiance was to humble the antagonist. The unnamed auctioneer (in fact Henry Montgomery) 'asked, as a favour from us, to correct his speeches as well before we published them'.[18] Blythe was beginning to master two important revolutionary skills: how to hunt in a pack, and how to achieve ascendancy through using one's wits.

Fraternisation among hacks even extended to Strangford Lough: Spencer Henry, secretary of the Newtownards Swimming Club, was doubtless responsible for Blythe's election to its committee.[19] This appointment may have reflected Blythe's political rather than sporting prowess: during summer in Bangor, he 'had time to bathe in the pool – I still could not swim – and I had time to sunbathe'.[20] A less predictable friendship developed with a Belgian Jew brought over from Scotland for a year as the *Spectator*'s reporter in Newtownards. In later life, Blythe would counter anti-semitic generalisations by stating 'that the only Jew whom I knew well was a fascinating, honourable and kind man'. Though 'proud of his race' and an abstainer from bacon for sanitary reasons, 'he did not subscribe at all to the teaching of the rabbis' or perform devotional duties.[21] Jacques Jellen's unique definition of his 'religious profession' for the census confirms Blythe's account: 'No particular denomination, but no atheist'.[22]

Blythe made few friends outside journalism during his year and a half spent cycling around the county to cover local meetings or checking proofs in the *Herald*'s Bangor office. Yet he quickly grew familiar with the social fabric of north Down through attending court sessions, meetings of local authorities, and religious services associated with the installation of a new minister or with the Orange and Masonic orders.[23] His work required daily briefings at the RIC barracks as well as frequent chats during court hearings, but in retrospect Blythe expressed embarrassment at having had to speak 'pleasantly and in a friendly way and even flatteringly with whichever constable was on duty in the day room'. Though primly claiming to have had 'enmity for them within the heart', he made a point of parading selected aspects of his background:

> I gave them, as a mental cover, far more information about myself than I would have given, had I been attempting to make friends with them. I told them where I was from and where I had been working previously, where I learned shorthand and the like. I made no mention of the Gaelic League, or of Sinn Féin.[24]

This account suggests how craftily strategic Blythe had already become in dealing with new acquaintances, a skill essential to anyone aspiring to a double life. Yet his assertion of underlying 'enmity' suggests an unconvincing attempt to deflect justified suspicions of duplicity.

Newtownards proved far more exhilarating than Bangor, supplying him with 'an abundance of local friends'.[25] His closest comrade there was Willie Doggart, a 'clerk and office-boy' at the *Chronicle* office, with whose family Blythe lodged throughout his two and a half years in Newtownards. Blythe's appreciative depiction of the Doggarts in

Trasna na Bóinne highlights the versatility required for survival in a country town dogged by endemic infectious disease and fluctuating trade. Willie's parents James Neill and Maggie, aged sixty and fifty-five in 1911, had not prospered: his father could not make an adequate living as a house painter, and ill-health had caused his mother to retire from teaching at the local 'non-sectarian' primary school. Five of her eleven children were dead, and the other six were all living at home in East Street, ranging from Jemima, a grocer's assistant aged thirty-two, to Ernest's favourite, Mabel, who at twelve was still a 'scholar'. Isabella and Fenella were both in their twenties with no occupation beyond helping out in the house and grocery shop, and Maurice, aged fourteen, was a railway clerk.[26] James Doggart supplemented his meagre income as a painter and shopkeeper by conducting the choir of the Second Presbyterian church (one 'interesting service of song' was mournfully entitled 'The Shadow of a Life').[27] But Jemima's failed attempt to set up her own shop had put the family in debt, prompting them to take Blythe as a lodger. The house was large enough to provide him with the use of an upstairs sitting room as well as a bedroom without extra charge, a saving in which the thrifty Blythe exulted.[28]

The Doggarts were teetotal Presbyterians much involved in youth movements and moral regeneration, though not conspicuously associated with Orangeism. Willie Doggart's presence on the platform on 12 July 1911 strongly suggests that he was an Orangeman, but his lodge has not been identified.[29] He became a Freemason only in 1921, after demobilisation, when he joined the newly formed Press lodge 432 in Belfast along with Bob Henry and most of Ulster's leading newspapermen.[30] It was James Jamieson, Blythe's other close friend in Newtownards, who brought him in contact with the town's interlocked fraternal networks. 'Jamesie' was a Scottish-born Presbyterian aged thirty-three in 1911, who had married a Newtownards woman and moved there after the birth of their first child.[31] Though a slater by training, he moved up in the world in Newtownards. In addition to conducting an embroidery agency (acquired from his mother-in-law), he spent three evenings a week manning the Free Public Library in the town hall.[32] Blythe offered an enigmatic account of his friend's outlook: a Freemason who was in some sense 'a radical' and 'nearly a republican', a supporter of 'Home Rule' who was uninterested in Irish nationalism.[33] He failed to add that Jamieson was also an Orangeman. His friendship with Jamieson encouraged Blythe to nurture his love of drama in two settings: the Newtownards Amateur Dramatic Society, and 'Volunteers' lodge 1501.

II

As a journalist, Blythe had ample opportunity to immerse himself in the political, social, and cultural life of north Down, however deficient it might seem by comparison with Dublin or Belfast. In Bangor, he joined the Literary and Debating Society, spoke in a few of its discussions, and was intrigued by a debunking lecture on spiritualism by 'Conall Cearnach', alias the Revd F. W. O'Connell. Few clergy of the Church of Ireland could match O'Connell's spiritual and professional versatility: product of a 'souper' family in Connemara, curate of St George's Church of Ireland in Belfast, lecturer in Gaelic Language and Literature at Queen's University, contributor to the nationalist *Irish News*, assistant director of the Dublin broadcasting station, and Catholic convert in late life.[34]

Blythe also developed a quizzical interest in suffragettes, attending lectures in Bangor by the Australian Muriel Matters[35] and Charlotte Despard (an incessant embarrassment to her brother Sir John French, future Chief of the Imperial General Staff).[36] Both speakers had recently addressed a rowdy demonstration in Trafalgar Square organised by the Women's Freedom League.[37] Having 'taken a liking to Muriel's talk', though rejecting her contention 'that women would be better and more intelligent voters than men', Blythe was 'delighted' to be sent to the house of a Bangor solicitor (George McCracken) to report the views of Mrs Despard. On finding himself alone among one hundred women in a crowded room, Blythe closed his notebook and fled, only returning when Mrs McCracken agreed to summon her husband to act as his chaperon. He 'enjoyed Mrs Despard's speech immensely. There was humour and sense in it, unlike the talk of some of the fanatics who were seeking rights for women at the time.'[38]

Blythe's uneasy fascination with suffragism continued after his move to Newtownards in September 1910. In January 1911, he reported his own contribution to a debate on women's suffrage organised by the First Presbyterian Church Guild and chaired by William Wright. Though an Episcopalian, Blythe could easily have passed as a Presbyterian and was often so identified in later life and after death. Blythe moved 'that we do not support the Representation of People Act [*recte*, Bill], 1910' under which it was proposed to enable female electors for local councils to vote in parliamentary elections, so enfranchising a million women.[39] Blythe's characteristically masculinist proposal was supported by the teacher and future Masonic historian David Orr,[40] but countered through an amendment by the formidable Dr Harriet Neill from Bangor, flanked by several members of the Irish Women's Suffrage League. As Blythe ruefully acknowledged: 'After a prolonged and interesting debate in which it was seen that Dr Neill's forcible arguments in favour of the enfranchisement of women had the sympathy of the majority of the audience, the question was put to a vote and Dr Neill's amendment carried by about 3 votes to 2.'[41] This outcome may have been influenced by the fact that the Revd William Wright was himself something of a suffragist, who in his zeal to solicit female support for the struggle against Home Rule told a heckler at the next Twelfth demonstration that 'Yes, they would give them the vote if they wanted it'.[42]

In his early columns as 'The Old Town Clock', Blythe expressed frustration at the lack of cultural amenities in Newtownards by comparison with Bangor. Whereas Bangor had 'fine reading and recreation rooms', essential for counteracting the appeal of 'liquor-drinking and the tavern', the Newtownards Reading Room was 'a dark, dirty, malodorous hole . . . littered with a confused mass of disintegrated newspapers'. Not yet reconciled to gambling, he deplored the absence of censorship: 'The evening papers are taken in without having the betting news blocked out, as is customary, and an undesirable type of reader encouraged.'[43]

The First Presbyterian Church Guild was one of the few local institutions able 'to give the people intellectual interests', a function performed 'in the South of Ireland [by] the Gaelic League, whatever may be said of its main object'. He lavished praise on the Guild that had brought suffragism into Newtownards:

> Besides its social value, it has a distinct educational utility. Its lectures and debates awaken the interest of members on many questions to which they would otherwise be oblivious . . . Such societies, no matter where they exist, are a public benefit, but it is in the country districts that the need for them is greatest. . . . If the minds of the people were stirred the multitude of things would acquire new interest, social life would become more zestful, and the country would lose its dulness [*sic*].[44]

A year later, 'Purple Star' would make a similar appeal for restoration of a 'healthy national life' through Home Rule, reinforcing the assumption that 'The Old Town Clock' was indeed Ernest Blythe.[45]

The tone of Blythe's analysis is also reminiscent of J. M. Synge's concluding prescription of 'Possible Remedies' for distress in Connaught, explored in a celebrated series of articles for the *Manchester Guardian* in 1905.[46] Yet Blythe, intent on avoiding any taint of nationalism in his work for the *Herald*, was distinctly less radical than Synge, for whom Home Rule was a more promising agency for social reform than Presbyterian guilds:

> One feels that the only real remedy for emigration is the restoration of some national life to the people. . . . If Home Rule would not of itself make a national life it would do more to make such a life possible than half a million creameries. With renewed life in the country many changes of the methods of government and the holding of property would inevitably take place, which would all tend to make life less difficult even in bad years.[47]

Blythe was more interested than Synge in practical economic initiatives and social reforms. In November 1910, 'The Old Town Clock' welcomed the establishment of 'several new factories' in Newtownards, marking it out as 'progressive' by comparison with the stagnation of 'too many of our smaller Irish towns'. He was particularly excited by the heavily capitalised Ulster Print Works Co., which would 'undoubtedly be a source of great benefit to the town, and we hope will bring worthy dividends to the shareholders'. The former boy clerk in the Department of Agriculture welcomed a forthcoming flax show in Newtownards, signifying 'the strenuous efforts being made to revive this historic Ulster industry'. He relished this official attempt to modernise agriculture: 'Expert itinerant instructors are employed to teach the farmers the best methods of culture; and experiments are continually being carried out in manuring, steeping, and scutching.'[48]

Blythe's authoritarian instincts were apparent in his comments on the Poor Law, reflecting 'an ever-depending conviction that the present method of dealing with destitution in these islands[49] is radically wrong and utterly unsuitable to present day conditions'. 'Various Continental countries' such as Switzerland practised a more equitable and efficient system than voluntary incarceration in workhouses:

> Labour colonies are established in suitable districts, and to one of them every able-bodied person who becomes unable to support himself is despatched. In the colony he is well looked after, and fully occupied with some kind of productive labour. He is detained for some months until he has acquired in some measure habits of industry.

After discharge with a small allowance, the pauper was allowed a few opportunities to secure regular employment; but if 'he comes back repeatedly he is treated as a criminal and undergoes a term of punitive imprisonment'. The future minister for finance noted that labour colonies 'would be cheaper than the present plan of entertaining the tramp fraternity'; the future fascist relished the prospect of 'suppressing the unemployable'.[50] Synge, famously besotted by the 'tramp fraternity', would have been appalled.

Blythe's social and economic commentaries exhibit his wide-ranging curiosity, analytical skill, and authoritative manner, striking achievements for a 21-year-old writing in a provincial paper for an audience accustomed to an easily digestible mixed diet of local news, reassuringly familiar unionist oratory, comical anecdotes in English or Ulster-Scots dialect, and syndicated snippets from the wider world. Blythe's column also reflected growing mastery of local alignments, tensions, and social nuances. Yet his work as a provincial reporter offers little insight into his political preoccupations, whether as a republican, a liberal, or an Orangeman. Of all these personae, the most closely veiled was Brother Ernest Blythe of the Newtownards 'Volunteers'.

CHAPTER SIX

'Humble Orange Brother'

I

E rnest Blythe, as already revealed, was admitted to Volunteers lodge 1501 in Newtownards on 14 September 1910, remaining an Orangeman for seventeen months until his resignation on 14 February 1912. Though the *North Down Herald* seldom reported ordinary lodge meetings, the occasion of his initiation was marked by a substantial if profoundly unrevealing account of the meeting, at which all lodge officers were re-elected. The five initiates were not named, but the four who survived scrutiny may be identified from the minutes of the next meeting of the district lodge. Blythe's fellow recruits were James Boyce (aged eighteen), son of a cotton weaver; Robert McCullough (twenty-two), a hosiery knitter whose father was a general labourer; and Thomas Stevenson (eighteen), a grocer's assistant. All except Blythe were to sign the Ulster Covenant two years later, but none became a Freemason.[1]

How important and effective was Orangeism in pre-war Newtownards? The town was overwhelmingly Protestant (only 9 per cent of the parish population were Catholics, three-fifths of the remainder being Presbyterians). This imbalance made it pointless to engage in active discrimination or offensive rhetoric against a placid minority without a single Hibernian division. In the absence of a strong and vocal nationalist opposition, compounded by local indifference to dissident Protestant alternatives such as the Independent Loyal Orange Institution, unionist organisers usually found it difficult to mobilise support. By comparison with the Orange heartland in mid-Ulster, Newtownards was not a strongly Orange town. Out of a population of almost 10,000 in 1911, less than 400 men belonged to the thirteen lodges within district no. 4, which had been restricted to the town since 1880.[2] The annual returns of district membership reveal fairly minor fluctuations from 1884 up to 1916, ranging from

265 in 1890 to 480 in 1884 and 450 in 1914 (Table 6.1). As elsewhere in Ulster, membership soared after both great wars, reaching 904 in 1921 and 667 in 1949. By 2001, the district's ageing membership had subsided to 366, four short of the number when Blythe became an Orangeman in 1910.[3]

Table 6.1. Membership of Orange Lodges in Newtownards, 1884–1927[4]

Year	Dist	1501	Year	Dist	1501	Year	Dist	1501	Year	Dist	1501
1884	480	16	1895	407	16	1906	311	26	1917	530	32
1885	402	17	1896	421	24	1907	420	27	1918	639	38
1886	412	26	1897	346	23	1908	344	21	1919	805	37
1887	313	27	1898	364	23	1909	352	31	1920	877	41
1888	358	26	1899	368	29	1910	370	30	1921	904	49
1889	329	26	1900	397	30	1911	358	23	1922	780	40
1890	265	18	1901	362	30	1912	359	28	1923	723	40
1891	309	16	1902	348	31	1913	435	26	1924	645	38
1892	276	15	1903	359	36	1914	450	34	1925	616	35
1893	369	20	1904	297	35	1915	401	32	1926	572	38
1894	412	22	1905	302	36	1916	423	30	1927	471	22

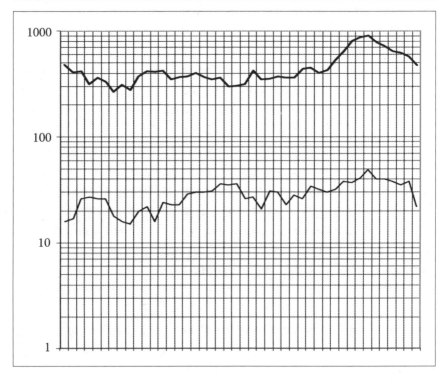

Blythe's own lodge had struggled to survive up to the mid-1880s, with several years in which no lodge return was submitted.[5] Its membership remained quite small up to 1917, varying between fifteen in 1892 and thirty-six in 1905. As the logarithmic graph demonstrates, the membership curve for lodge 1501 roughly paralleled that for the district, especially after 1909. Like the district in general, lodge 1501 would expand sharply as ex-servicemen returned to Newtownards in search of work and social contacts, rising to thirty-eight in 1918 and forty-nine in 1921 before dwindling to twenty-two in 1927. The true working membership was probably even smaller, as only sporadic attempts were made to discipline defaulters and absentees. Purges of lodge 1501 were carried out in 1904, 1909, and 1924, when long-term suspensions were applied to twenty-two miscreants in all, only one of whom (a clergyman) was eventually readmitted.[6]

Despite its small size, the lodge was pre-eminent in Newtownards Orangeism and a major force in local politics. In the year of Blythe's initiation, every district officer except the treasurer belonged to lodge 1501. Its most notable figure was the district master, Thomas Robert Lavery of Lakeview, who had served as a local magistrate ever since opening his first hem-stitching business in 1889. Lavery, a married but childless native of Armagh aged fifty-six in 1911, was ubiquitous in the town's tangled fraternal networks, including the Royal Black Institution, Apprentice Boys of Derry, and Baden-Powell's Boy Scouts.[7] Lavery had first been installed as master of lodge 1501 in 1883, finally surrendering the office in 1901 to James Mawhinney, a draper in Frances Street. Apart from the period from 1899 to 1906, he also presided over the district from 1894 to his death in 1940, his portrait having been prematurely unveiled in the Newtownards Orange hall three years earlier. In advanced age he served in the House of Commons and Senate of Northern Ireland, yet his most glorious achievement was doubtless to become vice-president of the 'Imperial Grand Orange Council of the World' in 1923 (unlike most holders of that honorific, he never made it to the top).[8] By 1911, Lavery was already a seasoned local politician and administrator, as chairman of the Board of Guardians and Urban District Council, member of the Technical Instruction Committee, School Board, and

Joint Hospital Board, and treasurer of the 'Sick Nursing Association (Non-Sectarian)'. Few political or social initiatives in unionist Newtownards were attempted without Lavery's blessing. He was even called upon to address a meeting to organise a branch of the North Down Women's Unionist Association in January 1912, though it was Mrs Lavery who became the first branch treasurer.[9] Blythe admired his style as chairman of the Guardians: 'Mr. Lavery is by habit and temperament a suave and courteous gentleman.'[10]

Lavery's deputy in the district was the draper James Mawhinney, whose business rival James Wright (master of lodge 1501 in 1910 and 1911) was district secretary. Wright's successor as lodge master, a barely literate 'grocerrer' in Little Frances Street named James Jamison, was on the district committee. The district chaplain was William Wright, minister of the Second Presbyterian church and a firebrand unionist orator playfully known as the 'Bishop of Newtownards', who joined lodge 1501 in October 1898.[11] According to Blythe, Wright had 'started his clerical life as a liberal' before becoming 'a normal unionist' and eventually 'the main unionist of the area'.[12] In 1886, he had denounced Home Rule before the Ulster Convention in Belfast and the Liberal Unionist Association, heralding his eventual passage to the standing committee of the Ulster Unionist Council (UCC). Wright was also a prominent Freemason and Blackman, belonging to Friendship Masonic lodge 447 and William Johnston Memorial RBP 307 (one of only two Royal Black Preceptories in Newtownards, where the rival Knights of Malta still held sway).[13]

Wright's assistant and later colleague as district chaplain was the ferocious English-born rector of Newtownards, William Twist-Whatham.[14] Though suspended from lodge membership in September 1924, the rector had the rare distinction of being readmitted to the Order in May 1928. He lacked finesse, as indicated by his botched attempt as workhouse chaplain to reclassify 'Protestants' and 'Episcopalians' entering the workhouse as 'Church of Ireland', in which Lavery had supported him. According to Blythe's tongue-in-cheek report on the acrimonious debate that ensued: 'As the chairman hinted if Rev. Mr. Whatham had made his request a little more tactfully, it is probable that the proposal . . . would have been carried.'[15] A few months earlier, the rector had displayed his abrasiveness in the inflammatory sermons that so affronted Elizabeth Bloxham.

Even without access to minute books for lodge 1501, which surrendered its warrant in 2015, we may identify ninety brethren who were admitted to the lodge or held offices between 1884 and 1918.[16] These included Thomas Corbett and William Mitchell-Thomson, who successively represented North Down in the House of Commons from 1900 to 1918.[17] Corbett had belatedly joined the lodge in October 1898, on the same night as Wright and Twist-Whatham.[18] A few weeks earlier, he had narrowly failed to defeat his landlord rival (John Blakiston-Houston) in a by-election for North Down. Corbett, a Clapham builder and London county councillor of Scottish birth, finally secured the seat two years later at the expense of another prominent unionist landlord (Robert Gordon Sharman-Crawford). He was supported by the Presbyterian Unionist Voters' Association, having 'deliberately sought the Orange and labouring vote' while making a virtue of his lack of landlord supporters.[19] District no. 4 had endorsed 'Brother Corbett' in 'his righteous efforts to put down the tyrannical clique which had been preventing the working men of North Down from having a voice in the selection of a candidate'.[20] Mitchell-Thomson, another peripatetic Scot with West Indian business interests who briefly became one of Ulster's local heroes, was admitted to the lodge in May 1910, immediately after his unopposed election for North Down following Corbett's death. He held important economic posts during and immediately after the Great War, subsequently becoming postmaster-general before elevation to the peerage.[21]

In addition to these notables, several members of lodge 1501 became local politicians, including two who joined Lavery on the Urban District Council. William James Ferguson, a handkerchief manufacturer like Lavery, headed the poll for Scrabo Ward in the 1911 election.[22] Another councillor in Blythe's time was Thomas Maddock, a mechanical engineer with no less than six sons who followed him into the same lodge. Ferguson spent seven years as lodge treasurer, while Maddock became worshipful master of RBP 307 as well as treasurer and master of lodge 1501. Entry to the lodge therefore promised easy access to some of the key figures in Down unionism, at both municipal and county level.

Equally important for a newly arrived journalist was familiarity with a broad social spectrum, providing rich source material for 'The Old Town Clock', the *Herald*'s column of Newtownards news and gossip.[23] Table 6.2 shows the occupation, age on admission, and religious denomination of most of Blythe's fellow recruits between 1898 and 1912.[24]

Of all ninety known members of lodge 1501, it has proved possible to match sixty-seven brethren with census returns for 1901 or 1911.[25] The resultant profile confirms the diversity of brethren in Blythe's lodge. Three-fifths were Presbyterians and one-third were Episcopalians such as Blythe, along with three Unitarians and a single Wesleyan Methodist. Over four-fifths were natives of County Down, with only four from other Irish counties (including Blythe, from Antrim), four from England, and three from Scotland. In fifty-seven cases, we may calculate age at admission from census returns and dates of confirmation. The median age at admission was twenty-five (four years older than Blythe), and three-quarters were under thirty when they joined the lodge.

Occupational details are available for sixty-four brethren, excluding four 'scholars' too young to be at work in 1911. The lodge elite comprised three with official positions (the two MPs and an army sergeant), seven professionals (three clergymen, a pharmacist, a solicitor, a mechanical engineer, and the journalist Blythe), and at least three in management (a laundry proprietor, a mill manager, and Lavery the factory owner). Nine members had 'white-collar' jobs as clerks, agents, or commercial travellers, while ten were merchants, wholesalers, or shopkeepers. The largest category included twenty-two skilled workers and tradesmen, ranging from seven textile operatives to an English-born 'steeple-climber' or 'steeple-jack'. By contrast, there were only eight unskilled workers (four labourers, an agricultural labourer, a carter, a paper-carrier, and a bread-server). Though an urban lodge, 1501 included two farmers. Several other members came from a farming background, which accounted for about one-quarter of identified fathers of brethren (including James Blythe).[26]

Table 6.2. Admissions to Lodge 1501, 1898–1912

Name	Occupation	Age	Religion
Frederick John Bloor (1898)	steeple-climber	37	Episcopalian
Thomas Lorimer Corbett (1898)	magistrate, later MP	53	unknown
William Laurence Twist-Whatham (1898)	clergyman	32	Episcopalian
William Wright (1898)	clergyman	42	Presbyterian
Joseph Robson (1901)	blacksmith	18	Presbyterian
John Robb (1903)	general labourer	21	Episcopalian
Isaac Arnold (1903)	bricklayer	29	Presbyterian
Joseph Palmer (1904)	labourer	21	Episcopalian
John Long (1904)	army colour sergeant	35	Presbyterian
Samuel H. Black (1905)	hardware merchant	32	Presbyterian
Collins Alexander Cooke (1906)	mill manager	19	Episcopalian
Francis Robinson (1906)	commercial clerk	19	Episcopalian
Robert James Colville (1908)	assistant clerk	25	Presbyterian
Andrew Malcolmson (1908)	laundry proprietor	33	Presbyterian
James McCully-Cherry (1908)	pharmacist	33	Presbyterian
James Jamieson (1909)	librarian, embroidery agent	31	Presbyterian
John Fullerton (1909)	bricklayer's labourer	26	Presbyterian
James Johnston (1909)	factory clerk	17	Presbyterian
Hugh Mawhinney (1909)	water inspector	26	Presbyterian
William Mitchell-Thomson (1910)	MP	32	Presbyterian
Ernest Blythe (1910)	journalist	21	Episcopalian
James Boyce (1910)	[cotton weaver's son]	18	Presbyterian
Robert McCullough (1910)	hosiery knitter	22	Unitarian
Thomas Stevenson (1910)	grocer's assistant	18	Methodist
John Doggart (1912)	commercial traveller	60	Presbyterian
Stewart Christie (1912)	commercial traveller, grocery	29	Presbyterian
William Martin Wright (1912)	bank solicitor	27	Presbyterian

The quality of housing, as reported by police enumerators for the decennial census, was correspondingly diverse. Three-quarters had decent 'second-class' accommodation, compared with seventeen in substantial first-class houses, two in the cramped third-class, and none in fourth-class mud cabins (no longer common even in the rural west). The median number of rooms was six, but one-quarter of the houses contained at least nine rooms (the size of the farmhouse in Magheraliskmisk where Blythe was staying with his family on census night).[27] Whereas three rooms sufficed for three brethren such as Fred Bloor the steeplejack, the Presbyterian minister William Wright had thirteen rooms, with fifteen each for Twist-Whatham the rector and the draper James Mawhinney. The grandest accommodation (with forty-six rooms and twenty-seven front windows) was reserved for a visitor to the county on census night, 1911, when William Mitchell-Thomson, MP, was staying at Crawfordsburn with Robert Sharman-Crawford, the liberal-minded unionist landlord defeated by Corbett in the general election of 1900. A substantial minority of Orange households (22 per cent) included servants, only one-sixth of whom (five out of twenty-nine) were Roman Catholics. The Blythe household was among the few employing a Catholic servant girl. At the other end of the spectrum, ten householders supplemented their income by taking in boarders (invariably Protestant). Admission to lodge 1501 supplied this newcomer of dubious credentials with privileged access to the inner workings and social complexities of Newtownards.

For many Ulster brethren, fraternal engagement went far beyond the Orange lodge with its monthly meetings, annual walks, and periodic church services. Tens of thousands of enthusiasts joined 'higher orders' restricted to qualified Orangemen, such as the Royal Arch Purple, the Royal Black Institution (with its eleven additional degrees), or the Belfast offshoot of the Royal Black Knights of Malta. Many other fraternities competed for their attention in early twentieth-century Ulster, seldom ostensibly 'political' but typically restricted to Protestants. The moral and social imperatives drilled into the brethren by Orange chaplains were indistinguishable from those espoused by temperance bodies such as the Good Templars and Rechabites, in addition to societies connected with particular Protestant churches. The Oddfellows, Foresters, and other 'friendly societies' offered a tempting amalgam of entertainment, moral instruction, and material benefits more securely funded than any available through Orange lodges, though the Orange and Protestant Friendly Society became a strong competitor in the Edwardian decade. The typical fraternity was restricted to adult men, but a growing array of youth organisations performed similar functions for both boys and girls, often transcending boundaries between the Protestant churches but scarcely ever admitting Roman Catholics. The Boys', Girls' and Church Lads' Brigades, eventually joined by the Boy Scouts[28] and Girl Guides,[29] offered valuable moral and physical training for Protestant children, and a launching pad into adult fraternities, paramilitary bodies, and the forces of the Crown.

Orangeism's oldest and most reputable competitor was the Order of Free and Accepted Masons, whose lodges, hierarchies, disciplinary regulations, and rituals had provided the main organisational model for the Orange Order. Despite the prohibition of political discussion in Masonic lodge meetings and the absence of a religious test excluding Catholics and Jews, a great many Protestant unionists belonged to both orders and derived similar social, moral, and material benefits from each. 'The Masonic', however, with its higher fees and charitable ethos, was widely regarded as a more respectable and exclusive affiliation than 'the Orange', which was still struggling to cast off its unsavoury reputation for insobriety, sectarian violence, and tolerance of corner-boys 'without a stake in the country'. The two orders had clashed intermittently in nineteenth-century Newtownards, conflict being fanned by the exposure of two alleged Fenians who were expelled from local Masonic lodges (though at least one Fenian Orangeman was likewise expelled).[30] By Blythe's time, however, the membership of both organisations was overwhelmingly unionist, Ulster liberalism was dormant, and Fenian sentiments were rarely voiced by brethren of any order.

The extensive overlap between Orangeism and Freemasonry may be revealed by matching members of lodge 1501 with nominal registers compiled by the Masonic Grand Lodge of Ireland, which aimed to list every recipient of its certificate of membership and every transfer from one lodge to another.[31] Of the ninety Orangemen, no less than thirty-seven (two-fifths) appear to have become Freemasons before

1922.[32] Those belonging to both orders mostly joined the Orange first, though nearly two-fifths were already Freemasons before joining lodge 1501.[33] Many Orange Masons were seriously fraternal, fifteen progressing to Royal Arch chapters and twelve serving as Masonic officers. At least six brethren held office in both orders: the Presbyterian minister William Wright, his son William Martin Wright (solicitor), William Ferguson (handkerchief manufacturer), Thomas Maddock (mechanical engineer), Samuel Black (hardware merchant), and William Anderson (a printer who served in the Great War). Blythe's close friend and fellow actor Jamesie Jamieson transferred from his Scottish lodge to Union Star 198 in July 1908, a few months before his initiation as an Orangeman. Jamieson remained a Freemason long after resigning from the Orange, transferring to a lodge in Saintfield in 1913 from which he resigned six years later.[34] Significantly, Ernest Blythe did not follow his Masonic example.

Some of the most prominent brethren of lodge 1501, such as Thomas Lavery and Thomas Corbett, were not Freemasons with Irish certificates, but William Mitchell-Thomson transferred to a Bangor lodge shortly after his election for North Down in 1910. A decade earlier, as an undergraduate, he had been initiated in Oscar Wilde's old lodge in Oxford.[35] When speaking to Freemasons in Moneyrea in December 1911, Mitchell-Thomson 'hardly dared to mention' that he 'was a working member of a lodge in England, Scotland, and Ireland at the same time. (Applause.) If he did that, somebody might begin to think there was some hidden political meaning in it.'[36] Well they might! Few affiliations were so useful to a politician as Freemasonry, notwithstanding its prohibition of 'politics' within the lodge.

In several respects, as indicated in Table 6.3, the members of Blythe's Orange lodge who became Freemasons were indistinguishable from those who abstained.[37] In both cases, three-fifths were Presbyterians, and over four-fifths were natives of Down. The median age of entry into the Orange was in the mid-twenties for both groups, and there was no tendency for those who became Freemasons to emerge from a later generation of Orangemen.[38] The Masonic Orangemen, however,

Table 6.3. Profile of Lodge 1501

Characteristic	All Brethren	%	Freemasons	%	Others	%
Census Matches	67		32		35	
Religious Denomination						
Presbyterian	41	61	19	59	22	63
Episcopalian	22	33	11	34	11	31
Other	4	6	2	6	2	6
Birthplace						
Down	57	84	27	84	30	83
Other Ireland	4	6	1	3	3	8
Britain	7	10	4	13	3	8
House Class						
First	17	23	11	33	6	15
Second	54	74	22	67	32	80
Third	2	3	0	0	2	5
Median Figure						
Rooms in House	6		8		6	
Front Windows	5		6		4	
Age at Admission (Years)	25		26		25	

were more likely to live in substantial houses and to follow skilled occupations. One-third of the group resided in first-class homes, 41 per cent were skilled tradesmen or operatives, and 16 per cent had professional employment. The corresponding proportions for non-Freemasons were only 15 per cent, 30 per cent, and 6 per cent respectively. Yet white-collar Orangemen such as clerks, officials, and shopkeepers were *less* inclined to become Freemasons.[39] Another unexpected contrast is revealed by matching both groups with those who signed the Ulster Covenant in 1912. Whereas 68 per cent of Masonic Orangemen were probably signatories, the proportion for non-Freemasons was only 55 per cent.[40] Far from attracting any political non-conformists within the Orange Order, the Masonic order seems to have been particularly congenial to orthodox unionists in pre-war Newtownards.

The more one unearthed about the brethren of lodge 1501 and their place in Newtownards life, the more frustrating it became to have so little insight into Brother Blythe's personal experience of the Orange. He was doubly bound to silence by his obligation as an Orangeman and, more decisively, by his need to avoid identification by fellow nationalists as an initiate. At a late stage of research, I stumbled on two compositions offering vital clues to his engagement with the Order, suggesting a less trivial connection than simply initiation in September 1910 followed by resignation in February 1912.

Just before Christmas in 1911, the *Ulster Guardian* published a satirical piece by 'Purple Star', facetiously entitled 'Dissension in the Orange Ranks. (A Doleful Disclosure.)' He was 'exposing their misdemeanours in this particular publication because it is read chiefly by rotten Protestants'.[41] The 'disclosure' related to evidence of disunity at the recent biannual meeting of the Grand Orange Lodge of Ireland, which, 'driven to desperation by the grumbling and clamour, the secret intrigue, and open mutiny, of those who should have borne it true and unquestioning allegiance, has exchanged its absolute authority for a nominal suzerainty'. Blythe was referring to its delegation of executive authority to Colonel R. H. Wallace's Provincial Grand Lodge of Ulster (the projected 'Dublin' counterpart was never formed).[42] He explained the origin of the supposed split:

> The Orangemen of Ulster have basely determined to desert their scattered, persecuted brethren of the South; and these latter, who should have learned the value of Freedom from their own sufferings, have still more basely determined to assist the Nationalist rabble in breaking the proud spirit of the North.

Worse still, northern Orangeism was itself fragmenting: 'An Orange Republican party is also being formed, and disagreements are arising between the passive resisters and military men.' 'Purple Star' delivered an elegant parting thrust, endorsing the Grand Lodge's call for unity:

I, as a disinterested outsider, would implore the brethren to adopt its recommendations and pay no attention to the factionist provincial lodges. Prepare to defend yourselves, and in doing so remember that in modern warfare it is long range which tells. Do not waste your money like the foolish Garvagh men on miniature rifles. Invest in Krupp cannon.

This advice presumably arose from a threatened collision on 'Lady Day', 1910, between Orange and Hibernian factions in Garvagh, County Londonderry, which had led to the proclamation and abandonment of both meetings, and the deployment of more than 400 policemen in a town with 600 inhabitants. It was reported that 'almost every man in Garvagh had provided himself with a revolver and a plentiful supply of ammunition'. Though a six-pounder cannon stamped 'N. L. Vady 1848' had been lent to the Orangemen to intimidate or bombard their opponents, it was rusty with loose bolts and thought more likely to damage the gunners than their opponents if fired. The prudent decision by county officers to abandon the demonstration disgusted the Garvagh lodge, which thanked 'the brethren of Limavady and Boveva for granting the use of their cannon'.[43] This incident highlighted the tension between cautious officers fearful that the 'Radical Government' would 'brand them as rebels', and an increasingly militant rank and file in much of Ulster. The substance of Blythe's portrayal of divisions within Orangeism was borne out by later collisions between southern and northern factions, suggesting that Brother Blythe was indeed privy to debates inaccessible to outsiders.[44]

However tongue-in-cheek, Blythe's satire suggests that he still viewed Orangeism as a potential source of both revolutionary violence and pragmatic alliance with nationalism. In addressing readers of the *Ulster Guardian*, his primary purpose was to boost liberal morale by stressing the divisions within militant unionism. Yet to achieve this aim, he needed to display the Orange connections which had enabled him to correct a bland report of the biannual meeting in the *Belfast Evening Telegraph*.[45] In stating his credentials, 'Purple Star' was careful to deny the key fact that would simultaneously have given full authority to his report and destroyed his reputation among liberal readers:

> Although I have not the honour – and I am well-nigh ashamed to admit it – of being a member of the Order, my most esteemed and warmest friends have all ridden the goat, which is a metaphorical expression meaning that they have been inducted into the Orange Order, and been initiated in all its rites and mysteries. Therefore, as readers of the *Guardian* will understand, I have special channels of information as to all the artifices, manoeuvres, and what are called wire-pulling operations by which Civil and Religious Liberty is preserved to us.

His alleged 'informant was an exalted brother of the Arch-Purple Degree and a Worshipful Black Knight – I could not refuse to accept his word, though I still cherish fondly in the secret chambers of my heart a hope that owing to the condition he was in he may have spoken with rather more emphasis than the circumstances warranted'. His friend had reported 'that the spirit displayed at the meeting was abominable – "bl–dy d–d-well awful" was his own racy and unmistakable expression of disapproval'.[46] Nowhere else, so far as I know, did Blythe explicitly deny his membership of Volunteers lodge 1501 in Newtownards. And nowhere else, with one exception, did he parade his familiarity with the Order so convincingly.

A week earlier, 'Purple Star' had contributed a remarkable poem in twenty rhyming couplets, 'Suitable for recitation at Unionist Club tea-meetings', entitled 'The Lodge'. This dramatic evocation of a lodge meeting at 'Carrick Orange Hall' was qualified by a sly footnote: 'Lest any brother should feel exultant without due cause, I desire to state that the name "Carrick" is purely a product of my own creative imagination.'[47] Not so his eye-witness account of lodge proceedings at dead of winter:

> . . . The brethren all have sworn an oath to guard their Faith and Home,
> And spend their blood to shield them from the Harlot-hate of Rome;

And so the old lodge musters in accord with ancient form,
Despite the minions of the Pope, the fury of the storm.

Within the hall a leaping fire sends forth a golden glow,
And circled soon around it are the brethren bending low;
Their frozen garments soften, and their shiv'ring limbs grow still –
The sternest stalwart deigns to jest, and laughs with right good will.

Anon the distant church clock strikes: the fated hour is come,
And all are in their places ere the pond'rous bell is dumb;
The chairs are ordered neatly, the scarlet cloth is spread:
The Master steps up haughtily unto the table's head.

The brethren deck their shoulders stout with sashes of the blue,
In token of the oath they've sworn and of the deeds they'll do;
And there as equals mingle, in their zeal for Truth and Right,
The humble Orange brother and the stately Black Sir Knight.

The Master lifts the Sacred Mallet, thrice he smites the board,
The faithful Tyler answers with the pommel of his sword:
What follows then by voice or pen no Protestant would tell,
And from the eyes of Papishes the secret's guarded well.

. . . So meets the Lodge as it has met since William set us free;
So shall it meet in future time defying Tyranny.
Home Rule may come, alas! and countless viler ills befall,
But loyal men shall ever meet in Carrick Orange Hall.[48]

Apart from being a rather good parody of kindred verses in *The Crimson Banner Song Book*, Blythe's poem is notable for declining, as the Orangeman's ritual of initiation required, to reveal the secrets of the Order to outsiders.[49] Even as 'Purple Star', three months before his resignation, Brother Blythe remained more or less faithful to at least one of his solemn promises.

CHAPTER SEVEN

'The Old Town Clock'

I

By setting the district lodge minutes beside Blythe's articles in the *North Down Herald* and other press reports, we may recreate something of the flavour of Newtownards Orangeism and unionism in this critical period. However guardedly, Blythe's work as a journalist also provides clues to his own opinions and judgements, typically conveyed through ironic asides or subtle changes of tone. Two months before his admission, Blythe reported that 'the night of the 11th was, as usual, the liveliest of the year', with drummers and revellers disturbing the sleep of 'staid, sober citizens' throughout the night. As a firm teetotaller, he remarked approvingly that 'Tuesday was in Newtownards pre-eminently a sober "Twelfth." ... there was nothing which would correspond to the rite of "drowning the shamrock" on St. Patrick's Day.' The same applied to the demonstration at Carrowdore, reflecting the Order's latter-day attainment of 'a high position in personnel and discipline'.[1] The platform party included at least six members of lodge 1501, in addition to its three district officers who had headed the procession to the field. Lavery, Wright, and Mitchell-Thomson proposed predictable resolutions in customary style.[2]

A few weeks after his initiation, Blythe was probably among the twenty-four members of his lodge who bought tickets to the district's annual soirée, unless he secured one of the complimentary passes sent to the three local newspapers.[3] The evening began with a concert and ended with dancing, one of the pianists being Blythe's Belgian Jewish colleague on the *Spectator*, Jacques Jellen. But the most dramatic entertainment was provided by the after-tea speakers. T. R. Lavery was relatively benign, remarking that 'the quality of the men in the Society at present was far superior to that of the men who formed it twenty-five years ago', partly because of the rigorous exclusion of men of 'intemperate habits'. But he regretted 'a certain lukewarmness' and warned 'every Orangeman' of 'more arduous duties which he would be called upon to discharge. (Applause.)'[4]

Blythe's innocuous report in the *North Down Herald* gave no hint of what was to come (as revealed in the *Chronicle*). William Wright, the Presbyterian minister, promised that 'in a very short time they would have taught their young men to resist Home Rule and also to handle arms. He thought there was no hope for them, except the hope of using arms.' Yet he also expressed confidence that 'English and Scottish soldiers' would never 'turn their swords against the men of their own kith and kin'.[5] It was the firebrand English rector William Twist-Whatham who did most to puncture the giddy atmosphere with apocalyptic warnings:

> Very few of the young people there knew anything at all about Home Rule, or of the political situation at the present time. If, as they were applauding the very fine impersonations [of Harry Lauder] of Mr. Fleming and the other items, the crack of rifles were heard outside and the windows of that hall were broken with bullets, they would have been greatly startled. In all probability that would happen in the near future. That might be the last time there would be a social gathering in that hall in connection with the Orange Institution, and he believed the next would be of a very different character. . . . [Home Rule] meant that their factories would be closed, their homes broken up, and everything that made life worth living would be lost. He urged them to be ready for the evil time, and to prepare to do their duty to their country and to their Churches and to their God. (Loud applause.)

The ignorant 'young people' soon recovered their good humour as 'the dancing continued to an early hour in the morning'.[6]

In February 1911, Lavery directed the district lodge to revive the 'long lapsed' unionist club in Newtownards, as part of a wider strategy for mobilising opponents of Home Rule who were unwilling or unfitted to become Orangemen. Blythe's report of an 'enthusiastic public meeting' in the town hall predicted that 'the Club will have a career of very useful activity in the strenuous days which are before us'. Its first president was Sharman-Crawford, with William Wright as chairman – 'both staunch Unionists, and excellent fighters'.[7] In fact, the unionist club did nothing over the next year, leading to a tongue-in-cheek rebuke from Blythe:

> Newtownards Unionist Club has at last awakened! and none too soon. It is now working with feverish energy to make up the headway which it has lost and to put itself in presentable condition for the rapidly approaching demonstration at Balmoral on Easter Tuesday.

The club had at last held its first drill meeting on 20 March 1912, and might yet 'make itself equal to the orangemen despite their several weeks start'.[8]

In retrospect, Blythe portrayed himself as a shrewd observer of the tactical pretences associated with the proliferation of such bodies. At the inaugural meeting of a Clandeboye branch of the Bangor unionist club, he noticed that the large and enthusiastic crowd included only a dozen local people, being stacked with visitors from the Bangor club:

> The trick worked well. . . . With regard to the people of Clandeboye, when they heard of all the strangers who had visited the area, a lot of them regretted not having attended the meeting, to see everything for themselves. Therefore the new club soon increased its membership.[9]

The *Herald*'s report of the meeting confirmed that the 'representative attendance of the inhabitants of Clandeboye neighbourhood' was also sparse. In proposing formation of the Clandeboye branch, the speaker remarked that 'they need not be dismayed at the comparatively small number of the inhabitants of Clandeboye present that evening. At the first drill in Bangor they had only sixteen members present. Now they had a regular attendance of over a hundred members and on Saturday afternoons between two and three hundred.' Those present could scarcely have missed the fact that 'contingents of about seventy each marched from Bangor and Helensbay and assembled outside the building'.[10] Contrary to his knowing gloss in *Trasna na Bóinne*, Blythe's report made no suggestion of pretence or trickery.

Blythe's tactfully balanced reporting justified the testimonial supplied by his editor, Harry Gaw (a Presbyterian of the same age as himself), when he left the *North Down Herald* in early 1913:

> A journalist of very pronounced ability. He is a reliable verbatim note taker, a good paragraphist, a discreet and polished writer on current local and general events. He is a man of high character, at all times courteous and obliging, and was exceedingly popular with the general public in this neighbourhood.[11]

Discretion was not a quality commonly attributed to Blythe in his later public career.

Blythe's columns and reports demonstrate his readiness to voice unionist sentiments, while occasionally resorting to irony for the benefit of friends in the know. When summarising an 'important lecture' by William Wright before 'a fair attendance' at the Orange hall in March 1911, Blythe appeared to endorse Wright's implacable opposition to Home Rule: 'The lecturer gave an interesting account of the Home Rule agitation from its origin at the break-up of the Fenian Movement, to the present day, and pointed out the moral with great emphasis and cogency.'[12] Seven weeks later, when Lavery induced the Urban District Council to present a loyal address to 'their Majesties' on their forthcoming visit to Ireland, Blythe remarked that 'it is a somewhat far cry from Newtownards to Dublin', yet 'surely not too far to go to present an address to the King':

> At this juncture when various Nationalist bodies are showing the inherent disloyalty of their political faith by refusing a proper greeting to their sovereign, it is well that the loyal voice of the North should be heard. Apart altogether from fulfilling our duties as citizens of the Empire by showing a fitting respect for the Sovereign, it will have a wholesome effect on the Radical

contrivers of paradoxes who have recently been trying to belittle the loyalty of Ulster.[13]

Few casual readers would have suspected that the author belonged to several of those disloyal 'Nationalist bodies', and was himself soon to become an adept contriver of such paradoxes as a regular contributor to the IRB's mouthpiece, *Irish Freedom*. In *Trasna na Bóinne*, Blythe recalled how easy he found it to compose disingenuous leading articles for Harry Gaw by comparison with his laborious essays for *Irish Freedom*:

> I was able to sit down, not having done any prior thinking at all, and have the main article ready for the printer within half an hour. A few times, for devilment, I would reproduce sentences which had been published in *Irish Freedom* – from my own pen – in order to prove that not all Irish nationalists would be satisfied with the limited Home Rule that the members of parliament were seeking.[14]

The devil's work, indeed! No passage in his autobiography reveals more clearly the psychological consequences of Blythe's double life, with its private jokes and perpetual deceits.

Blythe's first Twelfth as an Orangeman was celebrated at Ballyrea in 1911, with speeches and processions scarcely distinguishable from those reported in the preceding year. He had an unrivalled vantage point, being one of three journalists listed among the platform party (the others were Willie Doggart and Spencer Henry of the *Chronicle*). Their presence, though not in itself proof that all three belonged to the Order, clearly implied endorsement of its principles.[15] The *Herald*'s report was colourless by comparison with that in the *Spectator*, presumably the work of Jacques Jellen.[16] Whereas Blythe merely noted that 'the close proximity of the field to Newtownards conduced greatly to the extraordinarily large attendance of the general public', the *Spectator* expatiated on Ballyrea's adjacency to 'Strangford Lough, glittering like a sea of silver in the bright sunshine, and tinted with streaks of deepest blue'.

Yet, buried deep within Blythe's report were ominous words from William Wright exhibiting the growing militancy of Ulster unionism:

> They did not want to fight but if their leaders found it necessary to call upon them to fight for their rights and liberties they were prepared to go with them. . . . And would they who were living now allow future generations to say 'These coward forefathers of ours would not contend for their rights as citizens of the British Empire.'

Jellen's still starker summary of Wright's speech excluded the deferential reference to 'their leaders': 'They did not want to fight, but if their rights and liberties were threatened they would fight, until not a man was left, if needs be.' Long before Ulster Day, the revolutionary mood was already apparent. Yet the next instalment of 'The Old Town Clock' adopted a rather jaded tone in reflecting on the Twelfth celebrations: 'Whatever excitement they engendered has subsided, and whatever dislocation of business they occasioned has been rectified.' Blythe was delighted to report that 'practically no drunkenness was to be seen amongst the general public, and absolutely none amongst the brethren. Altogether the local demonstration was exceedingly creditable to the spirit and good sense of the North Down Orangemen.'[17]

Through observing loyal Newtownards from within, Blythe would have picked up some useful hints about the contradictions and internal rifts within Ulster unionism in the period of the Home Rule crisis. Whereas most southern nationalists despised Orangeism as a monolith, bound together by bigotry, ignorance, and 'Ascendancy' arrogance, Blythe in later life was clearly alert to more complex realities. Within Newtownards Orangeism, there had long been evidence of tension between 'democratic' and 'aristocratic' factions, most clearly expressed at election time but also evident in the eruption of the Independent Loyal Orange Institution in 1903. When extolling William Wright's 'good work for the Unionist Cause' after his death in 1919, Thomas Lavery recalled diplomatically that 'they had differed on occasions'.[18] Back in 1885, at Lavery's suggestion, the

district had withdrawn its invitation to 'the Revd. Mr. Right' to preach
on the Twelfth, in response to his opposing the re-election for North
Down of Lord Arthur Hill, the county grand master. This contest
had pitted a Protestant landlord (supported by Episcopalians such as
Lavery) against the Presbyterian linen merchant John Shaw Brown.
Brown, president of the Belfast Liberal Association and a temperance
advocate, opposed Home Rule but also opposed amalgamation with
the Conservative party.[19]

In later years, as Thomas Corbett's electoral career illustrates, the
determination of Orange and unionist leaders to secure aristocratic
endorsement led to recurrent opposition from many churchmen,
not always Presbyterian, who valued Orangeism as a forum for
promoting working-class social and moral reform rather than as a
tool for mobilising the masses behind Tory grandees. This perennially
radical strand within Orangeism encouraged nationalists like Blythe
to believe that Ulster unionism was inherently unstable, despite its
formidable appearance of mass solidarity.

Another useful lesson for a nationalist observer was the readiness
of Orangemen to prepare for armed resistance against the forces
of the Crown, contradicting the complacent southern belief that
Ulster's opposition to Home Rule was mere 'bluff'. In May 1886,
lodge secretaries in the Newtownards district had been asked to
fill out circulars relating to 'Rifles &c.', presumably listing available
weapons and brethren prepared to drill in preparation for possible
resistance if Home Rule were imposed.[20] Whereas preparations for
armed resistance in 1886 and 1893 were soon abandoned following
Gladstone's parliamentary defeats, the crisis initiated by introduction
of the third Government of Ireland Bill gave rise to concerted
drilling culminating in the formation of the Ulster Volunteer Force
in January 1913.

On 9 February 1912, all Orangemen of the district had been
summoned through the press to a meeting in the Orange Hall 'for
the purpose of further perfecting our arrangements in Defence of
Civil and Religious Liberty, which all of us know would be seriously
imperilled by the passing into law of any measure of Home Rule

for Ireland'. The meeting, attended by over 200 brethren including all local masters, resolved 'to make arrangements in our respective Lodges to have our members drilled in military form in accordance with instructions from Grand Lodge of Ireland, thus enabling us to take our stand in defence of our country, hearths, and homes, in event of "Home Rule" becoming Law'. All present raised their right hand and stood up to endorse the resolution. Twelve days later, the masters were reconvened to meet a drill instructor, 'relative to having members of this District Lodge prepared to march in military style' to the Easter Tuesday demonstration at Balmoral showgrounds. Lavery duly complimented 'the brethren on their good turnout on that occasion in good Order and military style', impressing 'not only our townspeople but strangers from a distance'. Drill continued every Tuesday and Friday night in a 'satisfactory' number of lodges, providing valuable preparation for future service in the UVF.[21] Blythe's report confirmed that the district contingent had marched to the railway station 'in good style' that 'would have done credit to a body of regular troops', and praised the 'discipline and bearing' of all but a few half-trained participants.[22]

II

Ernest Blythe did not directly witness the deployment of his Orange brethren or participate in drilling, of which he already had experience through membership of the IRB, Fianna Éireann, and Dungannon clubs. On 14 February 1912, five days after the inauguration of drilling, Blythe resigned. At the next district meeting, on 26 February, 'Lodge 1501 reported the resignation from the Orange Institution of Bro Ernest Blythe which was confirmed'. We may conjecture that drilling in defence of the Union, even in preparation for armed conflict with forces of the Crown, would have stretched his duality of allegiances beyond breaking point. His departure may also have been influenced by the resignation on 14 June 1911 of his close friend, 'James Jamison Jr (librarian)'. Jamesie Jamieson had been admitted to lodge 1501 in March 1909, six months before Blythe, and was surely responsible for drawing his new friend into the lodge. He should not be confused with the lodge's deputy master, James Jamison the 'grocerrer' of Little Frances Street, even though Jamesie lived in the same street.[23]

Though no longer an Orangeman after February 1912, Blythe remained a close observer of the drift towards rebellion in Ulster. He later reflected that inside knowledge, combined with emancipation from prejudice, gave him an ideal vantage point for clear-headed analysis of the 'Carson movement':

> As my own political opinions were completely different from their opinions and as I had rejected from my own mind most of the prejudices that they still had, I was able to look accurately at them without any clouding of vision affecting me.[24]

On Easter Monday 1912, the eve of the great Balmoral rally, he was unimpressed by the oratory of unionist heroes who had assembled in Conway Square to greet their parliamentary leader, Andrew Bonar Law. In retrospect, Blythe evinced 'no respect for any of the speeches, in terms of style or content', being particularly unimpressed by Carson, whose 'voice was hoarse'. Though 'a large crowd was present', Blythe recalled that 'no one was too agitated' by the event, to which the district's Orange lodges had been instructed to march in procession.[25] As 'The Old Town Clock', Blythe had made no disparaging remarks about the speakers, stating that 'practically the whole male population, as well as a very large number of ladies, assembled in Conway Square', while 'throughout the whole proceedings the utmost enthusiasm was manifested'.[26]

Likewise, he reported 'great manifestations of enthusiasm in Newtownards' on Ulster Day (28 September 1912), following packed services in the parish church (with a sermon by Twist-Whatham and lessons read by Lavery), the Reformed Presbyterian church, and the Second Presbyterian church (where William Wright was supported by the Methodist and other local ministers). Blythe evidently preferred the effervescent Wright to the grim Twist-Whatham, and his report shows how clearly Wright perceived the historic import and sacerdotal character of Ulster Day:

He said that every man who signed the Covenant would receive a parchment document, which he must return to-day; as the documents had to be compared with the signatures in the book. But they would be returned again to every man who signed to keep, he hoped, as a memento of the great history-making occasion. In asking them now to sign they, the ministers of the Protestant Churches in the town would sign at the head of the people. They were united in this matter.[27]

Despite its religious trappings and rituals, Ulster Day was viewed by many Orangemen as the first stage in a military campaign. A month beforehand, the district lodge had resolved 'that the Orangemen resume Drill immediately owing to meeting of 28th Sept next'.[28] The stewards responsible for directing the celebration included four members of Blythe's former lodge. 'The Old Town Clock' reported, perhaps tongue in cheek, that 'there has seldom or never been such a display of enthusiasm in Newtownards' as that aroused by a preliminary organisational meeting at the Guild Hall, preceded by a procession of speakers escorted 'by the members of the Unionist Club and Orange Order, as well as the Church Lads' Brigade Band, and a company of torch-bearers'. An outdoor meeting was held, part of the crowd being accommodated in the town hall. On Ulster Day itself, the town's traders closed for the afternoon ('practically without exception'), and 'the affixing of signatures proceeded very rapidly'. Blythe predicted, rather deflatingly, that 'a very respectable' number of signatures would eventually be secured.[29] Though there was no overt reference to dissent or apathy among the town's unionists, it is worth noting that less than half of the members of lodge 1501 can be matched (even tentatively) with Covenant signatories.[30]

Militarism became even more overt over the winter, as the drill parties formed by Orange lodges and unionist clubs were transformed into the UVF. Admittedly, training in the Newtownards district remained lax even after Ulster Day, following further attempts to revive regular drilling in conjunction with the unionist club in early October.[31] The district lodge was preoccupied with circulars endorsed by the Provincial Grand Lodge of Ulster concerning recruitment for the UVF and the new Ulster Signalling and Despatch Riding Corps, and with raising money for the 'Sir Edward Carson Ulster Defence Fund 1913'. Though slow to respond, lodge 1501 eventually raised 57s., more than any other lodge in the town.[32]

Less onerous displays of militancy were better supported. Despite 'drizzling rain' on 16 January 1913, dense crowds witnessed the burning of the Government of Ireland Bill in Conway Square, performed by Thomas Lavery. An 'authentic' copy of the bill was attached to a long pole and 'set aflame from the blazing tar-barrel and, as Mr Lavery waved it aloft, loud cheers greeted the action'. Blythe's report was positive as always, emphasising the 'most orderly character' of the procession and ceremony, and the tactful re-routing of the procession out of respect for the deceased 'Mrs McCall, the wife of Mr. Edward McCall, J. P., High Street, one of the most prominent, and at the same time, most highly respected Roman Catholic residents in our town'. Carrying the innuendo that some prominent Catholic townsmen were far from respectable, Blythe's salute to religious tolerance missed only one trick (Mrs McCall's mother was a Protestant, suggesting a 'mixed marriage').[33] Obliquely referring to his own predicament, Blythe contemplated a crowd 'who, if not all Unionists – we presume there may be some such individuals in the town – had ample evidence of the intense loyalty of thousands of the inhabitants'.[34]

Following Blythe's departure for Kerry in April 1913, surprisingly many brethren in County Down ignored the insistent drive towards militarisation headed by Colonel R. H. Wallace's Provincial Grand Lodge of Ulster. By June 1913, only 1,700 out of 9,742 Orangemen in the county (17 per cent) had offered their services to the UVF by signing what was euphemistically termed 'the forward movement declaration'. Lavery made repeated appeals to lodge officers to supply names and addresses, including those of 'members who had not signed'. Though the Newtownards district was less recalcitrant than the county in general, with 169 signatories out of 435 brethren (39 per cent), the majority remained 'aloof' and therefore 'unworthy to be a member of the Institution' (according to a resolution approved by the county grand lodge in November 1913).[35] Likewise, despite the fervent patriotism and zeal for recruitment expressed by Orange leaders after August 1914, most of Blythe's lodge comrades did not serve in the Great War. The Roll of Honour displayed on the walls of the Newtownards Orange Hall lists only eight members of lodge 1501, including William Mitchell-Thomson, MP, whose credential was an honorary lieutenancy in the Royal Naval Veterans' Reserve. No member was killed, though William Wright's son William Martin Wright, a lieutenant in the 13th Royal Irish Rifles, was 'seriously injured' at the Somme in July 1916.[36] By comparison with most Newtownards lodges, number 1501 contributed an unusually small proportion of its members to the forces.[37]

In retrospect, Blythe tried to trace his growing realisation that Ulster's campaign against Home Rule was more than a game of bluff in which mock soldiers with wooden guns performed a parody of revolution on behalf of their conservative masters. This was indeed his initial impression as a reporter in north Down, based on the popular belief that mass mobilisation would again, as in 1886 and 1893, suffice to thwart Home Rule. Blythe observed with fascination the creation of rifle clubs in Newtownards and Bangor, followed by an unofficial special constabulary in Lecale. He 'wrote a satirical piece about the Special Constables because . . . I found it difficult to take the opposition seriously and that is where I went wrong'. He was reassured by local reaction to a UVF march from Bangor to Groomsport: 'A lot of people on the footpaths and in the doorways saw them and they were hysterical with laughter the whole time that the awkward recruits were passing by with their fake guns slanted over their shoulders.' Yet Blythe, with hindsight, attributed the mockery not to political indifference, but to the persistent belief that political manifestations such as the Ulster Covenant would avert the need for armed conflict.[38]

As a result, the early UVF seemed timid and unprepared for warfare, as Blythe's brother James demonstrated in Magheragall:

> One afternoon, my brother, who was big and strong and who had some boxing ability, was driving a horse and cart on a narrow road when he saw thirty or forty of the Volunteers marching against him. For fun, he overturned his horse and cart across

the road, entirely closing it to the Volunteers. He waited without moving until they came upon him. Instead of attacking him or hitting the horse or doing something to open the passage for themselves, they climbed the fence into a field and when they had gone beyond the obstacle they climbed back on the road again.

Yet, as Blythe observed during various visits to Ulster after moving to Kerry in April 1913, the UVF were soon to become a serious fighting force, as their political leaders realised that exhibitions of mass democracy accompanied by military pantomime might not prevail against Home Rule:

> Later, after they had received their firearms, they had a totally different spirit. If anyone would attempt to pull my brother's prank on them, they would be thrown out of the way immediately and would probably get a beating.[39]

Far from alienating Blythe, their growing earnestness encouraged him to view the UVF as a potentially revolutionary force which, as his later contributions to *Irish Freedom* indicated, might even be harnessed to the republican cause.

Blythe connected the growing militancy of Orange Ulster with its most potent symbol, the defeat of an English king at the battle of the Boyne:

> If some of them thought about putting up a fight against the English army, they only thought of it as a fight against bad forces which had seized power over there. It was easy enough to develop the idea among them that they could fight against the English government without fighting against England itself. There wasn't an Orangeman in the country who did not have one historical fact among his thoughts, namely that King James was removed from his throne in England and that King William was brought over from Holland in his place in favour of the Protestants. As well as that, all the unionists were experienced in

listening to stupid nationalists, who reminded them that certain Orangemen threatened to kick Queen Victoria's throne into the Boyne if their ministers did something which displeased them.[40]

By 1913, armed conflict with the Crown forces already seemed an imminent possibility, eliminated only by the redirection of UVF and Orange militarism to the war effort after August 1914.

Blythe's decision to leave the scene of potential revolution before climax was taken with some regret. Such was his preoccupation with the Amateur Dramatic Society that his resolve to abandon journalism and become a farm labourer in west Kerry began to wobble. According to *Trasna na Bóinne*, he kept to his plan for two reasons: loyalty to friends who had welcomed his determination to master Irish in the Gaeltacht, and an arrangement with the *North Down Herald*, through Harry Gaw, to prolong his stay in Newtownards for just 'a couple of months' in order to avoid being posted to Donaghadee before production of *The Drone*. Wary of future unemployment, he solicited testimonials from Gaw, Bob Henry of the *Chronicle*, and W. H. Davey of the *Ulster Guardian*. Though Davey's reference was effusive, he set more store in Gaw's support. Yet it was Henry, despite his disapproval of a plan 'that he saw as strange and even stupid', who proved most supportive, writing out a cheque for £10 as well as an enthusiastic endorsement.[41] Blythe shed 'a few tears' on the train to Belfast after farewelling the Doggarts, especially fifteen-year-old Mabel, and ruminated 'that I would not be able to have a close relationship again with any of my unionist friends'. On his final night at Magheraliskmisk, where he stayed briefly before travelling south:

A sort of stage fright hit me just as had happened when I was sitting waiting for my cue to go on stage on the first night that we performed *The Drone*. It occurred to me that perhaps I would not find work in the Gaeltacht, that maybe my plan was extremely stupid and that I was making a fool out of myself.[42]

Few passages in Blythe's autobiography carry greater conviction, or convey so clearly his conception of revolution as drama.

CHAPTER EIGHT

'Uncle Dan'

I

Throughout his career, Ernest Blythe was a theatre man as much as a politician. Like so many members of Roy Foster's 'revolutionary generation',[1] he viewed politics as a form of theatre and theatre as a forum for politics. Blythe was already a seasoned playgoer and press critic when he moved to County Down. He first visited the Abbey Theatre in June 1905, greatly enjoying William Boyle's comedy *The Building Fund*.[2] Until his departure for Bangor in 1909, he 'never missed a single play' at the Abbey Theatre. He watched 'some of the short plays like *Cathleen Ni Houlihan*, *Riders to the Sea*, *In the Shadow of the Glen* and *Spreading the News* so often that I had them memorised from start to finish'.[3] Blythe invariably bought a cheap ticket in the gallery or back of the pit, as did IRB comrades such as Peadar Macken and Seán McDermott.

From 1907, he recalled sending unsolicited and unpaid reviews of 'every new play' at the Abbey to W. P. Ryan's *The Peasant and Irish Ireland* and its successor, entitled *The Irish Nation and the Peasant*.[4] These were always published, despite his anonymity and inexperience, perhaps because he had 'strong opinions and I did not restrain my pen'. He wryly recalled being unaware that reviewers were customarily given free seats, and maintained his critical independence by never reading reviews in the daily press.[5] The earliest review attributable to Blythe included a tribute to Synge, the Abbey's 'most artistically successful' writer of 'peasant plays', marked by 'their wonderful, never-wearying dialogue, and their humanity'.[6]

In May 1908, Blythe attended the first production of *The Drone*, a kitchen comedy with Ulster-Scots touches by 'Rutherford Mayne' (Samuel Waddell), performed by the Ulster Literary Theatre (ULT) at the Abbey.[7] This resulted in his only visit to the 'green room', where he gatecrashed a party to greet the Ulster visitors by buttonholing Seán

McDermott.[8] Like Blythe himself, those who wrote and acted for the ULT almost always lurked behind pseudonyms, supposedly to avoid being unmasked as 'playactors' by workmates or acquaintances.[9] The *Peasant*'s reviewer, 'Cnó Cúil' or 'Nut Corner', was again surely Blythe – sorely in need of a copy-editor:

> 'The Drone' is a delightful satire on the man who pretending to work at things beyond the comprehension of his associates passes the time in idleness and scheming, but whose company and 'crack' (according to the moral to be drawn from the conclusion of the play) is more preferable than [*sic*] that of a woman with a shrewish tongue.

He was particularly delighted by the 'facial expressions' and comical skill of the actor playing Uncle Dan ('the Drone'), the part that Blythe himself was to perform almost five years later in Newtownards. The reviewer's Ulster sympathies emerged in his barbed conclusion: 'The visit of these Northern playwrights and players should serve as a stimulating example to our local society with the pretentious name' – the Irish National Theatre.[10]

Blythe later adopted the pseudonym 'Cairbre', evoking the mythical poet and satirist of the Tuatha Dé Danann who bragged before the second battle of Moytirra that 'through the spell of my poem they will not be able to contend with warriors'.[11] Two reviews for the *Peasant* illustrate Cairbre's readiness to express 'strong opinions', both literary and political. In 1908, he contributed carping assessments of two Abbey plays by William Francis Casey, a future editor of *The Times* of London, bemoaning their triviality and concluding that 'a company of capable Gaelic players is an absolute necessity'.[12] Just before leaving Dublin, he wrote just as dismissively of Lady Gregory's version of Molière's *L'Avare*, which he compared unfavourably with her own curtain-raiser, that 'very powerful piece' *The Gaol Gate*.[13] This was among the 'patriotic' plays that had filled Sinn Féiners like Blythe 'with military fervour', more effectively than any 'bare propaganda'.[14]

Thereafter, all reviews by Cairbre concerned Belfast productions, confirming the censorious critic's imputed identity beyond doubt. In

May 1909, he attended a revival in Belfast's Grand Opera House of *The Drone*. Though 'the acting was simply magnificent' in the Belfast revival, Blythe regretted the addition of a third act which descended into farce.[15] Almost a year later, he noted the ULT's success in attracting a much larger audience, albeit for Mayne's *The Captain of the Hosts*, which he deemed inferior to *The Drone*. He was more interested in *The Mist that Does Be on the Bog* by 'Gerald MacNamara' (Harry C. Morrow).[16] This 'parody on the beautiful but artificial dialogue of Synge' was 'not appreciated' by an audience less conversant with the Abbey repertoire than the sophisticated Cairbre.[17]

Blythe was nonetheless an admirer of *The Playboy of the Western World*, whose Belfast première he had reviewed in August 1909. Though Synge's speech was 'no more the speech of the Connacht peasantry than the speech of Shakespeare was that of his contemporaries', Blythe delighted in Synge's 'big-mouthed phrases': 'His denunciations smite like a sledgehammer.' Blythe endorsed the prevailing view that *The Playboy* was a masterpiece and no 'libel on the Irish race', suggesting that 'very few ever thought it was' except 'the rioters in justification of their conduct' during the first production in 1907. He had been taken aback when one of those fined for rioting was welcomed into his own circle of the IRB without the usual inquisition, being 'congratulated with cheers and clapping' as 'a pure-hearted loyal patriot' who had defied the hated police.[18] Recalling his own presence at the first performance on 26 January 1907, Blythe remarked that even then the first two acts had been 'heartily applauded', disapproval being provoked only by 'one unfortunate phrase' in the third act:[19]

> It is said that considerable changes have been made since then, but at this distance I could detect nothing but two slight verbal alterations, neither of which should have been made. To my mind 'stitching my clothes' is not so good as 'putting a stitch in an ould shift', while the 'fifty women' phrase ['fifty women in their shifts'] – the cause of all the trouble – ought on principle to have been retained.[20]

Touché!

Though Blythe did not share the rioters' indignation at *The Playboy*, he clearly enjoyed the additional strand of drama that riots introduced, and had himself relished 'hissing, and shouting, and booing' at the Theatre Royal because of a presumptuous programme note asking the audience 'not to clap during the performance'.[21] Inspired by 'angry complaints' after the première of *The Piper* at the Abbey, Blythe recollected having gone 'to the Saturday matinée to see the play and, more than that, to be present when the rioting started'. Instead, he witnessed 'a very clever speech' from Yeats before the performance, which ensured that the play 'was quietly listened to and was heartily welcomed'.[22] Even mediocre productions could be transformed into high drama through heckling, rioting, Yeats in full cry, or (most exhilarating of all) an invasion of the pit by the Dublin Metropolitan Police.

Despite his enthusiasm for the theatre and his experience as a drama critic, Blythe had little personal contact with the actors and playwrights of the Ulster Literary Theatre in Belfast, apart from Bulmer Hobson, who had moved to Dublin before Blythe's arrival. An exception was Ernest Thompson, the 'distant relative' who had acted in two of the ULT's earliest productions of plays by 'Lewis Purcell' (David Parkhill).[23] When home on holiday during his four years with 'the Department', Blythe would visit Ernest's family in Woodvale, and it was the Thompsons who introduced him to the ULT by taking him to *Suzanne and the Sovereigns* by Purcell and MacNamara. This rollicking comedy of the Williamite wars became the group's 'most popular production', being devised 'with such light-hearted good spirits that it delighted all sections of its audience'.[24] Blythe recalled 'that two crowds were present, with packs of easily agitated members of both groups sitting like islands here and there throughout the audience'. Each party tried to outdo the other in 'cheers and clapping', creating a risk 'that punches would be thrown'; but the performance 'made everyone in attendance laugh far too much to allow the anger to build'.[25]

Ernest Thompson, as already mentioned, was the elder brother of Stanley Wellington Thompson, the future Presbyterian minister, Freemason, and Orange and Black chaplain. Ernest Thompson himself had recently become a Freemason, joining his father in Ulidia lodge 135, Ballymacarrett.[26] He became an estate agent, remaining in close contact with Blythe's sister Josephine in her declining years.[27] Like most members of the ULT he had wide interests, owning a painting entitled *Man in Green* which was displayed in the Royal Hibernian Academy and destroyed during the rebellion of 1916.[28]

Blythe's other ULT connection was W. R. Gordon, a member of Belfast's Dungannon club identified as 'Billy Gordon, Painter of Orange banner' in one of Blythe's notebooks.[29] Gordon was a man of many parts (artist, actor, folk singer, broadcaster), an agnostic reared in the Church of Ireland, who taught art at 'Inst' for forty-four years while running a banner-making business in Bridge Street. Along with James Hodgen and MacNamara, he had joined the ULT in 1904, from a drama group formed by the Sketching Club at the Belfast School of Art.[30] As 'Robert Gorman', he took the lead in Rutherford Mayne's *The Turn of the Road* at its Belfast première in May 1909, during a week-long festival in which five plays were presented by the ULT at the Grand Opera House.[31]

Gordon painted and supplied banners for all comers, including trade unions, Hibernians, and Orangemen alike. His shop was regularly advertised in the *Irish Nation*, patriotically offering 'BANNERS (*entirely Irish manufacture*)'.[32] Yet his customers included Churchill lodge 1951 at Bootown near Newtownards. In early July 1910, the lodge's 'handsome new banner' was unveiled by the London-born wife of Captain James S. Henry, proprietor of the *Newtownards Chronicle*:

> The banner is a most artistic production, and was executed by Mr. W. R. Gordon, Bridge Street, Belfast. It is of orange and purple silk, and bears on one side a painting of King William crossing the Boyne and on the other an admirable portrait of the late Bro. John Murphy, P. M., who was one of the original founders of the lodge in 1869.[33]

Though Blythe may have helped secure this commission, Gordon was well known in Newtownards through conducting evening classes

at the technical school, where his colleagues included Elizabeth
Bloxham.[34]

II

The focus of Blythe's social life in Newtownards became the
Amateur Dramatic Society that he founded with Jamieson, who had
performed in a comedy for a similar group in Scotland and suggested
producing the same play in Newtownards. It proved simple to enlist
a few members from the town's small Catholic minority, since 'there
was no hostility towards them worth mentioning'. These included
James Murnane,[35] who was preparing to emulate his father David by
becoming a district inspector in the RIC after topping the cadetship
examination.[36] Both father and son were Irish speakers, though in 1901
David was sceptical of ten-year-old James' mastery of the language,
remarking that he and two brothers 'are being taught to read Irish
and English in school; but their knowledge is as yet backward'.[37]

   David Murnane had been promoted from the ranks in 1901,[38]
benefiting from a recent reform designed to diversify the officer
force by reserving half of the intake for serving head constables
(mainly Catholics) rather than cadets (mainly Protestants).[39] Upon
promotion, he had been extravagantly praised by the magistrates
and lawyers of Carrick-on-Suir for his courtesy, honesty, and ability
as head constable.[40] As district inspector in Lisnaskea and Trim as
well as Newtownards, he was many times commended and rewarded
for dealing efficiently with cases of conspiracy to boycott, arson,
unlawful assembly, and cattle driving, and finally for suppressing a
riot in Trim in September 1918. David Murnane did not take kindly to
criticism from superiors, being once 'severely reprimanded, without
record, for neglect of duty in keeping warrant Regr, & for the highly
objectionable tone of his correspondence'.[41]

   As a Catholic and presumably a nationalist, he fell foul of
two Protestant magistrates at Brookeborough, who opposed the
customary resolution of regret upon his departure from Fermanagh.
The resolution, proposed by the two Catholic members of the bench,

fell through when the Protestant chairman decided to 'leave it to the local magistrates to settle'.[42] Murnane thanked his supporters; but, as to his detractors, 'the less said about them the better'. He declared that 'they cannot say anything to me that would go to show that I ever neglected or overstepped my duty. For their opinions I don't care very much, and I won't be a bit displeased with them, nor do their expressions make me any worse friends with them.'[43] David Murnane was clearly a formidable adversary, equally resistant to interference from headquarters and chastisement by local Protestant dignitaries.

James Murnane performed as a prosecuting counsel in the society's first production, in a Presbyterian hall, while Blythe played 'an unimportant part as an elderly witness'.[44] One of Murnane's last duties as honorary secretary was to organise a dinner and musical entertainment for thirty members and friends at Apperson's Commercial Hotel, at which the artists were thanked by Jamieson and the utterly unmusical Blythe, while Bob Henry of the *Chronicle* spoke for the guests.[45] Having discovered Blythe and his son rehearsing their parts in his house, Inspector Murnane warned James that 'that man was in the Irish Republican Brotherhood in Dublin'.[46] We cannot tell how many of Blythe's unionist friends in Newtownards were likewise aware of his other life.

As Blythe admitted in *Trasna na Bóinne*, the society's artistic mentor was the experienced and tactful Jamieson; yet, by the final rehearsal, 'I was the controller.'[47] The rules left little room for consultation with any other members except the governing 'Committee', consisting of the treasurer (Jamieson) and secretary (Blythe):

> Every decision of the Committee shall be reversible by the majority of the ACTIVE MEMBERS, except that in the choice of plays and the assignment and withdrawal of parts, its decisions shall be final. No new member shall be introduced without the consent of the Committee.

Members ceased to be deemed 'active' if they omitted to pay their annual subscription of 1s. 6d., refused parts, or persistently failed to memorise their lines.[48]

After the modest success of its first show, the Newtownards Amateur Dramatic Society decided to tackle *The Drone*, complete with its farcical third act and already a staple of amateur theatre in Ulster. Preparation was meticulous, and the society paid for visits from a 'distinguished actor member of the Ulster Literary Theatre' (James Hodgen), to observe rehearsals and make suggestions to the cast (which Blythe subsequently took it on himself 'to impress upon the others'). Hodgen had recently been described as 'one of the most brilliant actors that the Ulster Literary Theatre has yet produced', notable for his 'clear enunciation' when performing parts in dialect.[49] The society also borrowed Uncle Dan's 'original fan bellows', a 'quaint and wonderful contrivance, which . . . never fails to throw an audience into fits of laughter'.[50]

The Drone was twice performed at the Guild Hall, takings on the second night being bolstered by the presence of two journalists summoned from Bangor by Blythe to deter freebooters. They were Seán Lester and Davy Boyd, both Protestant members of the Belfast IRB who left Ulster in 1913 to work on southern newspapers.[51] Lester, a lifelong friend, was to become acting secretary-general of the League of Nations. Boyd moved to Dublin in 1913, reported for the Dublin *Evening Mail* on the dramatic delivery and dispersal of Volunteer arms at Howth in July 1914, allegedly tried to blow up a bridge after missing the 1916 rebellion, and then retreated to Waterford. Discarding republicanism, he joined the unionist *Waterford Standard*. As managing editor and later proprietor from May 1921 to its demise in 1953, Boyd fearlessly exposed sectarian discrimination in local appointments, accusations of 'unlawful carnal knowledge and indecent assault' of a thirteen-year-old by a Waterford theatre proprietor, and scurrilous criticism of a Protestant judge who had dared to criticise the Catholic dean of Waterford. Though brought to court in each instance, Boyd was only once punished for his exercise of free speech in the Protestant interest.[52] Despite his abandonment of public nationalism, Boyd too remained Blythe's lifelong friend.[53]

Blythe's dictatorial approach alienated members of the society who had been fired or excluded from parts, especially girls, and it proved difficult to fill the three female roles in *The Drone*. When May

Blevings[54] as Sarah McMinn withdrew after the Thursday première because the audience had jeered at her unattractive appearance and persona as the villain of the piece, Blythe tried to win her back by inducing Bob Henry of the *Chronicle* to publish his own review of the performance, singling out her handling of a challenging part. Since the *Chronicle* was a 'Saturday' paper and therefore published on the previous day, his review appeared in between the two performances, allegedly coaxing the actress to return to the cast after her tearful withdrawal on the Thursday night. Republished in the next edition of the 'Friday' *Herald*, it gave a glowing account of his friends' performances in *The Drone*, and especially of his own part as Uncle Dan Murray:[55]

> Mr Ernest Blythe presented it with splendid effectiveness, and difficult as it was, he carried the character through to success. If his accent was not altogether what we are accustomed to hear, his action and perception of the part could not well be improved on. An exceedingly clever character study was that of Mr Wm. Laird Doggart as John Murray, the farmer. Mr Doggart, in speech, manner and make-up, was practically perfect. . . . Mr James Jamieson, as Sam Brown, a labourer in the employment of John Murray, imparted a frequent touch of humour to the part.

The producer's presence on stage at the beginning of all three acts, in the person of Sam Brown, would have reassured inexperienced actors taking flashier parts.[56]

In *Trasna na Bóinne*, Blythe's review appears as a masterpiece of tactical plámás, indicating that Miss Blevings 'surpassed all the others with her acting skills', bringing 'to life a character who was completely contrary to herself. I recommended for everyone who had not seen the first performance to make sure that they saw the second one because it was rare that they would get the opportunity, even in the great cities of the world, to see acting better than that of Miss Blevings.'[57] In fact, Blythe's tepid and back-handed commendation must have made matters even worse:

> As Miss M'Minn, Miss May Blevings played a trying part with conspicuous ability. The part of the designing spinster is one that does not gain much sympathy from the audience, but Miss Blevings interpreted her part so effectively that the house was compelled to acknowledge the truthfulness of her portrayal.

Poor spinsterish Miss Blevings! Blythe's concluding appeal to attend the second performance, while vaunting 'one of the finest theatrical treats ever put before a Newtownards audience by local amateur actors or actresses', made no reference either to her brilliance or to the great cities of the world.[58] Blythe's private assessment of May's character was scornful of her social affectations: 'As she was a seamstress and was, therefore, on a level above the other girls, who worked in the factories or in the "mills", as they were called, we called her "Miss" always and I don't remember her first name.'[59]

Blythe's review was far more enthusiastic about the 'little Catholic girl' who played the heroine: 'That Miss Maggie McManus is no novice in the actor's art was quite evident, as her assumption of the role of Mary, John's daughter, proved. It was delightfully arch and captivating.' She had been poached from a rival dramatic society attached to the Catholic parish of St Patrick.[60] Maggie and Ernest appeared side by side in the cast photograph reproduced in his autobiography,[61] and he walked out with her 'once or twice' before, as usual, moving on to the next girl, apprehensive of being trapped. According to his characteristically cocky recollection: 'Despite giving pleasure to certain girls from time to time and letting them know that I liked them, as soon as I could control myself I would avoid them, for the fear of marriage.'[62]

Blythe recounted that a few days after taking an afternoon walk with Maggie, he received an anonymous letter 'denigrating her as a woman and an actor and stating that it was strange that a drama society couldn't be run without Papists. I don't think, however, that religious envy was entirely the cause for the letter.'[63] In fact, the letter from 'A Wellwisher' preserved in Blythe's papers sneered at Maggie McManus' class rather than her religion:

> I have often heard my pals speak about you concerning that girl named Macmanus. The password is fancy an Editor of an Newspaper keeping company with a doffer out of one of the mills.[64] The night of the play the audience thought she was going to devour all round her with her prominent teeth and her voice it is said is like a factory horn. . . . I wouldnt like to be very familiar with you but I shall finally express myself by saying you havent seen many girls.[65]

This jibe suggests that Ernest Blythe was not yet the self-denying potential ladykiller that he fondly imagined half a century later. He remained more comfortable in the company of impishly earnest young men like himself.

Producing *The Drone* was undoubtedly the climax of Blythe's period in Newtownards, leaving him exultant but drained. This mood was expressed in the *Ulster Guardian*'s review of a ULT revival at the Grand Opera House, before a full house only a few weeks later. The views of the anonymous reviewer closely resembled those of Cairbre, especially his objection to the additional third act as pure 'farce': 'As we have repeatedly pointed out, the Uncle Dan of the end of the play is a totally different character from the Uncle Dan at the beginning.' The reviewer had finally seen enough of *The Drone*: 'But if we may judge by one's personal impressions it would not be a bad idea to let the popular comedy now rest for a fairly long time on the laurels it has gained. Its appeal is slackening, whatever be the cause.'[66]

The same reviewer was far more excited by that 'masterpiece' (even 'miracle'), MacNamara's *Thompson in Tir-na-nOg*, in which an Orangeman blows himself up at the 'sham fight' in Scarva only to awaken in the company of Grania and the Fianna.[67] Four months earlier, after witnessing the first production, the *Ulster Guardian*'s reviewer had expressed confidence about Thompson's future conversion to nationalism:

> Beneath the burlesque Mr. Macnamara shows what we are sure he set out resolved in his mind to show – that Thompson, despite his ignorance of Irish history or his dwarfed and distorted idea

of patriotism, is at bottom as good an Irishman as the best, and if during his visit to Tir-na-N'og a war had taken place between its Ard-righ and, say, King Arthur, Thompson would, we are prepared to bet, have been found fighting shoulder to shoulder with Cuchulain.[68]

By March 1913, the reviewer was less sanguine about the prospect of a military alliance between Orange and Green, eloquently expressing Blythe's perennial ambivalence about Orangeism:

> We do not think there is a single Orangeman who would protest that Thompson is a caricature of the Order. Indeed, he makes a much better fight for Orangeism than the average Orangeman is capable of putting up. Nor have the other 'soort,' as Thompson refers to his opponents, much ground for complaint. . . . The play is a vocal triumph for Thompson, but it is a moral victory over the sour unreasonableness which makes Irishmen like Thompson proud of their Irish birth but ashamed of their countrymen and of their country's history. And of course with it all our sympathy goes out to Thompson, for we feel that his heart is in the right place if his head isn't, and that he is waging no mean battle according to his lights.

Perhaps, even now, ordinary decent Orangemen would break free from prejudice and redeem themselves as Irish patriots:

> And just as we get a peep of Thompson through a kindly haze that makes us indulgent to him, so the Thompsons in the pit and the gallery (we leave out the Thompsons in the stalls for they are beyond redemption) will by the sight on the stage of themselves as others see them come to a better appreciation of those shortcomings which keep them from being the best patriots in the world.

Blythe's authorship of this idiosyncratic critique is confirmed by the sly suggestion, a fortnight before his departure for the Kerry Gaeltacht, that 'with just a little care Uncle Dan, like Thompson, may stray into Tir-na-N'og'.[69]

III

Even if he tired eventually of playing Uncle Dan and watching *The Drone*, Blythe's infatuation with drama never wavered. By early 1914 he had established another amateur dramatic society among the farm labourers of Lispole in west Kerry, resulting in 'a variety entertainment consisting of Irish songs & dances & three short plays in Irish' in aid of the Christian Brothers in Dingle.[70] Blythe had evidently conquered his residual uneasiness about the Church of Rome. In the same year, he reasserted control in Protestant Newtownards:

> I spent about a fortnight at home up North. I visited Newtownards where the Dramatic Society, on advice that I had sent them from Kerry, were performing *The Turn of the Road* by Lewis Purcell [in fact Rutherford Mayne] and *The Lad from Largymore* by Séamas [Seumas] MacManus. I gave them some help and I stayed a few nights in the Doggart family home.[71]

His experience as an actor and his skill in voice production came in useful for Blythe as a public speaker. Though his delivery was unpretentious, he proved an effective canvasser for Sinn Féin before the South Armagh by-election of February 1918. The 'team' performed 'with true eloquence, too, for Bob Barton and Desmond Fitzgerald were orators, and Ernest Blythe could talk to the people in his sharp dialect, using their homely metaphors'.[72]

Blythe's theatrical taste was decidedly middle-brow, though he preferred plays with a political or social message to mere entertainments and 'farces'. As minister for finance in 1925, he declined to take over the ailing Abbey Theatre but introduced a modest yet vital annual subvention. Yeats was duly grateful: 'You have created the first endowed theatre in any English-speaking country, & as there are many people who would like to see the English government follow your lead I think once start the topic it will be taken up & spoken of far & near.'[73] Once out of parliamentary politics, the Irish National Theatre became his chief preoccupation. Blythe's performance as an Abbey director (1935–72) and as its managing director (1941–67), long ridiculed by those who regarded him as a philistine dullard, is belatedly being reassessed.[74] Apart from maintaining production after fire destroyed the theatre in 1951, eventually rebuilding it and balancing the books, his major contribution was to solicit and produce plays in the Irish language and to build up a troupe of competent 'Gaelic players', just as he had envisaged in 1908.

His own experiments as a dramatist were unadventurous: a translation into Irish of *Trial by Jury* by Gilbert and Sullivan, and a three-act comedy entitled *Rachel Ryan*, set in 1934 but never published and perhaps never performed. Set in 'an unpretentious suburban home' in Cuchulain Road, Dublin, the play centres on Bessie O'Neill's fantasies about her boy Charlie winning a fortune as a result of drawing a racehorse called Wytchwood Abbot for the 'Cambridgeshire'. She imagines the resultant news stories, interviews, and queues of eligible young ladies enticed by Charlie's promised £30,000. The play leaves us in suspense, the outcome of the race unrevealed. For a notoriously penny-pinching and book-balancing former minister for finance, presiding over an annual budget of barely £20 million, such dreams of easy wealth must have been wish-fulfilling.[75]

If Blythe's theatrical taste was plebeian, his judgement of artistic quality was surprisingly sharp. Unlike many Sinn Féiners and nationalist intellectuals, he had, after all, been bowled over by *The Playboy of the Western World* when he attended its first production at the Abbey Theatre in 1907. Twenty-one years later, when W. B. Yeats, Lady Gregory, and Lennox Robinson rejected Seán O'Casey's brilliant evocation of the Great War, *The Silver Tassie*, Blythe emphatically supported the old comrade with whom he had first explored Dublin's republican underground. O'Casey had been slow to send a copy to 'dear Ernie', treating him as a friend rather than a potential ally in his public tussle with the Abbey's directors, and boasting that 'it frightened hell out of Dublin's literary Chelsea men'.[76]

Blythe's response was equally warm:

> Thank you for sending me a copy of 'The Silver Tassie'. I have read it again and I think more than ever that it is a very moving and powerful play. I only hope I may be able to see it on the stage.

If the Directors of the Abbey had said they must reject it because they were afraid of a stupid riot in which their seats would get damaged and their curtain torn I could have understood their attitude. But when they decided to have none of it because it was not good enough for the Abbey and because it was unworthy of you, their minds worked in a way that is beyond my powers of comprehension.[77]

O'Casey responded excitedly that 'you probably know more about the Drama than those who are continually judging it. It is high noon time to realize that most of the art and literary deities of Dublin speak from a stand luminous with conceit and gorgeous with ignorance.' He looked forward 'with intense pleasure' to having Blythe to dinner at his London home (three years earlier, they had 'spent a vivacious evening talking of "old, and happy far off things, and battles long ago"').[78]

Blythe's appointment as an Abbey director on 9 March 1935 coincided precisely with publication of an article in *United Ireland* by 'An Old Supporter', almost certainly Blythe, in which he called for the appointment of three new directors (unspecified) whose presence would prevent 'undeniable mistakes in judgment' – such as rejection of *The Silver Tassie*.[79] The Abbey's reorganisation conformed closely to Blythe's prescription. When belatedly arranging with O'Casey to relaunch the battered *Tassie* at the Abbey a few months later, Yeats told him that 'I have just written to Blythe who is, now that Lennox [Robinson] is away, the most representative of our Board, telling him that you have permitted us to produce' the play. This production prompted a diatribe from the increasingly priggish 'Brinsley Macnamara' (John Weldon), another novice director who resigned from the board after failing to excise such 'wantonly offensive' passages as 'the travesty of the Sacred Office in the second act'. Blythe joined Yeats and the other four directors in refuting Macnamara's claims, especially his sneer that Abbey audiences had displayed an 'almost insane admiration for the vulgar and worthless plays of Mr. O'Casey'.[80]

In later life, O'Casey was dismissive of Blythe's management of the Abbey, claiming in 1950 that 'that fellow, Blythe, has done it in. I dare say, this was inevitable after the going of Yeats.'[81] Yet they remained 'fast friends',[82] tethered together by intersecting careers, shared secrets, and shared descent into splenetic old age. Among those shared secrets were memories of initiation into at least two brotherhoods. Above all, they were both men of the theatre. Had he been in a position to examine his own death certificate, Ernest Blythe would have been delighted by the description of his 'rank profession or occupation': not politician or journalist, as might have been expected, but 'Theatre Manager (Retired)'.[83]

PART THREE

Explanations

CHAPTER NINE

Some Questions

In making sense of Ernest Blythe's engagement with the Orange Order, and willingness to perjure his republican allegiance only three or four years after joining the IRB, we need to explore several hypothetical explanations:

I. As a young Protestant Ulsterman, did he join the Order as a *rite de passage* in accordance with family or neighbourhood tradition?

II. As a novice reporter, did he consider it his professional duty to penetrate the inner workings of Newtownards society by joining the town's elite Orange lodge?

III. Was he still uncertain of his political objectives and willing to try out any available option?

IV. Was he temperamentally drawn to the discipline, drama, and paraphernalia of secret societies in general?

V. Was he attracted by any movement that seemed likely to become involved in armed conflict with the Crown?

VI. Did the IRB's Belfast 'centre' enter lodge 1501 as a spy, hoping to collect information on Ulster's resistance to Home Rule and to entice brethren with potentially radical views into the IRB?

VII. Conversely, was he a loyalist spy in the republican camp?

VIII. Was he a police informer or an *agent provocateur*?

More or less plausible arguments may be presented in favour of each of these hypotheses. There remains a more comprehensive explanation for his conduct. Was Blythe, in some sense, a double agent?

I

Family tradition, so often the decisive impulse in fraternal enlistment, was surely a minor factor for Ernest Blythe. As shown in Part One, neither his father nor any close relative is known to have 'worn the sash', and his parents are portrayed in *Trasna na Bóinne* as displaying a dismissively condescending view of Orangemen. While the absence of nominal registers precludes verification of Blythe's own account, it has been shown that no identified older kinsman secured district office or became a lodge master apart from Thomas Blythe of Reilly's Trench, who does not figure in his autobiography. Furthermore, though he spent almost every weekend as well as holidays in Magheraliskmisk while living in Bangor and Newtownards, Blythe joined a lodge with no home or family connections.

II

As already suggested, membership of lodge 1501 was potentially useful for a journalist newly arrived in Newtownards, eager to penetrate the town's power structures and its social alignments and tensions. Blythe's coverage of local politics in the *North Down Herald*'s column 'The Old Town Clock' convincingly adopted the knowing tone of an insider. Yet Blythe was sufficiently alert, personable, and savvy to have mastered the town's political sociology even without *entrée* to the Orange hall. He had ample access to local preoccupations and gossip through his friendship with fellow reporters and participation in theatrical and debating societies. As a sociable teetotaller, he had a decided advantage over most journalists when fishing for information. However useful for intelligence gathering, membership of the Orange Order was not indispensable.

III

Another explanation for Blythe's duplicity is that, as a 21-year-old, he had yet to develop a settled political ideology and was still experimenting with sometimes wild alternatives. For many secret society men of his generation, political beliefs were less important than romantic preoccupation with the vestiges of Gaelic Ireland, whose language acted as a password into 'Irish Ireland' for those with even a rudimentary knowledge. Blythe's undoubted enthusiasm and missionary zeal for Irish, his great passion while still a boy clerk in the Department of Agriculture in Dublin, provided an obvious conduit into the IRB. The pre-war Orange Order was by no means immune to Irish revivalism, as illustrated by the Revd Richard Rutledge Kane's patronage of the Gaelic League and the Feis while grand master of Belfast (1884–98).[1] Even so, only an extreme optimist would have hoped to advance the cause of the language through joining lodge 1501, in which the only Irish speaker returned in 1911 was Blythe himself.

Many youngsters join a range of societies for a medley of motives, whether in search of variety, congenial company, or closer knowledge of the available options. Even for a committed republican, the appeal of radical republicanism was much reduced during Blythe's years in north Down by Sinn Féin's decline, the IRB's stagnation, and the apparent imminence of Home Rule. Yet, after four years of experimentation with most shades of nationalism (through the Gaelic League, the GAA, Sinn Féin, the IRB, the Dungannon clubs, even liberal and socialist societies), it seems implausible that mere curiosity would have prompted Blythe to enter such dangerous territory as an Orange lodge.

It might also be argued that Blythe's apparent duplicity was a typical symptom of the colonial condition, whereby citizen-subjects adopt multiple identities in order to serve two masters. As a citizen of an imagined Irish Republic, Blythe could discover something in common with the fellow-countrymen from whom he had been insulated as a child. As a subject of the Empire, he could take advantage of opportunities for employment as a civil servant or a journalist, and so gain access to a wider world. His simultaneous immersion in the IRB and the Orange might thus be interpreted as an extreme manifestation of colonial ambivalence. However, since few colonial contemporaries went so far as to penetrate two irreconcilable underworlds simultaneously, additional explanations must be sought for Blythe's aberrant expression of his multiple identities.[2]

There is ample evidence of Blythe's attraction to fraternal models of social and political organisation. This applied not only to the camaraderie and theatre of lodge meetings, but also to the methods by which brethren were recruited, disciplined, and mobilised. Fraternities such as the IRB, Ancient Order of Hibernians, and Orange Order were not self-absorbed elites but often the driving force in broader popular movements that they set out to infiltrate and manipulate. Though sharing conviction in their own moral and intellectual superiority and their entitlement to direct the uninitiated, these fraternities varied sharply in their methods and structures. By joining the Orange, Blythe gained access to the inner workings of a seemingly cumbersome organisation which had somehow managed to permeate a vast and highly effective political movement. This insight would have been valuable for any aspirant infiltrator, regardless of ideology. His later interest in 'semi-disciplined' bodies, eschewing the IRB's rigid centralisation, may have been influenced by his close observation of Orangeism in Newtownards.

In retrospect, Blythe stressed the simplicity rather than drama of his own initiation into the IRB in 1907.[3] He was fascinated by its code of discipline, according to which ordinary members knew none of their superior officers beyond their own circles, and in which the 'leaders' who occasionally inspected them were not identified. Even as a senior organiser, he remained uncertain about the identity of the putative 'president of the Irish republic' who headed the supreme council. He was impressed by the care taken by brethren to conceal their affiliation from outsiders, even friends or colleagues like Jack Shouldice under whom he worked in the Department of Agriculture. He strongly approved of the laborious character checks that preceded the admission of candidates (including himself), and the insistence on sobriety (though not total abstinence) as a prerequisite for discretion. Blythe's autobiography sets out the IRB's modus operandi in circumstantial detail, eschewing the coy reticence displayed by most ex-brethren even in late life.[4] The value he ascribed to its secretive discipline was political as well as moral, providing a model whereby a self-replicating elite could educate, energise, and control larger and less coherent movements.

Yet his experience of circle meetings in both Dublin and Belfast was that little was achieved beyond soliciting further recruits and raising small sums for buying arms.[5] As a provincial organiser in Munster and Ulster, he was constantly frustrated by the garrulousness, intoxication, and decrepitude of the old 'Fenians' whose names he had been given as potential centres or nuclei. By 1915, so he told me in 1972, he was no longer interested in the IRB, the open military movement having taken precedence since the split in the Irish Volunteers.[6] This account lacks an essential element: the systematic initiation of potential officers into the IRB, so that orders and information concerning the planned rebellion could be transmitted without recourse to the formal military chain of command. Blythe played a key part in expanding this clandestine network by personally initiating brethren during his tours, even as a paid Volunteer organiser. His preference for using a disciplined or semi-disciplined elite to control apparently open organisations was confirmed in the 1930s, when he espoused the fascist model of seemingly 'representative' vocational corporations superintended at every level by Blueshirt cadres.

Blythe applied similar precepts to the daunting challenge of 'language revival'. As an impassioned Irish Irelander with scanty Irish after almost a decade in the Gaelic League, he believed that propaganda and instruction alone were incapable of reviving its vernacular use. Having struggled to master the living language in the Lispole Gaeltacht at the beginning of the Great War, Blythe informed the League that it had 'absolutely failed' to preserve the living language by promoting its exclusive use: 'There is nothing of undoubted and indubitable value to show for the work of the past twenty years save a score or two of Irish-speaking children in places like Belfast and Dublin.' He believed it could 'be saved only in the Gaelic-speaking districts', not through conventional organisation or bribery but through a new body, 'under discipline as strict, and control as centralised as an army of soldiers or an order of priests'. This should 'carry on written and spoken propaganda, conduct schools and class[es], publish books and newspapers, run theatres and picture shows, fight elections, establish, assist and carry on industries', so integrating Irish speech with everyday life and national culture.[7]

Blythe's prescription for a Gaelic future involved the creation of self-sustaining communes under the iron discipline of strong leaders. Membership (including associates supplying financial support) would be restricted to Irish speakers, who would pledge themselves to speak only in Irish to fellow members and to 'bring up their children as Irish speakers'. Full members would have no 'private purse', relying on allowances to meet day-to-day requirements, and 'all shall conform to rule as to dietary and clothing, etc. and shall abstain from intoxicating liquor'. Only single men would be admitted to this missionary cadre, marriage being prohibited for five years, and all work in the commune would be conducted by its members 'except where unavoidable'. The commune's conduct would be 'solely in the hands of the President', who could be removed only by a two-thirds majority of members. The initial steps would follow the model of a religious mission, with three or four members visiting an Irish-speaking district to build a lecture hall, 'privately' win over between five and fifty likely lads, and finally announce the new organisation 'with a great flourish of trumpets'. Blythe's proposal was obviously inspired by his simultaneous work as a Volunteer organiser in Kerry, seeding local companies by first enrolling a few zealots into the IRB. Though ludicrously impracticable, this scheme confirms his preference for a secretive elite to mobilise and manipulate the masses in the national interest.

If Blythe revelled in the notion of an ascetic fraternity as an agent for mass conversion, he also enjoyed the drama and waggishness that typically offset such earnest aspirations. He shared these tastes with Seán O'Casey, who had introduced him to the IRB not long after his own alleged suspension from the Orange Order, having impulsively joined the green-sashed Irish National Foresters in an Ivy Day march to Glasnevin. O'Casey was particularly tickled by the elaborate rituals of the Royal Arch Purple.[8] Admittedly, Blythe had no liking for religious 'ritualism' (though Orangemen found no contradiction between denouncing ritualist clergymen and practising mock-religious rituals within the lodge). When first in Dublin, he had twice attended Mass out of curiosity, but found genuflection repellent and his presence as a Protestant impostor embarrassing: 'I decided in my mind that Mass is not as it is reported to be. I had no further curiosity about Catholicism for a long time.'[9] According to Leon Ó Broin: 'O'Casey had a predilection for the ultra-Catholic features of High Church Protestantism, whereas Blythe remained immovable in his inherited Low Church position. He was once assailed as a "Presbyterian bastard" and was able to retort that the accusation was "wrong on both counts".'[10] Yet, far from being repelled by O'Casey's ritualistic Anglo-Catholicism, Blythe identified it as a characteristically 'uncommon perspective' that only tended 'to increase the interest I had in all of his opinions'.[11]

Blythe was part amused, part intrigued by fraternal ritualism and hocus-pocus. A year or so before his Orange initiation, writing as 'Cairbre' in the *Irish Nation*, he poured scorn on the offer by delegates of the Ancient Order of Hibernians in the United States to send 14,000 Hibernian riflemen to liberate Ireland:

> Certainly the sight of two grown men coming over from America and trying to propagate a childish secret society with passwords and mysterious ritual, and giving themselves airs, calling themselves high-sounding names . . . was a very funny one indeed.[12]

The object of his ridicule was not the great sectarian brotherhood headed by Joseph Devlin's Board of Erin, widely regarded as the 'hidden power' behind Redmond's Home Rule movement, but its American counterpart, which had sponsored a rival faction in Ireland through an 'Irish–American Alliance'. Though deploring Devlinite Hibernianism even more than Orangeism, Blythe thereby acknowledged its chilling efficiency in mobilising nationalists behind a sectarian banner.[13] Blythe himself was of course disqualified from membership, since all Hibernian factions were restricted to practising Roman Catholics.

Yet two passages in his account of gaol life in early 1918, written in 1954 for the Bureau of Military History, suggest a typically playful fraternalist. In Dundalk:

> Paddy Sweeney organised a so-called secret society known as 'The Roughs and Toughs', with initiation ceremonies, secret signs and passwords. Someone got up an opposition body called 'The Ku Klux Klan', into which Dick McKee, Michael Brennan and I, amongst others, were initiated.[14]

After transfer to Belfast gaol, he found that 'all sorts of foolish and boyish tricks were played' by the resident republicans:

> The practice of forming so-called secret societies which had existed in Dundalk was also to the fore in Belfast. A 'No collar' brigade was formed and men went round the prison taking the collar and tie off anyone whom they found wearing them. . . . The result of the activities of the 'no collar' brigade was the formation of a society known as the 'collar and tie' society. One morning about half-past nine when the men were dismissed after the morning parade in the yard a large number of them suddenly disappeared. They came back wearing their shoes and trousers but nothing else except collars and ties round their bare necks. One friendly warder spoke to me about this incident and told me how humiliated he was at seeing men going around the yard like half-naked savages, as he said, 'with all them Orange warders looking at them'.[15]

Blythe was interested in dressing up as well as down. At Christmas 1915, the staff of the Irish Volunteers in Limerick city 'presented me with a Volunteer uniform, which I wore on all special occasions afterwards. In Limerick Australian hats were the uniform headgear.'[16] Blythe was delighted by his military persona, posing in his new uniform with a captain's three trefoil cuff-buttons and wide-brimmed hat, along with suitable props (blackthorn and cowering dog), for a photograph reproduced in his autobiography.[17] He stood as erect as permitted by his hunched posture, a bequest of recurrent childhood bronchitis allegedly induced by his witchlike grandmother, who had consigned him as a toddler to sleep in a damp attic store-room.[18] And in 1958, his friend Willie Doggart's little sister Mabel reminded Blythe that when her cousins visited their home in East Street, where Blythe was lodging, 'you used to slip their hats on your head and look at yourself in the mirror'.[19]

Like many Edwardian would-be dandies who were most comfortable in male company, the young Blythe might be described as a flirtatious misogynist. In the Fianna Éireann: 'The girls' Sluagh was a terrible thorn in the side of the boys because its existence caused them to be named "The Betsy Grays" up and down the Falls Road; but they were never able to get it abolished.' Being dominated by James Connolly's formidable daughters, Nora and Ina, the Betsy Grays were impervious to boyish jeers.[20] When languishing in Reading gaol over Easter 1916, Blythe found it 'almost impossible to read' the books by Mrs Henry Woods and Mrs Humphry Ward thoughtfully selected for him by the librarian warder: 'I left a note on my slate one day saying, "No more books by women, please". After that I got boys' adventure stories and detective tales, which were much better.'[21]

Blythe's preference for boys easily transmuted into contempt for women. Just after the civil war, when the chivalrous Kevin O'Higgins fulminated against the indulgence shown to national army officers who had assaulted and humiliated daughters of a doctor in Kenmare, Blythe was unexcited:

> Apparently, the girls were dragged out of their beds and were beaten with belts. No great harm was done to them, and the outrage was more an indignity than anything else.

Indeed, he was not 'particularly revolted at what seemed to me to be merely a case of a trouple [*sic*] of tarts getting a few lashes that did them no harm'.[22] Yet military witnesses reported that Florence and Jessie MacCarthy had been pulled out of their father's house in night attire and flogged with Sam Browne belts and had grease poured over their hair, a red mark being observed on Jessie's face.[23] Likewise, when told that his wicked grandmother Chelley had once been given 'a belt' by grandfather Robert 'that left a blue mark on her shoulder', Blythe's sympathy was entirely with the perpetrator: 'She spent the next two days going from house to house in the neighbourhood showing everyone the proof that her brute of a husband was after hitting her. The poor man was so ashamed that he never made any other attempt at rebelling, until he was on his deathbed.'[24]

So far, so bad: with such attitudes, Blythe should have fitted comfortably into most all-male secret societies. Yet, if fraternal proclivities were his primary impulse for joining the Orange, he would surely have used connections such as Jamesie Jamieson to introduce him to Freemasonry, which had even more exotic, intricately choreographed, and laddish ceremonies than the Orange Order. It was also the best organised of all fraternities, with well-honed procedures for inculcating moral precepts, vetting candidates, punishing offenders, raising money for charitable causes, and transmitting information throughout a large network of lodges. He had at least one Freemason in the immediate family, his father's youngest brother. Alfred Edward Blythe (1867–1956), who sent Ernest a droll postcard in 1909 which he never discarded, was a zealous Freemason during his long tenure as a national schoolteacher in Tynan, County Armagh.[25] Since almost all his fellow journalists in Bangor and Newtownards became Freemasons, Blythe must have been tempted to do likewise. According to his autobiography, he was 'leaning towards' membership, following approaches from Bob Henry and Jamesie Jamieson, until he learned that the fees would amount to pounds rather than shillings. In explaining his refusal of Jamieson's invitation, Blythe emphasised that he had no objection in principle: 'I did not believe any of the propaganda against the Masons that is widely accepted in Ireland.'[26]

The monetary explanation is not entirely convincing. Though Blythe might have found it difficult to afford both subscriptions on the salary of a junior reporter, his frugal habits (he 'neither smoked nor drank') should have enabled him to cover the fees for Jamieson's Union Star lodge 198.[27] Throughout his life, he deplored Catholic vilification of Freemasonry as bigotry. As he wrote to a priest in County Limerick in January 1925:

The 'freemason' slander which has been put around seems to be aimed at driving out every Protestant who occupies a responsible position in the Civil Service. The present Government will not stand for any form of political or sectarian test being applied to public servants.[28]

In a dyspeptic commonplace book replete with the scrawled expostulations of an angry old man, he extolled Freemasons as 'honest & honourable men', unlike the 'Knights of Columba' [St Columbanus] who were 'peopled by combinatn [*sic*] of idiots & chancers Catholic Sect to grab share of imagined graft from Masons'.[29] Yet, for an incorrigible politician like Blythe, Freemasonry in Ireland had a decisive defect: despite its sinister continental reputation, it seldom intervened in politics and had no recent record of infiltrating mass organisations.[30] From this perspective, the fact that Blythe did *not* join the Masonic is no less significant than his infiltration of the Orange. Attracted though he was by fraternal discipline and horseplay, Blythe had more valuable prizes in mind when he became an Orangeman.

v

Throughout his career, Blythe was excited by the allure of terror and violence as political weapons. When joining the IRB's Teeling circle, Blythe was attracted not only by its link with the Gaelic League but also by its sentimental commitment to making war upon Britain, though he deplored terrorism through assassination as practised by the 'Invincibles'.[31] As an Orangeman between 1910 and 1912, Blythe belonged to an organisation that seemed far more likely than the IRB to engage imminently in rebellion against the Crown. Like Pearse and MacNeill, he regarded the admittedly uncertain prospect of violent resistance against Home Rule as likely to benefit the national cause by bringing armed Irishmen, regardless of their professed motives, into collision with British forces.[32] If so, the Orange might even have qualified as one of those movements 'calculated to advance the cause of Irish independence' which the IRB was constitutionally bound to support!

Blythe combined his rhetorical enthusiasm for 'the doctrine of the sword' with personal abstention from violence. Above all a propagandist, he showed no inclination to act on his own incendiary advice. Many times arrested and imprisoned,[33] he never physically resisted his captors; though an indefatigable organiser of the IRB and Irish Volunteers, he never participated in 'engagements' or 'stunts'. Blythe's readiness to offer his own life as a 'bloody sacrifice' in April 1916 was not tested, as he had been imprisoned a few days before the rebellion upon failing to report to the Abingdon police as required by his 'exile' order. This act of defiance is perplexing. Before deportation from Dublin, Blythe was said to have been told by an executive member of the Irish Volunteers to lull police suspicions by obeying all such orders, so that he could be spirited back to Dublin in time for the show. His intimate friend from Kerry, Desmond FitzGerald, charitably inferred that Blythe had never received this instruction.[34]

Blythe's continuing delight in the *idea* of 'ruthless warfare' was evident in his advocacy of the slaughter of all those abetting the Crown forces, should conscription be imposed in 1918, and his robust defence of exemplary executions during the civil war.[35] In his celebrated manifesto published in *An tÓglach: Official Organ of the Irish Volunteers* a month before the armistice, and composed in Belfast gaol, Blythe revelled in the prospect of unfettered physical force in response to conscription:

> In our resistance we shall acknowledge no limit and no scruple. We must recognise that anyone, civilian or soldier, who assists directly or by connivance in this crime against us, merits no more consideration than a wild beast and should be killed without mercy or hesitation as opportunity offers. . . . Any man who knowingly and willingly does anything to facilitate the working of the machinery of conscription, must be dealt with exactly as if he were an enemy soldier. Thus the man who serves on an exemption tribunal, the doctor who treats soldiers or examines conscripts, the man who voluntarily surrenders when called for, the man who in any shape or form applies for exemption, the man who drives a police-car or assists in the transport of army

supplies, all these having assisted the enemy must be shot or otherwise destroyed with the least possible delay.[36]

This inspirational advice evidently delighted Collins, meriting republication after the armistice as a possible model for future 'resistance', and leading to Blythe's enlistment in army propaganda after his release from prison.[37] Typical of Blythe in pressing a proposition to its logical limits, however repugnant, it deserves inclusion in any manual for would-be terrorists.[38]

Blythe was equally ferocious in advocating executions and reprisals during the civil war. Though unruffled by General Paddy Daly's treatment of Dr MacCarthy's daughters in Kenmare, he favoured his removal from the Kerry command, 'mainly because he was not prepared to stand up to the necessary business of carrying out executions when they were justified'.[39] On 17 November 1922, Blythe made no apology for the first four official executions, for offences such as possession of a revolver: 'If a man carries a revolver in the street, when men every day are making attacks on the National Forces, then that man must know that he does it at his own risk.' As 'a member of the Government', he accepted 'the fullest responsibility for putting these men to death'. Once again, Blythe seemed to exult in the prospect of 'whatever bloodshed may be necessary':

> This Nation is now suffering from the effects of a deadly cancer. We must use the knife to cut it out, and it would have been better for us never to have begun asserting the will of the majority of the Irish people if we were not prepared to go through with it.[40]

When defending the execution of prisoners such as Erskine Childers, two days after the inauguration of the Irish Free State, he stated that all such killings were justified only by 'military necessity' and required no resolutions of the Dáil to legitimise them. He brushed aside the aversion to reprisals against prisoners expressed by Labour's 'very much respected' Thomas Johnson: 'Frequently nations are compelled, when they are faced with the commission of war crimes, to carry out reprisals on prisoners whom they have already in their hands.' Such actions should be judged by their results: 'If the Irregulars are falling away at the present moment is it because within the last week or two, we have been exceptionally clement and patient, or that we have been exceptionally drastic?'[41]

Blythe's eloquent advocacy of systematic violence against republican rebels reassured unionist observers, who had doubted the will and capacity of the new government to confront its yet more undesirable adversaries. Even his views on how to confront those abetting conscription, however obnoxious to Orangemen and unionists in 1918, had much in common with the apocalyptic rhetoric of Ulster's leaders in 1912–13 as they prepared for possible revolution. Yet the hypothesis that Blythe joined the Orange in order to promote ruthless warfare against the Crown falters when we consider the timing of his resignation, at the very moment when his lodge was first being drilled and trained for possible future action against the police or army. If his intention were to promote rebellion for its own sake, he would surely have remained in lodge 1501, signed the Ulster Covenant like his father, and joined the Ulster Volunteers.

VI

According to an alternative hypothesis, Blythe entered the Orange as a republican recruiting agent or spy, hoping to acquire insight into Ulster's preparations for possible rebellion and the mentality of those currently opposed to Irish republicanism. This is certainly consistent with his own admission that, while working in Bangor and Newtownards, he kept his nationalist views secret in both public and private, except when discreetly but ineffectually trying to identify potential converts to nationalism. Given the enrolment of many Ards Presbyterians as United Irishmen in 1798, and the occasional irruption of 'green lodges' and Fenian Freemasons and Orangemen, he may also have hoped to use lodge 1501 as a site for awakening national consciousness among the brethren, or even for IRB recruitment.

The zig-zag trajectory of the Independent Orange Order, founded in 1903, had demonstrated that evangelical loyalism was a volatile outlook, capable of transforming Robert Lindsay Crawford from the zealous Orangeman and editor of the evangelical *Irish Protestant* into a Home Ruler editing the *Ulster Guardian*, and eventually into an Irish republican activist in Canada.[42] By 1909, however, 'the revolt against the regular unionists was dying down', as Blythe learned from conversations with the proprietor of the *North Down Herald*, following his brief courtship of Independent Orangemen through the separate Belfast edition that reported and supported their campaign.[43] Republican infiltrators would therefore have found it even harder than usual to liberate Orangemen from their unionist shackles by exploiting divisions within the Orange. Even so, as indicated by Blythe's contributions to the *Ulster Guardian*, opportunities might yet arise to convert Orangemen into Irish patriots, to foster the fledgeling 'Orange Republican party', and to beckon the Thompsons of the Order in the direction of Tír na nÓg.[44]

As shown above, Blythe was strikingly unsuccessful in identifying and cultivating potential republicans in north Down. In Belfast, by contrast, republican agents had some success in transforming militant opponents into militant republicans. Rory Haskin, a Moravian British army veteran and Orangeman who had joined the UVF, was sounded out by Frank Wilson of the Belfast IRB, enrolled in the Freedom club, and introduced to the IRB by Blythe and Seán Lester.[45] Wilson's success in snaring Haskin was doubtless assisted by their common upbringing in small, close-knit religious coteries. Wilson, who refused to reveal his religion in 1911, had belonged to the 'Brethren' in 1901, though his father was Presbyterian.[46] Wilson became a drill instructor for the Irish Volunteers, and was interned in Frongoch after being caught in Tyrone in possession of a revolver and field equipment.[47] Blythe may have hoped to win over recruits with similar expertise in lodge 1501, which included at least one ex-serviceman.[48]

Wilson's previous conquests included his celebrated lodger Seán McDermott (1883–1916), initially a zealot of the Ancient Order of Hibernians who was introduced to the Belfast Dungannon club by Wilson and thence to the IRB. McDermott was paid by the Dungannon club to tour Hibernian divisions in search of recruits, and repaid his sponsors handsomely by betraying the Order's secrets:

'During his membership of the A.O.H. he furnished us with each new Hibernian password which was a source of great amusement.'[49] Larking aside, possession of the current password would have enabled republican spies to infiltrate divisions throughout the country in the guise of visiting brethren. Like Blythe, McDermott had no hesitation in perjuring himself for the greater republican good, having solemnly undertaken as a novice Hibernian 'that I will not divulge or allow to be divulged, the password of the Order, not even to a member of my own Division.'[50]

Blythe's resignation from the Orange Order after less than two years is consistent with the supposition that he had joined as an underground recruiting agent or a spy. The longer he remained a member, the greater the risk that the brethren would hear rumours of his continuing open involvement in Belfast republicanism and the Dungannon clubs, and eventually of his contributions to the IRB's *Irish Freedom* in Dublin and the liberal *Ulster Guardian* in Belfast. Blythe made some attempt to conceal his multiple identities. Since his contributions to the *Ulster Guardian* were either anonymous or attributed to 'Purple Star', his Home Rule persona would not have been obvious to colleagues or brethren in Newtownards. It is noteworthy that he was not recognisably a contributor to *Irish Freedom* until May 1912, three months after his resignation from the lodge. By using Irish forms of his name in *Irish Freedom*, Blythe thereafter made himself known to republican readers but not to monolingual unionists, to whom 'Earnan', 'Earnan na Blaghd', and 'Earnán de Blaghd' would have conveyed nothing. The fact that his sister Helen in Magheragall was a subscriber to *Irish Freedom* suggests that Blythe wished to avoid being caught with the incriminating journal in Newtownards.[51] On the other hand, when in Bangor he had a weekly order for *Sinn Féin*, *An Claidheamh Soluis*, the *Peasant*, and eventually the *Irish Homestead*, kept for him at the station news-stand by 'a girl who was a Protestant and a Unionist'.[52]

In writing of his 'double life' as a Belfast republican and an ostensibly unionist reporter a few miles to the east, Blythe indicated that he nevertheless managed to conceal his nationalist views from his friends and acquaintances in north Down. Yet it seems scarcely credible that brethren such as William Wright or Thomas Lavery, let alone Blythe's fellow journalists, remained oblivious to his other life in Belfast, and with each additional month in the Orange the risk increased of his being outed and ousted. Mabel Doggart recalled the suspicions of a neighbour in East Street: 'It seems while you would be passing her house she used to call out, There he goes again. He is an "Old Spy".'[53] Under these circumstances, resignation was an option preferable to expulsion leading to public exposure.

VII

It seems less credible that Blythe infiltrated the Gaelic League, the GAA, the IRB, the Fianna Éireann, and the Dungannon clubs as a loyalist spy, or that he remained a unionist mole even when serving as a minister in the revolutionary Dáil and the Executive Council of the Irish Free State. If so, one would expect Blythe to have been first an Orangeman, then a republican. A unionist mole would also have taken greater pains to conceal his Orangeism from republicans by abstaining, for example, from platform appearances at Twelfth demonstrations (as reported in 1911). Blythe was undeniably the subject of scurrilous rumours before, during, and after the revolutionary era, and was acutely aware of the suspicion with which all Ulster Protestants were regarded by many republicans. This may explain the long period of 'probation' to which his IRB candidacy was subjected after O'Casey's initial invitation in 1906, though Blythe challenged O'Casey's own explanation that, 'as a stranger to Dublin and unknown to the people with authority in the organisation, I should be kept under observation for some months'.[54] Republican doubts about his good faith may also have led to his premature removal as Belfast 'centre', though Blythe claimed to have been told by Hobson and McCullough that this was designed 'to enable McCullough to be elected to a higher office'.[55]

Such suspicions resurfaced in 1915, when Blythe was trying unavailingly to enlist Irish Volunteers in Templeglantine, County Limerick:

Tom O'Donnell's paper published a strong attack on me, stating that I was paid £600 a year by Carson, and that my object in Kerry was to entrap the young men into the Volunteers for the purpose of having their names available when conscription should be applied by the British.

According to Blythe, this oft-repeated slur was sufficiently absurd to be counter-productive, as about forty boys subsequently joined the new company.[56] Yet inspection of O'Donnell's *Kerry Advocate* reveals a different and even more damaging accusation, under the heading 'Carson's Agents':

> Two Orangemen from Belfast – men who twelve years ago were ardent supporters of Carson's campaign, are the paid organisers in Kerry of this newest form of treason to Ireland [the Irish Volunteers]. They are doing Carson's work more effectively than ever they did before. . . . If ever conscription is applied to Ireland, these men will be responsible, for not alone will they not fight themselves, but they will try to prevent others from doing it.[57]

Thus O'Donnell did not claim that the unnamed 'agents', Blythe and Alf Cotton,[58] were paid by Carson, and did not explicitly suggest that the Irish Volunteers were *deliberately* seeking or abetting conscription. Even if it were merely the outcome of guesswork or sloppy terminology,[59] O'Donnell's reference to 'two Orangemen from Belfast' was dangerously close to the bone.

VIII

By comparison with more recent Irish revolutionary movements, typically riddled with informers and *agents provocateurs* in their innermost circles, there is little evidence of successful infiltration of the IRB or Irish Volunteer command (as distinct from local units). This is partly attributable to the inefficiency and underfunding of the many disconnected counter-intelligence agencies associated with the police and armed services. Even so, despite the paucity of official documentation, it would be surprising if no infiltration occurred.

The prima facie case against Blythe rests on two facts. The first is the striking disjunction between his fiery advocacy of violence and his personal disengagement from fighting. Incendiary bluster is indeed consistent with the strategy of an *agent provocateur*, intent on beckoning zealots into public view to facilitate their identification and arrest. His wartime employment as a regional organiser for the IRB and Irish Volunteers in Ulster and especially Munster would have been ideal for such an agent. Yet the same disjunction between word and deed has a less serpentine explanation. Like many republican strategists, Blythe believed that blood-curdling propaganda was more effective than actual violence, and that co-ordinated threats of violence would not only intimidate the 'enemy' but encourage systematic mobilisation of local activists. If activists were arrested, their subsequent ordeals would provide valuable material for future anti-government propaganda. Blythe consistently preached the need for collective discipline and impressive shows of militancy, as distinct from practical preparation for warfare. If the masses were well enough organised in impressive military array, there might be no necessity for war.

The second relevant fact is his intimacy with policemen, especially in north Down, and his evident discomfort at such connections. When arriving at a hotel in 1917 to organise the Castletownbere Volunteers, Blythe was embarrassed to receive a letter of invitation from the district inspector of the RIC, James Murnane. While preparing to follow his father (and grandfather) into the force, Murnane had helped found the Newtownards Amateur Dramatic Society, being replaced by Blythe as secretary when he embarked on officer training at the Phoenix Park depot in March 1912. His father, as district inspector in Newtownards, knew all too much about Blythe, having warned James of his friend's membership of the IRB when in Dublin.[60] The Murnanes, though Catholics, would also have been well aware that Blythe had joined the Orange Order, a fact raising the possibility of blackmail leading to the provision of information on republican activities. James Murnane's record, though not unblemished, suggests a competent and courageous officer, who remained in the force until its disbandment in May 1922. He received two favourable records, including one for 'good duty' in Clonmel, County Tipperary, during the bloodiest phase of the guerrilla campaign in March 1921.[61]

Murnane amiably informed Blythe of his conspicuous appearance at the head of an old list of suspects to be arrested upon the outbreak of war, evidently published in the Dublin *Hue and Cry*:[62]

> I cut short the interview as soon as I could without insulting the man. I did not feel that it would be any help to me locally to have it reported over Castletownbere that on my arrival I had spent a long time closeted with the District Inspector.[63]

Indeed, even a short time closeted with a police officer might have served to bolster doubts about Blythe's true allegiance.

It is noteworthy that Blythe gave a variant account of this unsettling incident in his last volume of autobiography. In this version, it was Murnane rather than Blythe who desired discretion about their meeting, which occurred at Blythe's hotel when Murnane presented himself in 'a regular suit' rather than his officer's uniform:

> We talked a bit about people whom we knew in Newtownards, especially Jamie Jamieson, founder of the Dramatic Society, and Willy Quinn, who was murdered.[64] After criticising the Ulster Volunteers a bit, Murnane said that if we were to meet one another in the street the following day he would not let on that he knew me, and he said that it might be best if I wouldn't show that we were old acquaintances. I agreed with him, but I decided in my mind that I would have to tell the story of his visit to all the boys in case word spread that I was speaking with the district inspector about secrets.[65]

Whichever 'story' he told 'the boys', it was clearly designed to scotch the suspicion that he was an informer.

Blythe's acute sensitivity to the charge of fraternising with policemen is apparent in his account of meeting an older school contemporary who was training at the RIC depot in the Phoenix Park. During the half-year interval between O'Casey's invitation and Blythe's admission to the IRB, he was approached by his uniformed acquaintance in Fontenoy Street. Fearing 'that I might ruin my fledgeling nationalist reputation by staying and talking with constables in the street, just as I might ruin it as easily by bringing constables to my lodgings for tea', Blythe rather perversely proposed visiting a pub. As a teetotaller, this was his first such experience. They 'spoke kindly about our families, about people who were at school with us, and the like', but Blythe evaded the constable's proposal to go to the Tivoli while agreeing to write to him suggesting possible dates: 'It goes without saying that I never wrote him the letter.'[66] Why then did he need to say it?

One recalls his apparent fraternisation with the police in Bangor as a reporter for the *Herald*, and his denial, despite outward appearances, of having allowed polite acquaintance to develop into friendship.[67] According to *Trasna na Bóinne*, Blythe's involvement with the IRB in Dublin was known to the district inspector in Bangor as well as to David Murnane in Newtownards. Though Blythe's activities in north Down were carefully monitored, he was never challenged or charged by the RIC. When he pasted up half a dozen posters in Bangor mourning the executed Indian assassin Madan Lal Dhingra (his only public assignment for the Belfast IRB, in July 1909),[68] the police removed them overnight and made no reference to their existence next morning when he visited the barracks for the usual briefing. Blythe's account of this incident is tantalising: 'Though I did not assume, at the time, that I was suspected of having put the posters up, I was told something, a year or two later, that suggested that the constables knew well who had brought the posters to Bangor.'[69]

These passages suggest that Blythe's connection with members of the RIC was at times uncomfortably close, and that any sign of intimacy with the 'Crown forces' tended to arouse republican suspicions. Such suspicions may have intensified when he married Annie McHugh in the Catholic University church, St Stephen's Green, on 13 November 1919.[70] Annie was a teacher who, with Louise Gavan Duffy, had founded Scoil Bhríde (otherwise St Brigid's High School and Kindergarten on St Stephen's Green) as an Irish-language girls' school in 1917.[71] Her father Patrick and brother John had both been district inspectors, though John resigned from the force after less than two years' service in 1910, having been 'severely reprimanded' for absenting himself without leave 'in consequence of becoming intoxicated in the house of a resident in his district'.[72] Patrick McHugh, like David Murnane, had risen from the ranks, serving for no less than forty-two years before retiring on pension early in the Great War. His record was equally exemplary, resulting in favourable records arising from cases of housebreaking, 'clever frauds' (exposed through his 'detective ability'), obtaining money by false pretences, and rioting in Londonderry city in August 1913.[73]

When arrested a few months before his marriage, Blythe was carrying an unread letter addressed to Richard Mulcahy which 'advocated a system of attacks on the parents and relatives of R.I.C. men, which was something of which I completely disapproved'. It is noteworthy that Blythe voiced this opinion when the letter was produced at the preliminary hearing before his court martial.[74] According to Mulcahy, 'Blythe was in the position that during the Black-and-Tan period he was very outraged at this idea of killing police'.[75] The slur resurfaced in 1930, when Frank Aiken used a debate on the re-election of Cosgrave as president to blacken Blythe's name from the opposition benches:

> Mr. Blythe was very loud in his blood-and-thunder talk before the war about sword-tracks through the ranks of his enemies to freedom, but when the war started he was a peace-loving citizen. He was against the shooting of policemen. It was a case of: 'Oh, Shenandoah, I love your daughter.' He was very fond of their daughters and pleaded as to why they should get off.[76]

Blythe was clearly intimate with many policemen and their families, and was repeatedly embarrassed by such connections. Yet there is no compelling reason to infer that Blythe acted as a police informer or an *agent provocateur*, even if the Murnanes (and conceivably the McHughs) hoped he might do so.

1. Three faces of the young Blythe: sulky schoolboy, would-be dandy, and man-about-town trying to grow a moustache: EB, *Trasna na Bóinne* (1957); *Gaeil á Múscailt* (1973).

An teach inar tógadh an t-údar, mar atá anois

2. The Blythes' farmhouse, Magheraliskmisk: EB, *Trasna na Bóinne* (1957).

3. Main Street, Bangor, and Market Square, Newtownards (early twentieth century): W. A. Green Collection (HOYFM.WAG 3102, 3302), Ulster Folk and Transport Museum, © National Museums NI.

4. Orangemen assembling in Church Street, Newtownards (undated), and members of Volunteers lodge 1501 at 'the field' with banner depicting Revd William Wright (1947): Trevor McCavery, *Newtown: A History of Newtownards* (1994); Newtownards District No. 4 website. The former image is reproduced by courtesy of Dr Trevor McCavery, Newtownards.

5. Three luminaries of Volunteers lodge 1501, Newtownards: T. R. Lavery (1937), Revd William Wright (1909), and Sir William Mitchell-Thomson, 2nd Bt (1921): portrait in Orange Hall, Newtownards; *Belfast and the Province of Ulster: Contemporary Biographies*, ed. W. T. Pike (1909); gift of Bassano and Vandyck Studios (NPG x120990), © National Portrait Gallery London.

6. Blythe as Irish Volunteer organiser, flaunting his uniform in a Belfast street, with pistol, and in a country lane, with dog and blackthorn (*c.*1915–18): EB, *Slán le hUltaigh* (1970); *Gaeil á Múscailt* (1973).

7. Blythe with ministerial colleagues in the funeral procession for Michael Collins (28 August 1922, second from left, front), and in top hat and tails (*c.*1922, far right): NLI, W. D. Hogan Collection (HOGW 22); Hugh Kennedy Collection (KEN 4). These images are reproduced by courtesy of the National Library of Ireland.

8. Blythe as portrayed by Gordon Brewster for the Dublin *Evening Herald*, in 'The 'G' Man', as a detective gathering intelligence for a proposed tax on betting (28 January 1926), and in 'Hey Presto!', restoring the shilling docked from the old-age pension in 1924 (1 March 1928): NLI, Gordon Brewster Cartoon Collection (PD 2199, TX 20, 176). These images of the artist's original drawings and annotations are reproduced by courtesy of the National Library of Ireland.

CHAPTER TEN

Double Agent?

I

The possibility remains that Blythe was at least briefly a double agent, who exploited the knowledge and trust that he accumulated in both camps to try to mitigate the mutual misconceptions of loyalists and republicans. There is no direct evidence to suggest that he betrayed the secrets of the IRB to the Orange Order, or indeed the reverse. But it seems likely that he used his dual membership to try to spread national sentiments among Orangemen, and to persuade his republican brethren of the earnestness and revolutionary potential of Orangemen.

At this point, it is worth re-examining how Blythe himself construed his 'double life' in *Trasna na Bóinne*. Denying systematic deceit, he admitted merely to 'restraining my tongue a little':

> In my mind and in my room reading or writing, and in the company of just a few people in Newtownards who were very friendly with me, I strongly and without doubt was very much against the connection with England. In Belfast, I was a proclaimed Sinn Féiner, speaking in that vein with my fellow Sinn Féiners, and attending meetings. And as far as my fellow Sinn Féiners were aware, I wrote Sinn Féin propaganda in abundance. Among the local journalist fraternity, however, I was a news reporter who was friendly with everyone, without any distinctive sign that I was any different to any other local Protestants, and with nothing about me that would indicate that I had much interest in anything except collecting news. As a result of this, I would get invitations to join with the Orangemen and with the Masons. Even when the anti-Home Rule movement got heated and it was known that I refused to sign the 'Ulster Covenant', I was not met with enmity or with any coldness in the company of the people with whom I worked.

People who noticed that he held 'heretical opinions in terms of politics' would indulgently assume that Blythe was 'only a bit queer' in the head: 'The average northern Protestant at that time had all sorts of suspicions about any Catholic, but they had nothing but trust for a Protestant, even if he was a bit strange in himself.'[1]

To a surprising degree, he did indeed retain the trust of Orange and unionist friends. Long after his republicanism became generally known, former colleagues and friends remained notably loyal, never referring directly to his record as a pre-war Orangeman. When reporting Blythe's incarceration in Belfast gaol in August 1915, two and a half years after his departure from County Down, David Alexander's *Spectator* paid a carefully worded tribute to his 'essentially honest' character:

> Mr. Blythe was well known in Bangor, and his intellectual endowments and kindly personality won from him the friendship of numerous people in the locality, even those who[se] political ideas and aspirations differed from his own. A keen student, a widely read and cultured man and a writer of vigorous simplicity, he followed unhesitatingly the course of life adopted by his judgment. He is a Gaelic student of eminence, and a well-known writer in the Irish language . . . Whatever his political views were, he was essentially honest and free from materialistic considerations.

When publishing Blythe's account of his pursuit by the RIC in the *Newtownards Chronicle*, sent two days before his arrest, its editor Bob Henry recalled his 'very unassuming manner and a kindly way which made for him many friends in the district, including ourselves'. Henry also accepted Blythe's denial of claims that he had tried to evade arrest, pointing out that he had given his full current address for publication in the *Chronicle*.[2] Blythe remembered his support with gratitude:

> A few weeks later when I was sentenced to three months, Bob Henry published an editorial in the *Newtownards Chronicle* that was very amicable. He impressed that my friends in Newtownards

were sorry that I had gone down that road but that nobody who knew me thought that I was a scoundrel. They hoped that what had happened would not go against me in the future. I felt that it was very noble of him to write the note considering that the *Chronicle* was an Orange newspaper, that it was exclusively read by Unionists and that Bob himself was an ardent Orangeman. It would have been easier for him not to mention me at all.[3]

Further evidence that Blythe was not despised as an apostate is provided by a letter from his old housemate and *Chronicle* comrade Willie Doggart (a Covenant signatory), sent while awaiting demobilisation in France two months after the Armistice. Doggart applauded Blythe's electoral success as Sinn Féin's candidate in North Monaghan: 'Good old Uncle Dan. I was delighted he had gone in with such "A WALLOP". Give him my heartiest congratulations.'[4] When *Trasna na Bóinne* secured a literary award honouring Douglas Hyde in 1958,[5] the *Chronicle* likewise adopted an amused rather than censorious tone when recalling his connection with the town. The columnist had last met Blythe in the mid-1940s, when he was already managing the Abbey Theatre:

Despite the fact that he was in the course of rehearsing a play, he dropped everything and came bounding out to me. Off we went for coffee, with Mr. Blythe peppering me with questions about Newtownards and its people. He evinced a tremendous interest in the town's progress and activities. And he recalled with great hilarity the time when he was 'on the run' in Newtownards and he spoke with great affection of a certain well-known family here who secreted him until he was able to get away safely. And, by the way – just in case any of you can read Irish – I believe there are references in his book to those times when he was living in Newtownards and Bangor. I'll have to wait for a translation.[6]

This article was mentioned in an affectionate letter to Blythe by Willie's sister Mabel, who recalled 'two big policemen' standing at the yard gate during Blythe's clandestine visit to the Doggarts' home in East Street. Being young she was 'kept in the dark'; but she recalled how, in later years, her siblings 'used to laugh while relating some of your episodes to people'.[7] According to Blythe's account of this visit, Mabel was no longer an artless child:

> The Doggart family gave me a hearty welcome. Mabel, who was a schoolgirl when I left for Kerry, had grown into a young woman in the meantime, and had been working in a clothes shop for over half a year. I felt that she had a new opinion of me and I was struck with an urge to speak with her alone, but I never got the chance.[8]

Neither Mabel nor Blythe's fellow journalists are known to have referred to his past membership of the Orange Order, but this was not entirely forgotten in Ulster. In March 1963, Blythe received an anonymous postcard from Belfast addressed to the Abbey Theatre, featuring a portrait of William III, an arch, a scene from the Battle of the Boyne, and nostalgic slogans such as 'Civil and Religious Liberty' and 'Truth Unity and Concord'. The message was terse: 'See you on "Twelfth" John'. Blythe was sufficiently struck by this souvenir to preserve it with an oddly inapposite gloss: 'Obviously John Bull EB'.[9] Which John from his fraternal past had chosen to torment Blythe, half a century after his departure from Newtownards, is unknown.

Blythe, ever wary of being outed, took care to be as dismissive of the Orange rowdy as he was respectful of the quintessential Ulsterman. This dichotomy was already apparent in his writings for *Irish Freedom* and the *Irish Independent* in 1912–14. When lamenting Patrick McCartan's defeat by a Home Ruler in the South Armagh by-election of February 1918, Blythe (as editor of the *Southern Star* in Skibbereen) crudely denounced the triumphant 'Orange-Molly Alliance'. After his arrest and deportation to Ulster a few weeks later, the *Star* remarked that 'Cromwell's orders still survive in Ireland, the only variation being that instead of "to Hell or Connaught" it is now "to Hell or Ulster"'.[10] In 1954, when explaining the ineffectiveness of Belfast's Dungannon club, he protested that 'it was not possible to do much against the influence of Joe Devlin and the Hibernians on one side and the Orange mob on the other'.[11]

Yet Blythe would surely never have ridiculed his former brethren after the manner of the anonymous 'Thinking Protestant' from County Antrim whose letters to the press caused a ripple of republican and liberal approbation in July 1921. This writer claimed that at least half of all 'thinking Protestants in the North . . . would transfer if possible with infinite pleasure and a sigh of relief the whole Orange organisation to the wilds of Central Africa, the only place on earth for which its demonstrations were ever suited'.[12] Blythe's view of Orangeism was without contempt or rancour, at least in retrospect:

> Unlike some of the northern nationalists, I had no hatred whatsoever for the Orangemen or for any other of the northern unionists. . . . I looked on all the Orangemen as I looked on my own family, that is to say, as people who were misinformed, people who did not understand the Catholic outlook, but who were honest Christians and were usually without any desire to do an injustice to anyone else.[13]

If more republicans had shared Blythe's benign insight, could partition have been averted?

As one of Monaghan's representatives in the Dáil and minister for local government, in the immediate aftermath of civil war, Blythe intervened to ensure that Monaghan Orangemen could safely take part in their first Twelfth procession for many years. He informed Kevin O'Higgins (then minister for home affairs) that 'local people have been speaking to me about it', suggesting to him 'that it would be a good thing if the Civic Guard and the Military took special, but *unostentatious*, precautions, to ensure that no unpleasantness occurred on the occasion of the meeting'. The police report on this 'monster Orange demonstration' stated that 'everything passed off very quietly', despite the seizure on the public road of 'a large quantity of intoxicating liquor' and four consequent prosecutions.[14] Blythe's indulgent approach to Monaghan's Orangemen was doubtless influenced by his electoral vulnerability in the Monaghan constituency, demonstrated in 1933 when he was defeated by Alexander Haslett, an independent backed by the Orange Order who had also been returned at both elections in 1927. The fact that Blythe topped the poll in August 1923, the only election at which he exceeded the quota, suggests that his courting of Orange support had been effective (he easily outpolled the combined vote of the four independent candidates).[15] Yet Blythe's affirmation of the right of Orangemen to parade was surely an expression of conviction as well as expediency.

II

Throughout his public career, Blythe inveighed not merely against partition, but against unrealistic attempts to coerce or browbeat Ulster loyalists into accepting dictation from Dublin.[16] This outlook, based on his intimate understanding of Ulster Protestant realities reinforced by his brief impersonation as an Orangeman, led him to adopt many unpopular and controversial stances. In 1920, he offered a spirited challenge in the Dáil Cabinet to 'the imposition of the Belfast boycott':

> I thought that it was a most ridiculous and shortsighted proposal, and although there was nobody else on the Cabinet opposed to it, I had the advantage of having some knowledge of the North which none of my colleagues had, and I was firm in opposition. I argued so loudly & so strongly against the scheme that it was decided to take no action by way of Ministerial decision.[17]

His most histrionic opponent in the subsequent discussion in the Dáil was the Ulster Catholic Seán MacEntee (Monaghan's other deputy), while Arthur Griffith floundered. Blythe deemed Griffith 'as completely ignorant of northern conditions as the ordinary average Southerner who has never spent any time in the north-eastern area'. Blythe's argument against the boycott was characteristically terse:

> E. BLYTHE (Monaghan North) was entirely opposed to a blockade against Belfast. Such action should be taken against individuals only. To declare an economic blockade of Belfast would be the

worst possible step to take. If it were taken it would destroy for ever the possibility of any union. Belfast could not be brought down through the banks. They were there as a Government, and they could not afford to range any section of the citizens against them.[18]

Despite support from Constance Markievicz and Desmond FitzGerald, Blythe failed to carry an amendment limiting any 'commercial embargo' to individuals inciting 'the recent pogroms'. Griffith 'disagreed with both the resolution and the amendment', and Collins protested 'against the attempt which had been made by two deputies from the North of Ireland to inflame the passions of members'. Collins, reciting one of the shakiest shibboleths of republican rhetoric, pronounced that 'there was no Ulster question'. As the issue threatened to cause an embarrassing rift within the Dáil, Collins wrong-footed Blythe by having it referred back for ministerial adjudication, leading to approval of the boycott without further debate.[19] A few weeks later, in September 1920, Blythe seconded Griffith's motion for a Commission on Organised Opposition to the Republic, in which he was joined by old cronies such as Denis McCullough, Cathal O'Shannon, and George Irvine as well as 'Owen' O'Duffy and Seán MacEntee. The commission was one of several initiatives advocated by Blythe on the same day which came to nothing as revolutionary violence and counter-insurgency intensified.[20]

Blythe repeatedly experienced the frustration of being unable to convince ill-informed colleagues of policies which, for him, were self-evidently right. In November 1921, he was attracted by Craig's abortive proposal to establish two Irish dominions as a substitute for the two Home Rule jurisdictions defined in the 'Better' Government of Ireland Act. Faced with the menace that Northern Ireland would be subordinated to an all-Ireland parliament rather than Westminster, Craig boldly suggested re-establishing equity between the two regions by expanding the powers devolved to Northern Ireland – even at the cost of leaving the United Kingdom.[21] Once Ulster abandoned the Union, northern support for partition might wither away: 'It struck me that the proposition was an excellent one and would give us far more as a nation than if we went ahead on the basis that Partition could not be recognised.' Yet, still bruised by his defeat over the boycott, Blythe kept quiet. Apart from judging that so radical a proposal would not receive public acceptance without unanimous Cabinet approval, he 'felt, too, that after my fight against the Belfast Boycott I was not the best person to get support for such a policy'.[22] Since Craig's suggestion was curtly dismissed by Lloyd George, the Dáil Ministry and Irish delegates to the peace conference were exempted from offering a response. Blythe's version of his unvoiced opinion is intrinsically unverifiable, and may have been coloured by his much later interest in the potential value of a six-county dominion as a step towards reconciliation.

When supporting ratification of the Anglo-Irish Treaty in January 1922, Blythe spoke ambivalently about partition as 'the only member of the Dáil who comes of the people who are going to exclude themselves, or may exclude themselves, from the Free State'. While affirming 'that we have the right to coerce them, if we thought fit, and if we have the power to do so', he rather grudgingly accepted the pragmatic justification for de Valera's renunciation of coercion in advance of the peace conference. Believing that 'by suitable propaganda . . . these people could eventually be brought to the side of the Irish nation, as they were a hundred years ago (applause)', he urged persuasion: 'you cannot coerce them and comfort them at the one time'. Though Blythe often qualified his pragmatic preference for persuasion by affirming the right in principle to coerce, his exaggerated emphasis on entitlement in this fractious debate was probably designed to deflate lingering suspicions that he was a unionist apologist.[23]

In later years, his pragmatic approach, grounded on informed awareness of Ulster's deep distrust of Irish nationalism, was applied at critical moments to greater effect. Just before the killing of Michael Collins in August 1922, he drafted a celebrated memorandum which discredited all attempts to undermine the new northern state and led to the partial abandonment of Collins' dual northern policy of public conciliation and covert subversion. He informed colleagues that 'there is no prospect of bringing about the unification of Ireland within any reasonable period of time by attacking the North East, its forces or Government'; that 'economic pressure' and boycotts would be equally futile; that payments to northern teachers and 'all relations with local bodies' should be stopped; and that 'the "Outrage" propaganda should be dropped in the Twenty Six Counties'. Instead, they should display 'a perfectly friendly and pacific disposition towards the Northern Government and people' if they chose to opt out of the Irish Free State, implying 'that we shall influence all those within the Six Counties who look to us for guidance, to acknowledge its authority and refrain from any attempt to prevent it working'.[24]

Though subsequent governments never fully achieved that 'friendly and pacific disposition' and persisted with hostile propaganda, Blythe's other proposals were eventually implemented, leading to perpetuation of the existing border shortly after the collapse of the Boundary Commission in November 1925. Blythe considered the Anglo-Irish agreement of 3 December 1925 to be 'a very fair arrangement'.[25] On 19 March 1926, as minister for finance, he joined with Churchill to sign the 'Heads of the Ultimate Financial Settlement', part of the package that rescued both states from imminent bankruptcy at the price of mutual acceptance of their shared right to exist.[26] The settlement emerged from a 'tide of compromise and conciliation', propelled by Blythe's concessionary interventions at crucial stages of the final conference in London.[27]

As vice-president after the murder of Kevin O'Higgins, Blythe was the government's most coherent and unapologetic advocate of embracing the 'greater freedom and greater security' conferred by membership of the British Commonwealth of Nations, and abandoning the quest for a republic: 'as to whether we are aiming at an Irish Republic, we are not'.[28] It was this bold declaration that led Seán MacEntee to sneer two years later that 'in Deputy Blythe's case possibly it is a case of political atavism. He has merely been thrown back to the political opinions and ideas of his forefathers.' The same sentiment when uttered by Cosgrave, by implication a good native Irishman, was 'something much more blameworthy'. The only six-county Protestant in the Dáil was an easy target for such a jibe, zestfully delivered by its only six-county Catholic.[29] Despite their many conflicts, the 'only conspicuous adversary' to attend Blythe's funeral was Seán MacEntee, who arrived with a flourish in 'former President de Valera's ancient Rolls Royce' as his representative.[30]

Blythe's crucial objection to seeking a republic was its negative consequences for partition. When campaigning in September 1927, Blythe made his case before a 'large gathering' in Castleblayney, County Monaghan:

> If they could make this country a Republic to-morrow would it end partition? Would it not end for all time any chance of bringing partition to an end? ... 'If I could,' the Minister declared, 'turn the Free State into a Republic to-morrow, I would not lift a finger to do it, and, what is more, I would work with all my might against it. We have all that we want and all the powers and liberties that we want for the upbuilding of this country.'[31]

Though dismissed as 'a silly boast' by Cosgrave's biographer, Blythe's reasoned if contrarian objection to a twenty-six-county republic was widely shared by those who had once sworn allegiance to an all-Ireland republic.[32]

As for partition, he reaffirmed the principle of consent in March 1928:

> In regard to partition, our belief is that the end of that can only come by consent; that there can be no question of attaining it by either military coercion or coercion of an economic character. It can only come when conditions here have improved so much that it would be an attraction to people who are not in this State to come into a unified Irish State. We believe, furthermore, that that can never come about ... within a generation or two without the consent of Great Britain.[33]

A year later, in February 1929, he defended the right of the northern government to imprison de Valera when he violated an exclusion order to attend a function in Belfast organised by the GAA and Gaelic League. Any attempt to make 'the welkin ring' would only prolong partition. Even then, as in 1922, he did 'not say that one could not find historical justification for coercion, if coercion were possible; but I have believed for some time that coercion is impossible both now and in any future that can be foreseen'.[34]

Blythe maintained his opposition to all forms of military, economic, and political interference with Northern Ireland during his tempestuous Blueshirt phase, deploring Michael Tierney's sneering reference to a 'little simulacrum of a State' and his proposal for a twenty-six-county republic. Writing as 'E. B.' in *United Ireland*, he characterised reunion as 'a task of peculiar delicacy and difficulty', recommending 'a little patience and a little persistence, and even . . . a little tolerance towards a Government which has committed crimes and blunders but does not seem quite incapable of learning'. 'The best course', ideally, would be 'never to speak' of reunion, and 'to bend our minds and energies to making a big success of the Free State'. At this point, Blythe was careful to avoid prescribing a strategy for northern nationalists, tactfully urging 'consideration of what might be done by the Northern nationalists over a period of years towards facilitating a change of view amongst their Unionist neighbours'.[35] This was written in a period of mounting sectarian tension and continuing fragmentation of the Nationalist Party of Northern Ireland.

In July 1936, when a concerted campaign by Protestant churchmen was helping to avert a re-enactment of the previous season's riots in Belfast, he offered some provocative advice when speaking in Irish at a conference in Trinity College. According to the *Irish Times*, whose reporter had clearly found 'a full hour in Gaelic' a challenging assignment, Blythe recommended a nationalist electoral boycott in order to divide unionism:

> The proper thing for the Nationalists of the North to do was to boycott the Parliamentary elections, put forward no candidates, and record no votes. Not only would there be two Protestant parties in Parliament, but each of them would be doing its utmost to get the support of the Catholics. He was certain that in such circumstances the likelihood of the Catholics getting positions, fair play and education would be much greater if they ignored Stormont.[36]

Though a logical corollary of Blythe's belief that partition was sustained by sectarian mistrust rather than political ideology, it was perversely condescending to suggest that Catholics should disarm Protestant bigotry by simply renouncing political engagement. This proposal confirms that Blythe, so intent on placating his own 'Planter stock', still had scant sympathy or understanding for Ulster Catholics.

His ingeniously bizarre proposal for collective self-abnegation was bound to irritate unionists as well as nationalists, both already rent by internal divisions as well as mutual animosity. When opening an Orange hall at Lisnadill, County Armagh, Viscount Craigavon described the proposed boycott as 'a cowardly way which had never done any good, and it would not make a pin of difference to his colleagues or himself if there was not a Nationalist in the Northern Parliament'.[37] They would 'carry on just as usual and continue to give a fair deal to every citizen'.[38] Blythe's 'empty vapouring in Irish' was ridiculed at the Twelfth demonstration at Scrabo Hill, Newtownards, chaired by the venerable Senator Lavery of Blythe's old lodge. James Little, a controversial Presbyterian minister with an American doctorate who later represented County Down at Westminster,[39] informed the brethren that, if nationalists took up his advice of a boycott, 'matters ... would go on much the same without them'. Such futile gestures would make them 'a laughing-stock to the world. If all those petty intermeddlers from England and the Free State minded their own business there would be less ill-feeling and more goodwill'.[40] Blythe continued to intermeddle, but realised the need to construct a positive alternative to irredentist nationalism rather than simply to urge its dissolution. In later years, he suggested an alignment between nationalism and Labour, echoing the perennial dream that the sectarian element in nationalism could be subsumed in a broader social struggle.[41]

Long after his involuntary departure from parliamentary politics when the Senate was abolished in May 1936, when he was only forty-seven, Blythe continued to inveigh against the futility and hypocrisy of anti-partition campaigns which only intensified Ulster's long-standing distrust of southern motives. One of his most sustained analyses was a digressive memorandum of fifty-one pages circulated to politicians of several parties in October 1949, entitled 'Towards a Six-Counties Dominion?'[42] His aim was to halt the current non-partisan campaign against partition, designed to inflame northern nationalists and intimidate northern unionists without any weapons except propaganda, famously wielded by Conor Cruise O'Brien.[43] Blythe presented his credentials:

> I was brought up in a Unionist household in a strongly Orange area; I have always remained on good terms personally with my relatives and with my early friends, despite the widest differences of political opinion. I was in the North on the staff of a Unionist country paper from early 1909 till 1913 and saw at close quarters the preliminary stages of what is loosely called the Carson campaign, and the development of the Ulster Volunteers. On the other hand, I have been in the National Movement since very soon after I first came to Dublin as a boy, having joined the Gaelic League when I was a little over 16, Sinn Féin when I was 17, and the I.R.B. when I was 18.[44]

His proposals assumed that a more subtle campaign might induce the British government to offer dominion status to 'Ulster', as briefly hazarded by Craig in 1921, whereas imposed reunification was utterly impracticable. Such an imposition was 'unthinkable', not only because of 'Protestant bigotry and the size and concentration of the Orange population', but on account of 'the actual existence and strong democratic position of the Stormont Government'.[45] When the Labour politician Thomas Johnson demurred at his reference to 'bigotry' and loose use of the word 'Orange', Blythe accepted the rebuke: 'I am afraid that in doing so I was seeking brevity at the expense of accuracy and was perhaps half unconsciously writing down to the ignorance in regard to the North of some of those I was immediately addressing.'[46]

Even if Attlee's government abandoned its commitments and 'simply departed', the outcome of any attempt at revendication would be a 'bloody civil war', with the possibility that the North with its formidable engineering industry would 'manage rather easily to get the better of the struggle . . . like the Jews in Palestine'. Any form of 'direct action', or even a 'pre-coercion campaign like that at present in progress', was 'certain to fail' and also to make permanent partition even more probable. Northern hearts could only be won over by gentle and empathetic persuasion, since 'the true basis of Partition is religious bigotry, and the fears and suspicions that go with it', rather than any 'feeling of absolute oneness with the people of England'. Only since the later 1930s had Blythe realised that 'the roots of Partition . . . are pretty old and go very deep', and that 'Northern Unionists were certainly ready at any time between 1912 and 1922 to shed blood, or to sponsor bloodshed, for Partition'.[47]

No hope should be placed in American pressure, or the specious argument that Protestants had been well treated in the South, or Presbyterian nostalgia for the United Irishmen, or prolongation of the boycott of Stormont by northern nationalists. Instead, the Republic should amend the Constitution or place the territorial claim in 'abeyance', encourage 'Nationalist participation in public activities and in official social functions', and develop a 'plan of conciliation and social interpenetration'. Northern nationalists should avoid provocative displays of the 'Papal Flag', rise for 'God Save the Queen' when appropriate, and develop inclusive 'cultural practices'.[48] Blythe's proposals were too idiosyncratically radical to influence Irish politicians in 1949, but might have served as a blueprint for the peace strategy embodied half a century later in the Anglo-Irish and 'Good Friday' agreements.

For his detractors, such attitudes confirmed that Blythe had never cast off his Ulster Protestant blinkers, though no critic is known to have unambiguously revealed the guilty secret that might so easily have destroyed Blythe's glittering career and political reputation. Admittedly, dark hints of an Orange past eventually appeared in the Ulster nationalist press, outraged by his expressions of respect for the northern government and increasingly gentle references to the Orange Order. In response to a signed article entitled 'The Basis of Partition is Religious' (1950), a widely syndicated editorial landed a nasty parting thrust: 'Great will be the rejoicing in Lisburn at the return to the Orange orchard of the grower who once went a-foraging in the Republican desert'.[49]

The reference to Lisburn rather than Newtownards suggests, however, that the jibe was not based on specific personal knowledge. The writer was probably Anthony Mulvey, who had just emerged from fifteen years of 'abstentionism' to propagate the anti-partition cause at Westminster.[50] Mulvey edited an influential chain of mid-Ulster weeklies, whose managing director, Senator Louis Lynch, also wrote some of the leading articles.[51] Within the fractious Irish Anti-Partition League, Lynch was a key figure in the 'Omagh Group' of ex-Sinn Féin parliamentarians and journalists associated with his newspapers.[52] Yet, if anything united northern nationalists, it was surely the outrage occasioned by Ernest Blythe's advocacy of their extinction.

III

Blythe's primary motive in joining and leaving the Orange Order remains uncertain, despite ample evidence of his thirst for inside information, political adventurism, compulsive fraternalism, romantic attachment to rebellion, desire to recruit republicans through infiltration, respect for the determination of Ulster loyalists, and intimacy with policemen. Blythe's pursuit of a 'double life' in Belfast and north Down was most clearly evinced by his undeniable duplicity in belonging simultaneously to two incompatible secret societies, and his attempt to retain the trust of both parties even as he deceived them.

In later life, having left the Orange in 1912 and disavowed the IRB in 1919, he seems to have avoided the perils of oath-bound fraternal allegiance.[53] Yet Blythe, like all elected representatives of Sinn Féin including IRB brethren, went on to swear fidelity to the Dáil as the government of the Irish Republic.[54] During the Treaty debate in January 1922, he was notably dismissive of the binding force of that oath:

> I believe that in making my choice I am not fettered by the oath I took as a member of this Dáil. I believe that if I hold myself back from doing what I believe would be best for the Irish nation because it conflicted with the terms of that oath, it would

be doing wrong. . . . I would be false alike to the oath and the purpose of the oath if I held to the mere terms of it against my judgement of what was best for the Irish nation at the present time. Republicanism is with me not a national principle but a political preference.[55]

Blythe's cavalier attitude to oaths of allegiance was surely influenced by the conflicting commitments of his early youth.

Hints remain of a lingering double life in his idiosyncratic approach to partition, discussed above. By mitigating the counter-productive impact of policies designed to destabilise 'the North', and consolidating peaceful coexistence through the settlement of 1925–6, Blythe did his best to allay the fear and distrust of Ulster loyalists for the southern state. Whether deliberately or otherwise, his policies and proposals tended to reinforce the legitimacy of the northern state, and to oppose all attempts to subvert its authority from within or without. A master of ambivalence, subterfuge, and deceit, Ernest Blythe will continue to dodge the hounds of history even as they scent their prey.

When performing in *The Drone* in February 1913, Blythe had clearly warmed to his own part of Uncle Dan, that charming but lazy fantasist who proves shrewd enough to manipulate his family and pursue absurd experiments even as his deceits are exposed. For Mackenzie the Scottish engineer, Dan Murray is 'nothing short of an impostor'. For Sarah McMinn, grimly intent on wedding John Murray and taking control of his farm, her prospective brother-in-law seems 'an idle, good for nothing, useless, old pull a cork'. Yet John finds him 'always the best of company, and heartsome', while niece Mary gushes that 'he's got the whole brains of the Murrays, so father says, and then, besides that, he is a grand talker'.[56] As Blythe wrote in his review: 'Simple John has every confidence in his brother Dan, or ratherly [*sic*] he never questioned his bona fides, accepting them in simple faith, until the machinations of Sarah McMinn.' Despite this setback, Uncle Dan manages both to thwart his brother's marriage to Sarah and to perpetuate funding for his own inventions.[57] Like Uncle Dan, Ernest Blythe just about got away with it.

Fascist Echoes

I

T his book has displayed the startling diversity of Ernest Blythe's revolutionary education, and his readiness to adopt disguises in order to win the confidence and mould the political thought of disparate groups. Many of the ideas that pseudonymous young Blythes propagated in *Irish Freedom* and the *Ulster Guardian* reverberated throughout his political career, re-emerging during the revolution, his decade as a Free State minister, and the convulsions associated with de Valera's apotheosis in 1932. We have already traced the evolution of Blythe's idiosyncratic views on partition, and noted his romantic, even exultant attachment to the idea of violence during the revolution and civil war. In his liberal persona, Purple Star's detailed and thoughtful analysis of the financial implications of Home Rule proved surprisingly relevant preparation for his tenure as minister for finance (1923–32). Otherwise impeccably thrifty in his determination to balance the budget, Blythe indulged his lifelong passion for the Irish language with handouts that shocked his officials. Yet the most resonant echoes of his schizoid early career were reserved for the period after his departure from government and Dáil Éireann. In conclusion, let us consider some affinities between Blythe's early ideas and his controversial espousal of fascist precepts in the 1930s.

Blythe's crucial part in shaping and indoctrinating the 'Blueshirt' movement[1] no longer remains in doubt. He proposed the leader and the colour, drafted key policy documents, and was foremost in urging Eoin O'Duffy's followers to prepare for defensive conflict with de Valera's government or his IRA supporters. As O'Duffy's rhetoric became increasingly wild and uncontrollable, Blythe withdrew his endorsement, engineering O'Duffy's removal from the leadership of the League of Youth as well as the United Ireland Party (Fine

Gael) in September 1934.[2] Yet Blythe's thirst for radical alternatives to parliamentary democracy endured, as shown by his advocacy of Ned Cronin's anti-O'Duffy Blueshirts (1934–6) and Gearóid Ó Cuinneagáin's abortive 'Resurrection' movement (1940–4).

In embracing many of the tenets of Italian fascism, while disavowing the label, Blythe reverted to preoccupations expressed as a youngster, such as delight in violence, celebration of youthful virility, impatience with parliamentary democracy, and reliance on organised militant elites as an essential intermediary between government and people. While a minister, Blythe twice promoted the creation of semi-autonomous paramilitary forces with official sanction. He endorsed Séamus Hughes' proposal for a citizens' militia (July 1922), and introduced an additional military reserve only nominally drawn from ex-soldiers and charged with preserving public order (November 1929). Few recruits joined either the Citizens' Defence Force or the Volunteer Reserve, and both proved ineffectual as instruments of state control.[3] Despite contrary claims, he did not favour a military *coup d'état*, regarding the national army as a strictly subservient arm of the state. He deplored the conspicuously insubordinate involvement of serving officers in the National Defence Association in October 1930, intervened to stifle a putsch by Major-General Hugo (Hugh Hyacinth) MacNeill in autumn 1931, and played no reported part in O'Duffy's attempt to induce senior officers to overthrow de Valera's new government in March 1932.[4]

Only once did Blythe waver in his rejection of a military takeover. In March 1930, the weekly unofficial organ of Cumann na nGaedheal published an unsigned Irish-language leading article entitled 'An t-Arm'. On the basis of translated extracts in the *Sunday Independent*, this was widely identified in the republican press as the work of Blythe, and as proof of his abandonment of democracy.[5] In fact, the article affirmed that 'the Army will be loyal to the Government of the people's choice, irrespective of what Government it is. The soldiers are servants of the people.' Under certain conditions, however, 'the Army would be bound to subdue a political group for the welfare of the people in general'. This would apply if a party sought 'possession of governmental power by violence'; if an incumbent government failed 'to yield up the reins of office when a new Government had been chosen'; or if a future (Fianna Fáil) government 'set about changing the Constitution against the will of the people . . . with a view to depriving the people of their supreme authority'. Such a government would constitute 'a tyranny'.[6] Reverting to the quaint terminology of his address to the Belfast Freedom Club in 1912,[7] Blythe mused that it might be necessary to apply the doctrine of the 'sword':

> It is difficult to destroy a tyranny except with sword and rifle. If it should become a duty to destroy a tyranny in the Saorstat, it would be the duty of the soldier to move first, as he is best equipped for the work. Thus, the position is: Fianna Fail has nothing to fear from the Army if they are good boys; but if they are bad boys, the Army will be highly dangerous to them.[8]

This analysis clearly implied that the army would not be entitled to maintain the current government in office if defeated by Fianna Fáil, unless that defeat could be attributed to violence. It was widely misrepresented by political opponents, echoed by some historians. The IRA's organ, *An Phoblacht*, seized the opportunity to denounce Fianna Fáil for naively supposing that the bloodthirsty 'Cosgravian junta' would 'surrender all at the bidding of the electorate'. It inferred from the article that 'the Free State Army will suppress the Free State Dail and set up a military dictatorship' if a new government were to 'displease' Cumann na nGaedheal.[9] Selectively quoting from the translated extracts in the *Sunday Independent*, three future Fianna Fáil ministers offered a similar interpretation, invariably ignoring the list of specific circumstances under which military intervention would be justified.[10] For Seán Lemass, it endorsed 'mutiny' in the face of 'a policy of which it disapproves'; while Seán MacEntee vainly demanded to know if the repudiation of democracy had been composed by Cosgrave, Blythe, FitzGerald, or Mulcahy.[11]

In April 1932, *An Phoblacht* contrasted it with Blythe's recent statement that the army was 'entirely professional in its outlook and without any inclination to dabble in politics'. It was claimed that 'general rumour credited [Blythe] . . . with authorship of the article

– and Mr. Blythe made no denial'.[12] By March 1934, when the *Irish Press* resurrected the article in deploring the Senate's rejection of the Wearing of Uniforms Bill, it was 'generally accepted to have been written by Mr. Blythe'.[13] The process by which admitted ignorance of authorship mutated into 'general rumour', followed by firm attribution with no additional evidence, provides a salutary warning for detective historians. Nevertheless, the article's serpentine style strongly suggests the hand of Blythe.[14]

This article was clearly the origin of an incoherent outburst from de Valera when addressing the Senate during the debate just mentioned. Notorious for his own inflammatory prediction of 'wading through blood' in March 1922, de Valera seemed almost in awe of Blythe's blood-lust as he contemplated the Blueshirt menace:

> There is the fundamental, sinister threat which is felt by everybody to lie in this movement. It would be a threat if the movement were organised by anybody, but it is particularly a threat when it is organised by such a gentleman as Senator Blythe. Senator Blythe's history is well known to us. We know how he can write and how callous he can be. We know that that same Senator, with all his talk of democracy here, preached very different things a very short time ago and preached them, not in the old days either, but later, when he suggested very definitely that the Army were to be the arbiters here. . . . It was, of course, very cleverly done. More than anybody I ever heard of, the Senator can be callously brutal in his suggestion that it is only by combat, bloodshed and slaughter that political objectives can be won.

De Valera's main source for this appraisal was 'an article in Irish', which he could read 'sufficiently well to be able to know what was meant'.[15]

As in his youth, Blythe deployed an armoury of pen-names (as well as anonymity) for his articles in both languages, enabling him to address different audiences with different arguments in different registers.[16] He had not forgotten the arts of disguise, all the more necessary after his uncontested election to the Senate in January 1934.[17] Blythe's multi-faceted engagement with fascism is best understood by examining his pseudonymous contributions to party weeklies between 1930 and 1935, along with a handful of policy documents preserved in his papers.[18]

In April 1930, the *Star* published a much-quoted contribution by 'P.A.P.', again ascribed to Blythe, headlined 'Masses unfit to rule themselves?'[19]

> The success of dictatorship in Italy and Spain, and the frequent break-down of Parliaments, has given many democrats furiously to think whether, after all, the gods of democracy have not feet of clay, and whether or not that system of government, local and national, should be mended or ended. . . . The franchise in the hands of an ignorant, foolish populace is a menace to any country.

Far from prescribing dictatorship as a general solution, he goaded his readers by extolling the British monarchical variant of democracy: 'that seemingly incongruous system of compromise which avoids extremes and yet combines all of them has admirably suited the genius of the British people and will stand comparison with any or all of the systems of the world'. Blythe's long-standing impatience with political idealism called Pope to his mind:

> For forms of government let fools contest,
> Whate'er is best administer'd is best.[20]

In less stable societies, stability was threatened by 'the multitude' and 'the mob', which usually took up 'a wrong-headed, ill-informed attitude, swallowing sophistries, and refusing to listen to reason and sense'. It would always 'be true that those who think must govern those who do not think, and naturally that government must be fatherly and not representative'. Advances in the Irish Free State had been achieved despite, not through, the popular will:

Apathy and indifference are evidence of the unfitness of the masses to govern themselves. Is there a mandate from the mob for protection of our industries, for the revival of our language, for public health reform, for that wonderful scheme of electrification which is the admiration of the world?

'P.A.P.' concluded that 'it is in administrative spheres that democratic rule is most defective'. No specific reform was proposed beyond applying the 'managerial system' to local government, with a merely advisory role for a few public representatives.[21] Though expressing contempt for parliaments which 'do the talking' while experts 'do the real work', the article did not advocate the 'abolition of parliamentary institutions' as claimed by *An Phoblacht*.[22] Its central message still resonates today: the urgent need to find ways of transforming a fickle populace into an electorate of informed citizens, and to devise efficient systems of administration insulated from reckless meddling.

For Blythe and many of his ministerial and party colleagues, de Valera's electoral triumphs in 1932–3 signified the demagogic triumph of 'the mob' and the consequent risk of indirect dictatorship by the IRA, on whose support de Valera was assumed to be dependent. In February 1932, Blythe told a 'very large meeting' that 'the worst tyranny in the world to-day was perpetrated in Republics, such as Soviet Russia, Spain and Mexico'. He warned 'that if Fianna Fáil got into power they could not control the gun bullies', whereas if 'beaten this time they would break up'.[23] During his final election campaign in January 1933, he again downplayed the immediate threat posed by the IRA while warning of dire consequences if de Valera prevailed:

> They had been told there would be a renewal of armed revolutionary activity if Fianna Fáil were not returned to power. The people need not be alarmed about the I.R.A. If they had a de Valera Government, the time would come when the I.R.A. would become dangerous. The I.R.A. had recently been allowed its head to drill, arm and train, but if ever it fell out with Fianna Fáil he thought they would see a good deal of disturbance. With a Cosgrave Government there would be no trouble.[24]

The question of how to resist any oppressive alliance between the IRA and a Fianna Fáil government was not raised.

The nearest Blythe came to violent action against the state was when ordered to surrender his protective weapon in July 1933, as part of de Valera's attempt to disarm Blueshirt leaders. Shortly after Blythe's defeat in the general election six months earlier, the firearm certificate that he had held ever since the murder of O'Higgins was revoked, ostensibly because there was 'no good reason for requiring the firearm'.[25] Such was Blythe's attachment to revolvers, despite his poor aim and lack of combat experience, that when visited by detectives he refused to surrender it, having 'no intention of voluntarily making myself a defenceless target at the behest of Mr. de Valera or any of his colleagues, acknowledged or unacknowledged'. He informed the *Irish Times* that 'I still have the weapon, illegally if you like, and will not give it up without a big fight'. He again held to his gun two days later, yet agreed to seek renewal of his certificate when handed an application form. He declined the kind offer of 'an armed guard placed on his house and a detective to go with him', protesting that such protection would be 'rather ineffective, especially as he would probably have to travel a good deal by motor, and he could not always find transport accommodation for the guard'. Blythe's home was among those thoroughly searched for arms four months later, in the presence of Annie Blythe, but 'nothing was found and nothing was removed from the premises'.[26]

II

On April Fools' Day 1933, 'M. G. Quinn' (Blythe's persona as a political philosopher) lambasted the framers of the Free State Constitution for naively endorsing unfettered parliamentary democracy, laughingly suggesting that they deserved to be doused in 'boiling oil'. De Valera should not be blamed for the success of his 'lying campaign': 'Obviously the Fianna Fáil Party with its record of destruction could never have persuaded the people to return it to power unless it made use of its constitutional right to bamboozle them.' An alternative Irish solution must be found, creating 'an associative state', if the country were to be saved: 'We may learn from Fascism but we must not attempt any close imitation of it.'[27]

This article offered an acute analysis of the manner in which the revolutionaries had become dupes of their own propaganda, always centred on British abuses of democracy:

> We had been carrying on what was partly a small heroic military struggle, but what was principally a vast propagandist campaign against the British. . . . It often happens that the originators and disseminators of propaganda are even more affected by it than those to whom it is addressed, and so we were blinded by our own fulminations; we grew to think that there was a special sanctity attaching to all but a few of the formulae which make up the British Constitution. We saw none of the faults of the demagogic Parliamentarian State. We tried only to give it a more extreme, or, as we thought, a purer form than it had in England. By the sort of State we created, we made the developments of the past year, or something like them, inevitable.

Home-grown values, temporarily supplanted by those borrowed from the old enemy, must be reasserted.

A fortnight later, M. G. Quinn set out a model for 'a Diast, an organic democratic State adapted to Irish conditions', implicitly inviting comparison with communist as well as fascist precedents.[28] His choice of the obscure term 'Diast' (perhaps an acronym for 'democratic Irish associative state', or else a corruption of 'diaster', a double star) helped to distance his proposals from any external model. Though published in the party organ, his suggestions were designed to provoke debate rather than to herald a pre-determined policy change. Protesting rather too much, the editor noted that 'the proposals made above are, however, so far away from anything that could be adopted by Cumann na nGaedheal, that we are afraid that we cannot give our contributor much, if any, further space for them'. Parliament would exercise reduced powers, and 'the electorate would be protected from the misrepresentations and machinations of corruptionists and mountebanks by the interposition of a great national patriotic organisation which would be maintained as part of the constitutional machinery of the state'. This would ensure that nine-tenths of deputies 'would, in practice, be chosen by an organisation constituting a Mass Commission of defence and guidance'.

The 'Diastal Union or League' would incorporate 'the cream of the nation representing every social class', and would occupy 'a privileged position in the State'. No indication was yet given of what organisation would be selected, how it would be constituted, or by whom it would be supervised beyond self-regulation. Members of the Diastal Union 'would be required to set an example to their fellow-citizens of good citizenship and patriotic conduct', and those found guilty by 'its own disciplinary tribunal' of abusing their position would be 'ruthlessly' punished by 'expulsion and perhaps by fine'. While the Army Comrades' Association was not explicitly equated with the Diastal Union, M. G. Quinn reflected a few weeks later that 'there is one body in existence that might, perhaps, be turned into the sort of organisation that is needed', though 'a new society' would be formed if this unnamed body were 'not prepared to take up the burden'.[29]

Such an organisation would 'have roots in Irish history. Great popular, semi-disciplined organisations, which were rather combative public service bodies than political parties in the ordinary sense have had no small part in making the Ireland of to-day. Our people have a genius for combination and intelligent mass action.'[30] Blythe was obviously referring to the role of Sinn Féin and the Irish Volunteers in controlling and manipulating the democratic campaign for 'self-determination', and to antecedents such as the Land League. He prudently made no allusion to the only Irish example of such an organisation acting as the driving force within a functioning parliamentary system. Ever since partition, the Orange Order had exercised a powerful influence at every level of unionist and state organisation, ensuring that all but a handful of parliamentarians were brethren, and acting as moral arbiter for the state. The northern House of Commons, though democratically elected, exercised minimal constraint on a government locked in a symbiotic embrace with this 'Mass Commission of defence and guidance'.[31]

Characteristically, Blythe did not take public responsibility for translating his model for a one-party state into practice, yet within his party executive he was active in drafting and discussing documents on how 'Vocational Corporations' and 'Planned Economics' might operate.[32] The blueprint for 'vocational corporations' involved compulsory conciliation, prohibition of strikes and lock-outs, and heavy penalties for offenders.[33] During O'Duffy's year as leader of both Fine Gael and the Blueshirts, ending in September 1934, Blythe explicitly identified the Blueshirts as the basis of the future Diastal Union. The proposed 'agricultural corporation', constituted as a pyramid rising from parish branches to the Department of Agriculture,[34] resembled the model promulgated in *Irish Freedom* two decades earlier, which involved 'confederated' as well individual 'co-operative parishes'.[35] But there was an essential extra element in Blythe's draft proposals in 1934: the proviso that Blueshirts should convene the preliminary meetings, form the majority of every parish organising committee, oversee all higher divisions, and approve the appointment of all delegates.[36]

It is noteworthy that almost all specific references to Blueshirt supervision and control were deleted from the preliminary 'basis of discussion', annotated and presumably drafted by Blythe, except a vague provision that the corporation would involve 'a voluntary disciplined public-service organisation like the National Guard again become non-political'. This replaced Blythe's insistence on oversight by 'a disciplined public-service organisation such as the late National Guard was. If an Agricultural Corporation is to be formed it is, in my opinion, absolutely essential that it be, from the point of view of politics and personnel, under the Guardianship of the Young Ireland Association.' These changes indicate that Blythe's preference for control by a paramilitary organisation resembling the *Fascisti* was unacceptable to the majority of the Fine Gael executive.[37]

In one respect, however, the revised proposals were closer than Blythe's to the advanced corporative model that was about to be introduced in Italy. After eight years when separate corporations for employers and workers had operated within each sector, Mussolini finally decreed in February 1934 that each sector should have a single corporation headed by a council with equal representation for both groups.[38] Such developments in Italy were closely followed in Ireland.[39] Blythe's draft provided for separate organisations representing farmers and labourers at every level of the 'pyramid', whereas his colleagues preferred an integrated structure embodying the very latest Italian style.

In October 1933, M. G. Quinn expressed satisfaction that O'Duffy's Fine Gael was 'moving towards the formulation of a real political policy' based on 'a distinctive political philosophy'. Though welcoming Professor James Hogan's recent advocacy of 'economic corporations' transcending class-based bodies, he likened Hogan's scheme to 'an arch minus the keystone' (a metaphor central to both Freemasonry and Orangeism). The missing part was 'a political corporation . . . which will permeate, connect and balance all the economic corporations'.[40] Otherwise, Hogan's scheme differed little from Blythe's own writings on vertically organised vocational bodies which would sustain a corporate state organised by Blueshirts. Blythe's views delighted an Italian fascist agent during his visit to assess Blueshirt and Fine Gael leaders just before O'Duffy's ejection as leader. Whereas O'Duffy was a 'second-rater' and Cosgrave 'completely permeated by democratic principles', Blythe impressed him as 'an exceptional Irishman'. He seemed 'methodical, calm and quick-witted', well read in fascist texts, impatient of elections, and willing (in Keogh's paraphrase) 'to take Ireland along corporatist lines'.[41]

M. G. Quinn expressed dissatisfaction with the failure of Fine Gael's national executive to link 'economic planning' with 'constitutional change' enabling 'economic corporations . . . to be run successfully and on business-like lines':

> It might be achieved by the organisation of a great national party which would have a special status giving it an easy supremacy over such fractional or dissident parties as might continue to exist. A national party of the kind could accomplish the necessary task of damping down party warfare and of basing politics on realities without claiming anything like the monopoly position

which has been attained by certain new-type parties on the Continent.

Blythe stressed that the National Party should not 'be given the sole right to nominate candidates which the Fascist Party, in conjunction with the National Corporations has in Italy. On the other hand, it should have certain powers of veto, in regard to candidates proposed by other groups.' Likewise, though its leader would have 'great responsibility and great powers', he should not carry 'the authority of Mussolini in the Fascist Party'. He admitted that most Fine Gael leaders 'at present reject the idea of a national one-party system, but it is in the air'. Recent debates about franchise reform, educational tests for candidates, and 'any other such naive or out-of-date schemes' could not offer comparable 'hope for a satisfactory national future'.[42]

III

Like his titular leader O'Duffy, Blythe repeatedly extolled the need to mobilise young people, as in the 'League of Youth', just as when himself young he had extolled the Irish Volunteers, Fianna Éireann, and even Young Liberals. The most obvious model for a state in which the populace was organised, patrolled, and disciplined by a paramilitary network of relatively young toughs was Mussolini's Italy, but similar systems had developed in Germany, the Soviet Union, Turkey, and beyond. While the unorthodox 'M. G. Quinn' stirred up political debate among Treatyist intellectuals, the party organ also published his weekly column of exhortation and practical advice for Blueshirts over the pseudonym 'Onlooker'.

Six months before Cosgrave surrendered his political leadership to O'Duffy, Onlooker was hard at work welding the nascent Army Comrades' Association into 'a disciplined non-party association organised for public service', composed of companies that 'would be merely militant, not military'. The term 'company does not necessarily connote militarism', even if it 'does recall the Volunteer organisation to mind'. Rejecting 'the undisciplined habits of a loose-knit political organisation' (such as Cumann na nGaedheal, for so long an irritant to Blythe as a minister), its members would be expelled for wilful absence from monthly meetings. Companies were encouraged to form boxing clubs and hold classes in the Irish language and history; but card games, having no moral or educative value, should only be played 'outside amongst non-members, whom they might be able to convert or influence'.[43] Onlooker later recommended 'Volunteer' rather than 'Comrade' or 'Private' as a form of address in the Army Comrades' Association, since 'the fact that Socialists and Bolsheviks use comrade as a title of address almost rules it out for us', while 'Private' would be inappropriate since it was 'not a military organisation'.[44]

It is instructive to compare Onlooker's depiction of a 'militant, not military' organisation with Senator Blythe's denunciation of the Wearing of Uniforms Bill a few days earlier. Until the dissolution of the upper house in May 1936, he customarily performed the part of a statesmanlike critic of government proposals, offering measured advice on the basis of his unsurpassed administrative experience. In the Senate, he offered few hints of the romantic wildness and radicalism that inflamed his concurrent writings as a Blueshirt propagandist. In response to Thomas Johnson, the former Labour leader, Senator Blythe smoothly explained that the League of Youth was 'being organised along entirely civil and political lines, with political objects and political methods'. There were 'no military titles': after all, there were 'captains of football teams and of boat clubs, in fact all sorts of captains', and 'all sorts of uniforms, from the ordinary garb of the clergyman, which do not produce anything in the way of a military spirit'. The Blueshirts were in no way comparable to the IRA, 'whose principles are to force the people to carry out their will irrespective of the majority. The Blue Shirts is composed of men whose whole past has been given to asserting the principle of majority rule'.[45]

As for the accusation of fascism, Blythe the canny debater intimated that not a 'shadow' of this ideology hovered over his party:

> There has been a good deal of talk about Fascism.... Some people mean the corporative organisation by it, other people

mean the earlier events which occurred in Italy under the leadership of the present head of the State there, but with reference to it I would just like to say this: the whole plan and scheme of Fine Gael is a plan and scheme dependent entirely and aiming entirely at convincing the majority of the people by argument and discussion that what is proposed is in the best interests of the community, and not the application of a scheme of economic or other reform by any sort of force or *coup d'état*. . . . If the Senator's idea of Fascism means some sort of march to Dublin or a scheme to impose, by force or by arms, reform upon the people, then we are not Fascists and have no shadow of Fascism attached to us.

He acknowledged that the 'corporative policy was suggested to the leaders of Fine Gael by the experiment that is being made in Italy', but reasserted 'that although the general idea was founded in Italy there was no suggestion that it would be slavishly followed, adopted, ready-made and put down here, but it was said that it must be varied and modified to suit Irish conditions so that a wholly Irish scheme could be put up'.[46]

The quintessential Irishness of the Blueshirts was affirmed in Onlooker's first column in O'Duffy's *Blueshirt*. He was 'glad' that O'Duffy had 'made it clear that the National Guard is not a Fascist organisation', being 'purely the product of Irish needs and conditions', while 'anything that it may have borrowed from abroad is incidental and subsidiary'. He denied that 'the National Guard is Nazi or anti-Semite', declaring that its constitutional restriction of 'membership to Irishmen who profess the Christian Faith' did not imply that it was 'out to persecute, injure or attack those who are not Christians'. Onlooker placed the Blueshirts in the mainstream of Ireland's national history:

The political history of Ireland for several generations back has been the history of its great voluntary, disciplined, or semi-disciplined, organisations. The Fenians, the Land League, the Gaelic League, the Volunteers and Sinn Féin made the tradition out of which the National Guard has sprung.[47]

Onlooker often compared the Blueshirts to the socially inclusive Irish Volunteers, advising that each company should be 'a place for the tough and the toff. Like the Irish Volunteers it is open to all men who are willing to submit to discipline and to make sacrifices for their country's good.'[48] Though 'veterans of the national struggle, men who were mature even before 1916, have their place in it', the Blueshirts 'must be and remain primarily a young man's organisation'. Officers 'on the wrong side of fifty' tended to be unsatisfactory (Blythe was forty-four). He was insistent that Blueshirts act within the law, securing permits for any arms and abstaining from military drill: 'Men may be taught to fall in and march smartly so that A.C.A. parades may be seemly and impressive, but military evolutions should be avoided.'[49] Thus Onlooker echoed the outlook of 'Earnán de Blaghd' in *Irish Freedom* that mastery of 'the goose-step' was more valuable than 'the science of ducking behind bushes'.[50]

As a connoisseur of smart uniforms and pageantry, Onlooker gave close attention to the colour and fabric of shirts, the need for black berets rather than 'other headgear', and the selection of a 'distinctive flag'.[51] Blythe evidently proposed the blue shirt and the blue flag with its red Cross of St Patrick,[52] and as Onlooker normally offered his 'personal' opinion a week or so before it was endorsed by the executive. In mid-May 1933, he called for 'a rallying song that members may sing at times of exaltation and conflict when the National Anthem would be inappropriate'.[53] A week later, he extolled an anonymous 'March of the Comrades', 'to be sung to the air of "O'Donnell Abu," the finest of all our martial tunes. I hope that some of our companies will begin to chant them before or after the National Anthem at their meetings.' If chanted, these verses might have been greeted with derision, especially by their 'fork-tonguéd' target de Valera:

> Softly our voices are lilting in rhythm,
> Muted our step on the road we must go.
> Smould'ring, we brood on the viper whose venom
> Withers our substance with fork-tonguéd flow.
> > Comrades in duty high –
> > *Service* our battle-cry –

> Seeking no guerdon, bespeaking no prize,
>> Forward! preserve the State!
>> Flinch not from Hell's own Gate!
> Strike like the lightning that startles the skies![54]

Among those who responded to the call was W. B. Yeats, though his 'Three Songs to the Same Tune' (again 'O'Donnell Abu') failed to achieve publication in *United Ireland* or adoption by the Blueshirts. Three months before their first outing in the *Spectator* on 23 February 1934, Yeats sent Blythe typed drafts with various amendments, stating that he had gone through most verses 'syllable by syllable with Larchet[55] & got his general approval of the rest, but a singer might want some other changes, which I should be always ready to make'.[56] Experiment shows that Yeats' refrain is barely singable to 'O'Donnell Abu', being adapted from a ballad with a quite different metre. This was clearly the notorious Yeomanry anthem 'Croppies Lie Down', ending with variants of 'Down, down, croppies lie down', though neither Yeats nor his biographers drew attention to the embarrassing inspiration of Yeats' refrain:

> Down the fanatic, down the clown;
> Down, down, hammer them down,
> Down to the tune of O'Donnell Abu.

Yeats' third song was so sanguinary ('Justify all that have sunk in their blood') that he presumed that 'there is no question of its being sung'. Yet, when his songs were eventually published, *United Ireland* offered a guarded welcome to the ferocious third song in particular, which 'would be not unsuitable for occasional singing at League of Youth functions, though possibly that is to some extent ruled out by the fact that the official rallying song is to the same tune'.[57] Blythe, presumably the reviewer, may have been taken aback by an exhibition of verbal violence even wilder than his own youthful performances. As published in the *Spectator*, the third song included the notorious expostulation 'What's equality? – Muck in the yard'. The chosen anthem was a revised version in five stanzas of Blythe's preferred

'March of the Comrades', rechristened 'The March of Youth' and ending 'On, Youth of Erin; the Blueshirts Abu!'[58]

As the Blueshirts multiplied and violence escalated, Blythe began to contemplate a paramilitary as well as a 'militant' future. On polling day in January 1933, a tussle occurred between tallymen for the two main parties in Ashburton, County Monaghan, leading to the arrival of 'a lorry load' of Fianna Fáil reinforcements who 'chased Mr. Blythe's men from the booth' and 'placarded the polling station with their posters'. The disturbance was not quelled until a detachment of soldiers donned gas masks and prepared 'to use tear-gas bombs to drive off the disturbers'.[59] Such incidents, though not uncommon in earlier Irish elections, lent credibility to Blythe's prophecies of mounting conflict if Fianna Fáil prevailed.

Within a few weeks of Fianna Fáil's emphatic victory, Blythe was among those who interpreted the dismissal of O'Duffy as commissioner of the Civic Guard as a sign that de Valera was edging towards despotism, necessitating disciplined resistance through the newly formed Blueshirts. In late May 1933, Onlooker insisted that the salute of a 'civil organisation' such as the Blueshirts 'should not be military. Until I get orders to the contrary, I intend, myself, to salute by raising my right hand full length above the shoulder, with the palm to the front'.[60] Faced with criticism that this movement was 'somewhat similar to the salutes given by certain Continental organisations', he countered that it 'is said to have been common in ancient Ireland', and should be called 'the Victory Salute'.[61] In its final version, the right arm was to be raised at an angle of forty-five degrees above the shoulder with the palm 'facing forward and downward', a rather limp gesture.[62]

Two months before the Blueshirts' promised March on Dublin to mark Commemoration Day (13 August), Onlooker declared that the Army Comrades' Association must be prepared to use violence if attacked:

> Established to meet a dastardly attack it relies not on persuasion but on combat. It is organised for combat and it wants members who will not shrink from combat if the sight of preparedness fails to frighten off attack.[63]

A fortnight later, he reminded members that 'the A.C.A. is a peace-loving and law-abiding association but it is also a fighting one when attacked'.[64] It was essential to create a cadre of 'intelligence officers' who would 'protect the people against a subversive body which has a large supply of arms'. Blythe, having been largely responsible for enlisting the dismissed commissioner of the Civic Guard as the new Blueshirt leader, looked forward to 'an extraordinary growth in the strength and influence of the organisation'. In addition to O'Duffy's personal qualities of 'energy and thoroughness', he had 'no association with any existing political party or with any particular type of politico-economic policy'.[65] Like Yeats, Blythe clearly viewed his former fellow deputy for Monaghan as a malleable frontman whose reputed charisma would arouse enthusiasm for policies devised by more subtle minds. Despite O'Duffy's meek abandonment of the March on Dublin once declared illegal, Blythe remained of this opinion when pressing Cosgrave and other waverers to accept O'Duffy as the leader of the new United Ireland Party (Fine Gael). Blythe was not excited by the fascist fetish of the great leader, being more concerned with how a pliable demagogue could be deployed to political and administrative advantage. Nor did he ever demonstrably aspire to political leadership himself, preferring to exercise control from behind the scenes.

When the National Guard (successor to the banned Army Comrades' Association) was amalgamated with Cumann na nGaedheal and the National Centre Party to form Fine Gael, the Blueshirts retained a separate identity as the Young Ireland Association, itself soon banned and replaced by the League of Youth. Blythe kept a foot in each camp, becoming a typically middle-aged member of Young Ireland's organising committee as well as the Fine Gael executive. Onlooker remained preoccupied with outward appearances, filling his second and final column in O'Duffy's weekly *Blueshirt* with paragraphs on the garish new St Patrick's Cross badge (coloured in red, blue, green, and gold), how to prevent a beret looking like a pancake, and how to avoid covering one's face when saluting.[66] In *United Ireland*, he enthusiastically endorsed the new 'women's parade dress', which featured a blue dress of 'finer and softer material' than the men's shirts, along with black belt, tie, and beret. Men were urged to remove their black berets when indoors, but never to doff them when taking the salute or standing for the national anthem. Concerned that many Blueshirts were still 'unable to march with the smartness or click their heels with the precision which I would desire', he urged all units with halls to arrange 'physical drill classes' over the winter. Ever emphatic that 'the Young Ireland Association is not a Fascist body' and that 'its members do not model themselves on the Fascisti', he nevertheless urged them to 'learn a lesson from the history of the Blackshirts'. This was always to keep one's blue shirt on, just as 'the wearers of the black shirt, in spite of frequent murderous attacks and constant danger of death, went about everywhere in the uniform of their organisation'.[67] Blythe's reiterated denial of fascism was itself symptomatic of fascism, whose rituals and rhetoric were typically embedded in national histories or mythologies rather than foreign models.

As O'Duffy's defects as leader, thinker, speaker, and organiser became apparent, Blythe and most of his senior colleagues realised their mistake in endorsing him. Blythe has been widely condemned for the manner in which he set up O'Duffy as leader of the Blueshirts and then of Fine Gael, only to manoeuvre him out of both offices a year later.[68] O'Duffy himself was outraged by Blythe's 'brazen hypocrisy', accusing him of 'going from County to County making shocking falsehoods and vile slanders against me'.[69] Recalling Blythe's initial eagerness for his appointment, O'Duffy remarked perceptively that 'Mr. Blythe as usual tried to take all sides and keep in with everybody'.[70]

Yet, from Blythe's viewpoint, O'Duffy had failed in his performance as a charismatic puppet, so he snapped the strings. When mustering support for Cronin's faction of the League of Youth in October 1934, Onlooker explained that O'Duffy's 'stock has been falling during the past eight or nine months, chiefly because of the irresponsibility and imprudence of many of his utterances'. He had rejected advice 'to deliver his speeches from manuscript in future so as to avoid the absurdities and contradictions which had so often embarrassed and shaken the confidence of supporters'. These 'absurdities' doubtless included O'Duffy's explicit endorsements of fascism, crowned by his proposal to spend six months in Italy 'to study the corporative system', so subverting Blythe's presentation of the Blueshirts as a home-grown public service organisation.[71]

In November 1934, Blythe and Cronin (unlike O'Duffy) rejected invitations to an international congress of fascists and fellow-travellers at Montreux, 'the Blueshirts not being a fascist organisation'.[72] This episode was one of several that generated venomous exchanges between Blythe's *United Ireland* and O'Duffy's *Blueshirt*, as the two factions of the League of Youth devoted themselves to puncturing each other's grandiose claims. In denying Blythe's objection that the congress was 'a secret one', the *Blueshirt* observed that 'even in this country it is usual to have at least one private session at all conventions. Yet, nobody gets the feeling that such conventions are held "in Lodge".' Never had an opponent come so close to exposing the secret of Blythe's Orange past.[73]

Onlooker continued to publish his 'Blue Flag Notes' until the demise of *United Ireland* in July 1936, three months before Fine Gael's summary ejection of Cronin and dissolution of his moribund League of Youth. His final column gave priority to the evident collapse of 'the factionist element which split from the League of Youth nearly two years ago'.[74] Blythe's espousal of the 'corporate system of industrial organisations' was now ostensibly grounded 'on the general principles laid down in the great Encyclical *Quadragesimo Anno*', and Blythe no longer called for the curtailment of parliamentary power but merely for the delegation of 'certain tasks of an economic kind to subordinate bodies with specialised experience'.[75] Adept as ever in appealing to disparate potential allies, this unregenerate Low-Churchman shamelessly cited the encyclical of 1931 as an authoritative pronouncement of 'fundamental principles', which all League captains should purchase from the Catholic Truth Society for twopence to 'read and discuss . . . with their men'. Having grasped these principles, 'proposals for applying the Corporative System in the Saorstát can be studied from week to week in UNITED IRELAND and easily understood'.[76] His new-found fidelity to papal prescriptions was nicely lampooned in the *Blueshirt*: 'The Holy Father will, no doubt, be highly honoured to have Mr. Blythe write a commentary on *Quadragesimo Anno*.[77]

Onlooker still espoused Cronin's League of Youth as 'a voluntary, disciplined organisation whose members are banded together for public service';[78] but he no longer depicted it as a potential instrument for state control at every level of society. And when 'Gerald Smith', successor to 'M. G. Quinn', returned to the issue of 'an agricultural vocational organisation' in January 1935, no reference was made to oversight by any 'public service organisation' such as the Blueshirts.[79] Blythe, once a tireless kite-flyer of radical alternatives, had prudently reverted to orthodox defence of established Fine Gael policy.

When drafting his 'Blueshirt Memories' a few days after O'Duffy's death on 30 November 1944, Blythe set out to explain why an organisation 'of great strength and abounding vitality' collapsed within 'a matter of months' after de Valera's government declared the IRA an illegal organisation in June 1936. The transformation of the Army Comrades' Association from 'a social and fraternal organisation' into a 'militant' body was attributable to the widespread belief 'that a compact existed between Fianna Fáil and the military organisation to its left'. In retrospect, Blythe judged that this belief 'was ill-founded and that the intention of Fianna Fáil, from the beginning, was to preserve freedom of speech and democratic institutions'. With the IRA under interdict, 'the Blueshirt organisation . . . lost its *raison d'être* and its power of survival'. He believed, however, that 'the strength and even aggressiveness of the Blueshirts had the salutary effect of hastening very substantially the Government's decision to tolerate no illegal or extra-legal organised forces'. He ignored the fact that 'Blueshirtism' had been in crisis and decline ever since its division into squabbling factions upon O'Duffy's ejection from Fine Gael, nearly two years *before* proscription of the IRA. In retrospect, Blythe belittled the impact of 'the rudimentary corporative programme' which 'came later' than the upsurge of militancy: 'It was not, however, the programme which brought in recruits.'[80]

Yet, as revealed by his subsequent flirtation with the Ailtirí na hAiséirghe ('Architects of the Resurrection'), Blythe was still liable to revert to fascist prescriptions when the stability of

parliamentary democracy seemed vulnerable. He belonged to
Gearóid Ó Cuinneagáin's Craobh na hAiséirghe, the Gaelic League's
'Branch of the Resurrection', formed in 1940 when a German invasion
seemed quite possible. Presented like the Blueshirts as a home-grown,
Christian counterpart to fascism, the Resurrection movement was
overtly pro-Axis and anti-semitic, and its leader privately dubbed
Craobh na hAiséirghe as his 'Hitler Youth Movement'.[81] Though not
known to have formally joined the political party that emerged from
the divided branch (the 'Architects'), Blythe helped draft its policy
documents.[82] Articles attributed to Blythe in the *Leader* displayed
a rather condescending interest in radical groups such as Córas na
Poblachta as well as Ó Cuinneagáin's movement in 1941. He again
espoused the principle of 'vocational organisation', predicting that the
current 'decline in the popularity of democracy' would continue after
the war, regardless of its outcome. 'Parliamentary democracy . . . may
actually go near to disappearing altogether during the next ten years',
while 'vocationalism' ('another name for economic democracy')
would combine nicely in future with 'political authoritarianism'.[83]

With James Joseph Walsh, his boss at Clondalkin Paper Mills and
former colleague on Cosgrave's Executive Council, Blythe was held
responsible by British agents for '23 clubs for children' and lectures 'to
the youths on Nazi lines' in spring 1943.[84] Just before the June general
election, the *Leader* mooted the possibility of an unofficial *coup d'état*,
offering gnomic advice to the prophet of the Resurrection:

> Unless he desires to get into government at some future point,
> he shouldn't bother with electioneering at all. But if, however,
> he does want to get into government he should understand by
> now that there are only two roads to office, by means of the Dáil
> chamber or of the shedding of blood.[85]

Despite the apparent implication of this passage, Blythe (if indeed its
author) did not condone the second option. He warned 'Gearóid' that
'if he turns towards violence, then violence will be used to subdue
him', deeming him 'smart enough to realise that the Architects
have no hope whatsoever in attracting the crowd to them if it is not

clear to the public that they will do their work without breaking the law'.[86] As in 1930, he used Irish to express his more outrageous ideas, side by side with innocuous editorial reflections in English on the prospects for a coalition government.[87] Once again, Blythe became disenchanted with the leader's O'Duffy-like ineptitude, confirmed by the party's abject electoral failures in June 1943 and May 1944,[88] and he lost interest in yet another mutation of fascism.[89]

Such involvements led various intelligence agents, echoed by historians, to classify Blythe as a 'potential Quisling'. The only cited 'evidence' that Blythe would have entered government as a German puppet ruler is therefore imaginative inference from gossip and press reports, the stock sources of political 'intelligence'. He was one of four ex-Blueshirts so labelled by the Irish army's intelligence branch (G2) when contemplating Irish responses to a German invasion.[90] A report for the Secret Intelligence Service identified Blythe as one of the 'outstanding men' who might 'use' O'Duffy as a Quisling. Blythe was described as '100% Nazi', 'well-educated and cultured', with 'outstanding mental qualities' and 'lots of character, moral courage and determination', placing him 'head and shoulders above any other pro-German in Ireland' in 1941.[91] The credibility of this report was somewhat undermined by the baseless claim that he was a 'wealthy businessman'.[92] Blythe and Walsh were again named in 1943 as 'potential Irish Quislings' by whom Ó Cuinneagáin was being 'run'.[93] The puppet theatre was overflowing with incongruous candidates, as the 'potential Quislings' included not only ex-Blueshirts but Fianna Fáil ministers such as Blythe's calumniator Frank Aiken, a senior civil servant (Joseph Walshe of the Department of External Affairs), and IRA leaders such as Seán MacBride.[94] One can but imagine the number of broken heads that would have resulted if they had been invited to form a Punch-and-Judy government. In any case, Blythe was by temperament not a puppet but a puppeteer.

IV

Blythe's fascism was as idiosyncratic as his youthful republicanism, echoing many of the contradictions that make his life worth telling.

The young Blythe could preach republicanism, liberalism, and even unionism with equal conviction, deploying different names and personae to encourage each audience to work together in militant and disciplined movements. It was immaterial to Blythe that most republicans, liberals, and unionists believed themselves to be mutually and irreconcilably at odds. At least until 1914, he believed that any militant assertion of 'self-determination', whether by the IRB and Irish Volunteers, or by the Orange Order and UVF, tended to increase the likelihood of a bloodbath in which Irishmen would eventually find common cause in rejecting British control. As a journalist and politician in the early 1930s, Blythe again used different voices to energise Blueshirt activists, Catholic intellectuals, and conventional politicians in his attempt to reverse the disintegration of the ramshackle Treatyist alliance.

The elements of continental fascism that attracted Blythe all echoed his youthful preoccupations with virility, discipline, romantic espousal of violence and sacrifice, and fraternisation in paramilitary organisations. In 1913, he had proclaimed that only armed force could protect citizens against tyranny, including the tyranny of elected representatives:

> The only guarantee of freedom is the ability of the ordinary citizen to resort to arms in preservation of his rights or for the destruction of tyranny. Franchises and constitutions are but means of using that to which the sword gives title. Rulers, whether they be kings, aristocrats, oligarchs, or elected persons with their never-ending audacity, are preserved from the temptations of their position only by fear of the people.[95]

And 'fear of the people' could only be whipped up by disciplined organisations such as the Irish Volunteers. Two decades later, when addressing a rally of the League of Youth to commemorate a Volunteer killed in County Limerick in June 1921, Blythe declared that the Blueshirts 'were the successors of the Volunteers'. They should complete the revolution by helping 'to secure for the whole of Ireland one State and one Government', remaining in 'permanent existence' to perform 'national tasks' once Fine Gael had returned to power. These tasks might include 'the supreme sacrifice' if attempts were made 'to establish a Communistic regime or a dictatorship on a Mexican model'.[96]

Though the advice he gave the Blueshirts was reminiscent of that once offered to the Irish Volunteers, Blythe's vision of their future role in serving the state was surely also coloured by his intimate knowledge of the workings of the Orange Order. In Newtownards, he had observed how effectively a small group of disciplined Orangemen had permeated every public institution and political organisation. As already noted, he must also have been aware of the pervasive 'public service' role of the Order in the conduct of government and unionist politics at all levels in Northern Ireland. There was also an affinity of style. Like most Fascists and indeed Orangemen, Blythe the theatre buff delighted in the performance of militaristic rituals. These were designed not merely to proclaim efficiency and discipline, but also to create a dramatic link with the Irish past, as expressed in his choice of salute and anthem. On such matters, Blythe was not a tepid or moderating influence, but the most enthusiastic and committed fascist in the old guard of Cumann na nGaedheal.[97]

In other respects, Blythe did not conform to the admittedly fuzzy stereotype of a European fascist. He was only mildly interested in denouncing the abstract threat of communism, except as a stratagem for enhancing Catholic hostility to de Valera and the IRA by whipping up a 'Red Scare'. He was not demonstrably anti-semitic: when asked by an Irish Jewish leader about Fine Gael's position, Blythe assured him that 'your apprehensions concerning the attitude of the United Ireland Party towards the Jewish community in the Irish Free State are quite unfounded', since the party stood 'for toleration and full liberty for all law-abiding citizens of every denomination'. Rumours of future victimisation were 'absurd and malicious'.[98] Since anti-semitism had not yet been fully embraced by Mussolini, admiration for the Italian model did not yet carry any such implication. Like most pre-war Irish fascists, Blythe avoided endorsement of German National Socialism, which was widely regarded as anti-Christian and virtually ignored in Blueshirt and Fine Gael publications. Even O'Duffy seems to have avoided explicit endorsement of German expansionism and Nazi anti-semitism until after his return from Spain in 1938.[99]

Blythe was decidedly non-racist in his conception of Irishness as an attribute of almost all persons born in Ireland, including those of 'Planter stock' like himself.[100] Onlooker's proposal to limit the presidency to 'persons born in Ireland of parents domiciled in Ireland, one of whom was Irish-born', was an *ad hominem* jibe at de Valera rather than evidence of Blythe's xenophobia.[101] The issue had been raised by a correspondent who pointed out that only a native of the United States could become its president, whereas 'we have Mr. de Valera in the highest office in the State; and in 1927 we were threatened with the election of Senator Johnson, an Englishman, to the Presidency'.[102]

He did not contribute to the cult of any Irish Duce or Führer, aiming to use fascism to achieve greater administrative efficiency rather than greater glory. Nor did he consistently back Italy in international disputes, as shown by his support for international sanctions against Italy following its invasion of Abyssinia. When supporting de Valera's League of Nations Bill 'without hesitation' in November 1935, Senator Blythe noted that 'there are a great many people who have a certain feeling for Italy'. But he found the humanitarian pretensions of 'Italian propaganda' repellent, and declared that it was in the interest of 'a small nation' to support the pursuit of 'a rule of law amongst nations'.[103] His support for the League's stance may have been influenced by his long-standing friendship with Seán Lester, with whom the Blythes stayed during Lester's stressful assignment as the League's high commissioner for the 'free city' of Danzig, now Gdansk (1934–7).[104] It is true that Blythe retrospectively endorsed Japan's invasion of Manchuria in 1931 as a justified pursuit of *Lebensraum*. Four years later, he told the UCD Gaelic Society that 'over-populated nations had to expand. In his opinion, the driving of Japan out of the League was a great mistake.'[105] Once again, his mentor may have been Lester, for whom the Japanese invasion was 'no more amoral than the action of other Powers in the past'.[106] But the Lester connection would also have discouraged any endorsement by Blythe of German expansionism, which Lester was valiantly but vainly attempting to thwart in Danzig.[107]

While Blythe's trajectory before, during, and after the Irish revolution was in some ways unique, it also illuminates deeper affinities between republicanism and fascism. Republicans, particularly those trained in the IRB and the Irish Volunteers before 1916, were generally contemptuous of parliamentary democracy as a path to freedom. Even those caught up in the popular crusade for self-determination viewed parliamentary elections as an essential propaganda tool rather than an assertion of popular sovereignty which republicans were bound to respect. So long as activists retained popular support, there was no apparent contradiction between proclaiming democratic values and attempting to create a nation state as prescribed by Sinn Féin ideology. As the self-determination movement fragmented in response to the *fait accompli* of the Anglo-Irish Treaty, affirmation of democratic values ceased to be expedient for the minority, which reverted to the elitist republicanism of the old IRB. Likewise, when the Treatyists lost power in 1932, they too considered abandoning parliamentary democracy in its current form in order to regain power. In each case, the minority sought to educate, discipline, and control the supposedly deluded majority through incendiary propaganda coupled with largely non-violent paramilitary organisation. Such efforts proved ineffectual, whether practised by 'abstentionist' republicans in 1922–6 or by the Blueshirts a decade later. Once a practical electoral strategy for regaining power emerged, the more pragmatic minority leaders drifted back into conventional politics.[108]

In debating the appeal of fascism in the new Irish state, historians have concentrated on the extent to which democratic values and practices had permeated Irish 'political culture' in the period of the Union. Most maintain that the survival of the parliamentary system was a symptom of successful Anglicisation, dismissing Blueshirt and IRA challenges to democracy as representing small disaffected minorities. Conversely, it has been argued that Irish democratic values were skin-deep, because Ireland under the Union had remained in practice a colony rather than a full participant in parliamentary democracy. Thus the initial appeal of the Blueshirt and Resurrection movements was symptomatic of widespread rejection of the parliamentary system, their failure being attributable to inept leadership.[109] Blythe's career suggests an alternative perspective, focusing on the revolutionary education of activists rather than abstract suppositions about 'political culture'.

Though the major parties in the Free State eventually accepted the constraints imposed by democratic elections, many revolutionary veterans of all factions deeply distrusted the democratic credentials of their opponents and remained in readiness for renewed civil war and some form of dictatorship. This entailed support for paramilitary organisations such as the Blueshirts and the IRA, which could be mobilised to defend democracy against each other. Fascism (along with communism) supplied the most highly developed contemporary model of a tight-knit, paramilitary vanguard movement, making it attractive to ex-revolutionaries accustomed to harnessing the popular will through militant combinations.[110] Not every Irish fascist was a former revolutionary, and the typical revolutionary was not demonstrably a proto-fascist. Yet the anti-democratic legacy of the Irish revolution remained powerful, even if a majoritarian model of democracy in fact prevailed. Ernest Blythe, for all his oddities and contradictions, was a man of his age.

Abbreviations

AOH   Ancient Order of Hibernians
BMH   Bureau of Military History, MAI
BNL   *The Belfast News-Letter*
BP   Blythe Papers, UCDA
BPUD   *Belfast and Province of Ulster Directory* (*BNL*, annual)
CIFS   Census of Ireland, Family Schedule (accessible online)
DED   District Electoral Division
DEPD   *Dáil Éireann, Parliamentary Debates: Official Report*
(D)GC   (Deputy) Grand Chaplain
(D)GCI   (Deputy) Grand Chaplain, Ireland
(D)GM   (Deputy) Grand Master
(D)GMI   (Deputy) Grand Master, Ireland
DI   District Inspector, RIC
DIB   *Dictionary of Irish Biography*
DIFP   *Documents on Irish Foreign Policy*, ed. Michael Kennedy *et al.*
EB   Ernest Blythe (Earnán de Blaghd)
GAA   Gaelic Athletic Association
Gaeil   Earnán de Blaghd, *Gaeil Á Múscailt* (1973)
GOL(I)   Grand Orange Lodge (of Ireland)
GRONI   General Register Office of Northern Ireland
HCP   House of Commons Papers
IF   *Irish Freedom*, Dublin
IN   *Irish News*, Belfast
INP   *The Irish Nation and the Irish Peasant*, Dublin
IRA   Irish Republican Army
IRB   Irish Republican Brotherhood
IT   *The Irish Times*, Dublin
MAI   Military Archives of Ireland, Dublin
NA   National Archives, Kew

NAI	National Archives of Ireland, Dublin
NC	*The Newtownards Chronicle*
NDH	*The North Down Herald*, Bangor
NLI	National Library of Ireland, Dublin
NS	*The Newtownards Spectator*
NUI	National University of Ireland
NW	*The Northern Whig*, Belfast
ODNB	*Oxford Dictionary of National Biography*
OED	*Oxford English Dictionary*
PRONI	Public Record Office of Northern Ireland, Belfast
RBP	Royal Black Preceptory
RIA	Royal Irish Academy, Dublin
(R)IC	(Royal) Irish Constabulary
SEPD	*Seanad Éireann, Parliamentary Debates: Official Record*
SIS	Secret Intelligence Service (MI6)
Slán	Earnán de Blaghd, *Slán le hUltaibh* (1970)
TCD	Trinity College Dublin
TD	*Teachta Dála* (member, Dáil Éireann)
Trasna	Earnán de Blaghd, *Trasna na Bóinne* (1957)
UCD(A)	University College Dublin (Archives)
UG	*The Ulster Guardian*, Belfast
UIL	United Irish League
ULT	Ulster Literary Theatre
UUC	Ulster Unionist Council
UVF	Ulster Volunteer Force
WS	Witness Statement, BMH

Notes

PROLOGUE: INITIATIONS

1   Lodge 1501 (in district no. 4) normally met monthly on the second Wednesday in the Orange Hall, Newtownards, implying a lodge meeting on 14 September 1910: Co. Down GOL, *Annual Report for the Year ending 31st December, 1912* (Downpatrick, 1912). Such a meeting was reported in *NDH* (23 September 1910), stating that five members had been initiated, corresponding to the four admissions from lodge 1501 confirmed at the district meeting (the fifth having been overturned or postponed). All cited reports and confidential prints were viewed at Schomberg House, Belfast.

2   *NDH* (28 October 1910).

3   Orange Institution of Ireland, *Laws and Ordinances* (Dublin: pr. Br. James Forrest, 1896), 3, retained with minor variations in the next edition (Belfast: pr. *Northern Whig*, 1924), 3.

4   *NDH* (23 September 1910). Frank Robinson, a commercial clerk, was the lodge secretary.

5   Orange Institution of Ireland, *Ritual of Introduction to the Orange Order* (Dublin: Abbey Printing Works, 1908), 4–6.

6   Amended Constitution (17 March 1873), transcribed in T. W. Moody and Leon Ó Broin, 'The I.R.B. Supreme Council, 1868–78', 314, in *Irish Historical Studies*, xix, 75 (1975), 286–332.

7   EB, WS 939 (12 April 1954), 4A–5.

8   After initiation, Blythe returned to a front room packed with would-be initiates, where he and three or four other recruits 'were asked to stand up and let themselves be seen by the meeting': EB, WS 939, 3.

9   *Trasna*, 109–10.

10 Amended Constitution, 314.

11 *Trasna*, 114–15.

12 Amended Constitution, 314–16.

13 Constitution ('1914') as transcribed in Capt. H. B. C. Pollard, *The Secret Societies of Ireland: Their Rise and Progress* (Kilkenny: Irish Historical Press, 1998; 1st edn 1922), 229. This version was in fact drafted by Thomas Ashe, Diarmuid Lynch, Con Collins, and Michael Collins in early 1917, when the references to a majority decision and to 'peacetime' arrangements were dropped: Leon Ó Broin, *Revolutionary Underground: The Story of the Irish Republican Brotherhood, 1858–1924* (Dublin: Gill & Macmillan, 1976), 176.

14 *Trasna*, 181.

CHAPTER ONE: ORIGINS

1   Magheragall signifies the Plain of the Church; Magheraliskmisk may signify
     the Plain of the Fort of the Drunk.

2   The four children of James Blythe and Agnes Thompson were Ernest (1889–
     1975), James Alexander (b. 1890), Josephine Chelley (1891–1969), and (Mary)
     Helen (1893–1943).

3   *BNL* (25 April 1892). James Blythe had been elected to the select vestry in
     1889 and remained so in 1897, becoming a parochial nominator in 1894 and a
     churchwarden in 1895: *BNL* (12 April 1890, 25 April 1892, 6 May 1889, 5 April
     1894, 11 May 1897). Sources for John Thompson's office in Legacurry appear in
     note 25, below.

4   Mary Blythe (1854–1906) married Francis Brady (b. Co. Down, *c.*1852) in the
     parish church on 13 July 1883. The childless couple, living in a house with
     6 rooms and 4 front windows, were returned as Methodists in 1901. After
     Mary's death, Francis shared the house with his widowed sister, nephew,
     2 nieces, and a nephew-in-law, all members of the Church of Ireland: CIFS
     (1901, 1911). On 3 January 1872, also in the parish church, Mary's elder sister
     Helena (b. 1853) had married John Watson (a farmer in nearby Broomhedge).
     After his death in the Belfast District Lunatic Asylum on 19 June 1892, Helena
     married Thompson Hewitt (an Episcopalian farmer in Legmore, Moira) on 18
     October 1894 in Lisburn cathedral.

5   *Trasna*, 65, 41.

6   In 1901, the Episcopalian proportion in Magheraliskmisk was 61%, and the
     Presbyterian proportion in Deneight was 68%; the Catholic components were
     21% and 3% respectively: Census of Ireland (1901), enumerators' abstracts
     (digitally accessible).

7   The townland's 27 Catholics comprised 8 heads of family, 3 wives, 10 children
     (including a step-daughter), 1 sister, 3 servants, and 2 boarders.

8   Based on digital search for these townlands: CIFS (1911).

9   According to Griffith's Valuation (1863), the value of Robert Blythe's holding
     ranked second out of 19 farms in the townland leased or rented from the
     Marquess of Hertford (the estate passed on his death to Sir Richard Wallace,
     Bart). The holding of almost 83 acres was valued at £92 per annum for land
     and £4 for buildings (raised to £10 10s. in 1902). There were also 11 sub-tenants,
     mainly in cottages which occasionally had small gardens.

10   See, for example, *Belfast Weekly News* (6 August 1859, 8 August 1885); *Belfast
     Telegraph* (27 August 1880). As addresses for prizewinners at Lisburn shows
     were seldom given, it is possible in some cases that the prizewinner was
     Ernest's uncle (though the reference to 'Robert Blythe of Magherafelt' in 1880
     was probably a compositor's error for Magheragall).

11   Thomas Thompson (1812–99) and his brother James (1811–86) were the
     largest resident landholders in Deneight, which contained 23 tenants of the
     Mussenden estate and 30 sub-tenancies (3 of the tenants, including 2 with
     much larger holdings than the Thompsons, were resident elsewhere). Thomas

Thompson held 31 acres assessed at £34 for land and £3 for buildings, virtually the same value as his brother's holding. Only 6 of Mussenden's 23 tenancies in Deneight were valued at more than £30 per annum, compared with 16 of Hertford's 19 tenancies in Magheraliskmisk.

12 These amounts appear in the annual Calendar of Wills and Administrations for Ireland and Northern Ireland (PRONI: accessible online), referring to deaths in 1881, 1886, 1895, and 1900 respectively. No probate record has been traced for Thomas Thompson. The disparity between families was not evident in the next generation. James Blythe left 'effects' (personal estate) valued at £397 on his death in 1941, compared with £263 for Agnes' brother John Thompson (1937) and £419 for John's widow Sophia (1941). All assessments have been rounded to the nearest pound.

13 As documented below, Agnes Thompson's identified brothers in Belfast were Hugh (bricklayer's labourer) and Thomas (carter). James Blythe's brothers were Thomas William (gardener, farmer, and labourer in New Zealand), Robert (farmer in Aghalee), and Alfred Edward (teacher).

14 Their marriage certificate indicates that Robert Blythe, bachelor (1819–95) was resident in the parish of Magheragall, while Chelley Gawley (1829–1900) lived in Aghalee, in whose parish church they were married on 24 May 1850. A press notice gave Robert's address as Ash Grove, Magheragall: *BNL* (28 May 1850). Their children, as recorded in the Magheragall parish registers, were Thomas William (1851–1939), James (1852–1941), Helena (b. 1853), Mary (1854–1906), Henry (b. 1856), Robert (b. 1857), Jemimah (1860–86), a baby who died unbaptised (1861), Jane Ellen (1865–6), and Alfred Edward (1867–1956): PRONI, MIC 1/76A/1. Blythe states that they had twelve children, presumably including Robert's illegitimate offspring Sabina and Robert: *Trasna*, 38.

15 Wills of Chelley Blythe (16 August 1900, died 7 September 1900, probate granted 28 September) and Mary Brady (5 March 1906, died 7 April 1906, probate granted 13 June), in PRONI (accessible online). Chelley Blythe also bequeathed houses in Burnaby Street, Distillery Street, Agnes Street, and two in Riga Street, all in inner west Belfast. Blythe Street was reputedly so named for a sister of Robert Blythe upon her marriage to the builder of its first house: *Trasna*, 65. Since 'New Street' was renamed 'Blythe Street' only in 1876, whereas Grandfather Robert's documented sisters were married in 1848, 1850, and 1854, the story is implausible.

16 William Gawley (aged 85), death notice in *Belfast Weekly News* (3 January 1874).

17 The rateable occupancy of William Gawley's three holdings in Aghalee on the Hertford estate, comprising 26 acres valued at £31 15s. per annum for the land and £4 10s. for buildings, passed to Robert Blythe in 1873, Thomas William Blythe in 1875, and Robert Blythe (jun.) in 1884 (a small portion being sublet): PRONI, Valuation Revision Books, DED Aghalee (accessible online), VAL/12/B/9/2/A–E (1863–1928).

18 *Trasna*, 12, 39.

19 *Trasna*, 40.

20 *Trasna*, 24; EB, WS 989, 7. When Blythe visited his Thompson relatives in Belfast in 1914 after working as a farm labourer in Kerry, 'I remember one of the girls was surprised at the hardness of my hands when I shook her hand': *Slán*, 51.

21 Even Agnes' mother, still living in 1899 according to Thomas Thompson's death certificate, has not been firmly identified, and no baptismal entries have been located for her siblings (Hugh, Agnes, Thomas, and John were born in about 1841, 1850, 1852, and 1860 respectively): CIFS (1901).

22 Thomas Thompson of Deneight, tenant of Daniel Mussenden, was registered as an elector in Hillsborough on 15 January 1813 on the basis of a lease for the life of Thomas Thompson, perhaps his infant son (who died aged 86 in 1899). He was again so registered on 14 July 1815: Lists of Freeholders, Barony of Castlereagh, County Down, in PRONI (accessible online). On 27 October 1834, occupiers of titheable land in 'Dunaight' included Thomas Thompson (13 plantation acres valued at £1 per acre) and 'Jno Thompson or Thos' (24 acres): Tithe Applotment Books, 'Parish of Lisburn or Blaris', in PRONI, FIN/5/A/57.

23 Legacurry Congregation, Session Minutes (31 October 1847): kindly made available, along with registers not accessible on microfilm in PRONI, by the Revd A. Liddle, minister of Legacurry. It is possible that the new communicant was her grandfather.

24 Legacurry Session Minutes (26 December 1847, 22 October 1848, 30 December 1849, 19 May 1850).

25 Legacurry Session Minutes (4 April 1892, 1 January 1894, 6 January 1901).

26 John Thompson's eldest child was baptised in 1824, 2 years before his marriage to Mary Patterson, the next baptism being in 1829 (9 were recorded between 1824 and 1841). William married Jane Cordner in 1832, 4 baptisms ensuing between 1833 and 1842. See Registers of Baptisms and Marriages for First Lisburn Presbyterian church; Register of Baptisms for Christchurch, Lisburn (Blaris): copies in PRONI, MIC 1P/159/1; MIC 1/3.

27 *Trasna*, 65–6; EB, Address Book, *c*.1905–15, BP, P24/2181, listing J. Thompson of '46 or 26' Sandy Row; *BPUD* (1902–51), listing M. Thompson, draper (later dressmaker) of 46 Sandy Row. The Presbyterian household in Sandy Row (no. 46 in 1911, with 7 rooms and 5 front windows) included Thomas Thompson (48 in 1901, carter from County Down), his wife Zillah (44, from Antrim), Maud (20, dressmaker), James (14), and five other children: CIFS (1901, 1911). Thomas Thompson (Deneight, farmer, son of Thomas, farmer) and Zillah Williamson (Lisburn, daughter of Arthur Williamson, farmer, of Magheraclave, Dunmurry) were married in Lisburn on Christmas Day 1877, and had at least 11 children (born in Lisburn up to 1891 and thereafter in Belfast), of whom 4 died in infancy: marriage certificate and indexes to registers of births, deaths, and marriages, GRONI (accessible online). Thomas' marriage, like that of his sister Agnes Blythe, was celebrated in Lisburn's Railway Street Presbyterian church and was not witnessed by any Thompson.

28 Hugh Thompson (1841–1907), son of Thomas, married Agnes Allister (b. 1844), whose father was also a Deneight farmer, in the College Square Presbyterian

church, Belfast, on 8 November 1872. On the death of uncle James Blythe in 1886, his farm was divided between John and Hugh Blythe, who occupied 12 acres of land with no house until 1893. The family lived in Snugville Street, between the Shankill and Crumlin roads, during the final decade of Hugh's life: marriage entry, GRONI; Revision Books, DED Blaris, VAL/12/B/20/6D; *BPUD* (1897–1907); CIFS (1901, 1911).

29   *Trasna*, 64–6, 134; *Slán*, 51.

30   Samuel B. Thompson (1835/9–1917), son of William Thompson (farmer, Dromore, County Down), married Annie Baxter (from Banbridge) in Belfast on 10 April 1879. His precise relationship with Blythe's mother is unknown. The effects of Samuel Thompson of Edenderry House, Woodvale Road, following his death on 11 October 1917, amounted to £1,066: grant of probate, 5 December 1921, in PRONI (accessible online). His son Samuel Ernest occupied Edenderry House for more than 4 decades, whereas Samuel had occupied at least 6 other properties in Belfast since 1868: *BPUD* (1868–1965).

31   In a striking short poem entitled 'Chonnac Corp' ('Seeing the Body'), Blythe wrote that 'Because of some family fighting that would happen / I did not know the corpse', being puzzled at his mother's sorrow: Earnán de Blaghd, *Fraoch is Fothannáin* (Dublin: Oifig an tSoláthair, 1938), 36. Though Thomas Thompson died on 25 May 1899, when Blythe was 10, the poem indicates that he was only 5.

32   *Trasna*, 13–15, 22.

33   *BNL* (6 May 1889, 3 December 1892).

34   PRONI, digital index to signatories of the Solemn League and Covenant and the Women's Declaration (accessible online). James Blythe gave his address as Magheragall but signed up in Donaghadee, a seaside town to which Ernest often cycled as a reporter.

35   No Blythe has been found in published lists of Yeomanry officers (1797–1805), the only tentative connections being David and John Wright, lieutenants in the Lower Iveagh (Hillsborough) cavalry and infantry respectively, both commissioned in 1803. A Margaret Wright was the first wife of Robert Blythe's uncle Adam Blythe (d. 1870).

36   *Trasna*, 12.

37   This may refer to the landowning though untitled family of W. H. H. Lyons of Brookhill, the future Grand Master of Ireland, who succeeded his father in 1887. The estate in Antrim comprised 1,641 acres valued at £4,040 p.a.: U. H. Hussey de Burgh, *The Landowners of Ireland* (Dublin: Hodges, Foster & Figgis, 1878), 284.

38   *Trasna*, 29.

39   *Trasna*, 29–30.

40   This ordeal, usually not involving live goats, was associated with the ritual of the Royal Arch Purple Order, not those prescribed for the Orange or 'Plain Purple' degrees.

41   *Trasna*, 30.

42　In 1901, John Clarke (a 35-year-old farmer's son, Church of Ireland) was living in the household of his father Thomas (aged 80) in a second-class house with 3 front windows and 5 rooms; he remained unmarried in 1911: CIFS (1901, 1911), Magheraliskmisk. In 1903, he succeeded Thomas Clarke as rateable occupier of Magheraliskmisk (no. 20), with 15 acres valued at £16 for land and £2 10s. for buildings: Revision Books, DED Magheragall, VAL/12/B/8/13D.

43　Lodge 1180 (Mullaghcartan) had 80 members in 1851, and submitted returns until 1912, having dissolved by 1922 after several years of 'not working'. Clarke remained master to the end, also heading Brookhill Star and Garter RBP 579 in 1910: Co. Antrim GOL, *Annual Reports* (1851–1922); Grand Black Chapter of Ireland, *Annual Report* for 1910 (viewed at Brownlow House, Lurgan).

44　*Trasna*, 24.

45　James Johnston (an agricultural labourer of the 'Irish Church' aged 25, with a wife of the same denomination and 2 children) lived in a house with 2 front windows and 2 rooms in Ballynalargy (Magheramesk parish): CIFS (1901). No such expulsion was confirmed in the annual reports of Co. Antrim GOL (1851–1931).

46　*Trasna*, 24–5. Robert Walsh (a 29-year-old farm labourer of the Church of Ireland, returned by James Blythe as able to read and write) appeared on the Blythes' census return in 1901 but not 1911.

47　*Trasna*, 25–7. The names of the couple were withheld, uncharacteristically, by Blythe. Matthew Beckett (a Church of Ireland general labourer, aged 41) lived with his wife in Ballynalargy (Magheragall parish) in a house with 2 front windows and 6 rooms: CIFS (1911). Matthew Beckett secured a new labourer's cottage in Ballynalargy from the Rural District Council in 1906: Revision Books, DED Magheragall, VAL/12/B/8/13D–E. His name does not appear as a lodge master in the Magheragall district.

48　*Trasna*, 22–3.

49　*Trasna*, 27.

50　*Trasna*, 27–9.

51　*Trasna*, 31–2, 67. Thomas Fleming (a Catholic farmer aged 66 in 1901) lived with his family in Mullaghcartan (Magheragall parish, bordering Magheraliskmisk) in a substantial house with 5 front windows, 8 rooms, and 11 out-offices: CIFS (1901). No son named William appears in the census return, which lists only 3 of his wife's 10 children. His 3 farms included that next to the Blythes in Magheraliskmisk (no. 5, formerly belonging to John Connor, jun.), which he acquired from Samuel Taylor in about 1897: Revision Books, DED Magheragall, VAL/12/B/8/13D. It contained 31 acres valued at £35 for land and £4 10s. for buildings.

52　Alfred Edward Blythe (1867–1956), schoolmaster, joined Phoenix lodge 210 (Caledon) on 13 June 1894 and resigned in 1933, probably when (still unmarried) he retired and moved to Holywood, County Down, where his brother James and other relatives had settled. He became master of the lodge in 1906: information from Grand (Masonic) Lodge registers (accessible online) and officer lists, in Freemasons' Hall, Dublin.

53 *Trasna*, 11. Thomas Blythe (1815–95), father of Thomas Blythe the district secretary, and probably Robert Blythe (1819–95), Ernest's grandfather, were among ten children of Thomas Blythe (1785–1851) and Helena Magarry (1792–1860), though Robert's baptismal entry has not been located: Hillsborough Parish Registers, microfilm in PRONI, MIC 1/62–4.

54 The Hillsborough lineage has been reconstituted from church and civil registers and press reports, following up leads from family trees made public through ancestry.com. Though most Hillsborough Blythes were Episcopalians, the children of two branches were baptised as Presbyterians and Moravians.

55 Co. Down GOL, *Annual Reports* (1883–1919). Thomas Blythe was not elected as secretary of district no. 1 (Lower Iveagh, north-east) between 1892 and 1895, and held no other senior office in the Orange Order.

56 The Masonic registers record Thomas Blythe's initiation in Annahilt True Blues lodge 683 (12 August 1882), his transfer to lodge 356 at Maze, Hillsborough (31 December 1887), and his being 'struck off' (1895).

57 Mark Blythe joined lodge 188 (Hillsborough) on 1 July 1842; Arthur J. Blythe joined lodge 356 (Maze) on 23 December 1893; and Robert Blythe, a grocer, joined the same lodge on 15 February 1902. Thomas was a great-grandson of William Blythe of Lisadian (1754–98), as was Arthur John; Mark was William's grandson, but Robert's affinity is unknown.

58 Thomas, son of Thomas Blythe and Anabel Boreland (both single), was baptised 19 months after his birth on 17 October 1849; Mark, son of Mark Blythe (evidently in between his two marriages) and Kitty Hall (single), was baptised on 1 June 1834; and Mary, daughter of William Blythe and Mary Donaldson (both single), was baptised on 16 December 1838.

59 Likewise, none of the three Thompsons returned as district or county officers in Belfast between 1888 and 1912 were natives of rural Down, and no identified kinsmen were among the ten other Thompsons returned as private lodge officers in 1912: Loyal Orange Institution of Ireland, *Report of the County Grand Lodge of Belfast Meetings* (annual, 1888–1912), in GOLI Archive, Belfast.

60 Stanley Wellington Thompson (1886–1964), son of Samuel Thompson and his second wife Annie S. Baxter (a bleacher's daughter from Banbridge); returned as clerk (1901) and BA, student of theology (1911); assistant, Fisherwick Presbyterian church, Belfast (1914–15); ordained minister First Dungannon (1915, united with Second Dungannon 1928); YMCA chaplain, France (1917–18): obituary in *Presbyterian Herald* (September 1964); CIFS (1901, 1911); registered marriage entry for Samuel Thompson (widower) and Annie Baxter (St Enoch's Presbyterian church, Belfast), 10 April 1879; cuttings from *BNL* enclosed in Jo[sephine] Blythe to EB, 1 July 1964, in BP, P24/1679.

61 *Trasna*, 134–5. Sister Josephine's letters to EB (5 November 1958, 22 December 1960, 31 December 1967) indicate that she remained in frequent social and professional contact with the Thompson family of Edenderry House, and Ernest preserved a Christmas card from Stanley's sister Mabel Elizabeth sent in 1914: BP, P24/1679, 1539. He recalled spending a night in Belfast 'with my relatives, the Thompson family' (including 'the girls'), when visiting Ulster

from Kerry in 1914: *Slán*, 51. The Thompsons lived in Vignette Terrace for a decade, before moving a few doors up the Woodvale Road to Edenderry House in 1916 (thus expanding from 6 to 16 rooms): *BPUD* (1906–17); CIFS (1911).

62 Stanley Thompson, a member of lodge 1657, Dungannon, was elected as DGC for County Tyrone in every year between 1920 and 1964: GOLI, *Half-Yearly Reports*. He was admitted to Masonic lodge 9, Dungannon ('The Muses'), in 1918, joined the associated Royal Arch Chapter, and remained a member of lodge 289, Belfast, until his death in 1964: Grand Lodge Registers.

63 See ch. 9.

64 Information on lodges, masters, and returns of expulsions, etc. is gleaned from the annual reports of the Co. Antrim GOL. Though in County Down, the Deneight lodge and Lisburn district fell within County Antrim's jurisdiction.

65 Joseph Thompson was probably the 28-year-old labourer (son of John, a farmer) who married Jane McAteer (daughter of a weaver from Largymore, adjacent to Deneight) in the Lisburn registry office on 30 July 1864 (he was expelled from lodge 756 on 9 December 1864). Though this Joseph was currently working in Drumalig, Saintfield parish, he was surely the son of John Thompson and Mary Patterson of Deneight, born on 30 November 1835 and registered by the minister of First Lisburn Presbyterian church. It is likely that this John Thompson was either a brother or an uncle of Agnes' father Thomas.

CHAPTER TWO: FAMILY SECRETS

1 *Trasna*, 38. Thomas William Blythe in fact preceded his brother Robert as occupier of the farm at Aghalee, before emigrating in about 1884.

2 Sabina, daughter of Robert Blythe of Magheraliskmisk (mothers were not yet named in the parish register), was baptised in Magheragall on 28 November 1847, more than two years before Robert's marriage as a bachelor. Robert, son of Robert Blythe of 'Magheragall Parish' and Jane Cooney (single woman), was baptised in Hillsborough on 10 November 1850. Since the name Robert was reused in 1857 for the future farmer in Aghalee, this 'love-child' probably died young.

3 *NW* (13 January 1860).

4 For the eviction of 'some O'Connors' from Hallstown, see *Trasna*, 11–12. John Connor, jun. occupied a smaller holding (no. 5) of 31 acres, valued at £35 for land and £4 10s. for buildings, next door to Blythe's (no. 4) in Magheraliskmisk until 1879; John Connor, sen., probably his father, occupied 64 acres. (no. 1), valued at £68 10s. for land and £2 10s. for buildings, until 1877: Revision Books, DED Magheragall, VAL/B/8/13B.

5 *BNL* (29 June 1900).

6 Revision Books, DED Magheragall (1863–1928): VAL/12/B/9/2/A–E; Irish Land Commission (Purchase of Land (Ireland) Act, 1891), *Return of Advances*

under the Act during the Year ended the 31st March, 1899, 19, in HCP, 1899 (354), lxxix. In that year, Blythe was advanced the purchase price of £651 for three holdings amounting to 44 acres, valued at £59 10s. p.a. and currently held at a judicial rent of £32 11s. 6d. Louis Garrett, who had succeeded Blythe as the occupier of two of his holdings in Aghalee in 1907 and 1909, was occupying Blythe's former house in 1911: CIFS (1901, 1911).

7   *Trasna*, 38. The legacy was given as £200 on the following page.

8   *Thames Star* (20 July 1899); *Auckland Herald* (3 January 1881); *New Zealand Herald* and *Auckland Star* (15 September 1944). An earlier 'Missing Friends' notice dated 17 October [1897] had repeatedly appeared in the Wellington *New Zealand Times* (27 April to 22 June 1898): 'News is sought of Thomas William Blythe, who left Maragall, Lisburn, Ireland, about fourteen years ago for Auckland.' All New Zealand newspapers have been consulted digitally through 'Paperspast' (National Library of New Zealand).

9   In fact 49, his age was given as 45: *Auckland Star* (26 June 1890).

10   *New Zealand Herald* (18 November 1939). Documents located through ancestry.com include Electoral Rolls for New Zealand Parliament (1896–38); New Zealand Cemetery Index (for interment in Shortland Cemetery, 30 November); and printed Returns of Deceased Estates by the Public Trustee (filed 14 December 1939).

11   Will of Chelley Blythe, 16 August 1900, with notice of grant of probate, 28 September 1900: PRONI (accessible online). Her sons James and Alfred Edward Blythe were named as executors.

12   *Trasna*, 39–41.

13   James Alexander married Harriett Christiana Hill (a farmer's daughter from Carnlougherin, Magheramesk) in Broomhedge Methodist chapel on 30 January 1919.

14   In 1911, Harriett Christiana Hill (a typist aged 22) was living with her father Joseph (a farmer aged 53), her mother (45), 7 younger sisters, 2 pre-school brothers and her widowed grandfather Joseph Hill (an 88-year-old retired farmer); the entire family was Methodist and born in Antrim, inhabiting a first-class house with 7 front windows and 11 rooms to accommodate its 13 members: CIFS (1911).

15   *Belfast Gazette* (28 July, 1 September 1922). The composition of debts had yet to be completed in early 1923: *NW* (14 July 1922, 11 January, 2 February 1923).

16   James A. Blythe, Court Records, p. 22, in PRONI, ANT/1/2C/32/50 (file released at my request). These sureties by James Blythe, retired farmer, 4 Moffett's Terrace, Holywood, and Joseph Hill, farmer, Carnlougherin, Magheramesk (28 June and 18 July 1922), in default of the defendant's own surety of £200, related to summonses to petty sessions in Lisburn and subsequently to the Belfast assizes.

17   *BNL* (28 June 1922, 28 February 1923); *NW* (1 March 1923).

18   *BNL* (22 November 1923).

19   The births of John Alexander and Annie Elizabeth on 25 December 1920 and 27 March 1922 were registered in the Lisburn district, while James Ernest was

born in Blackpool on 1 August 1925. Annie (Betty Hezlett) died in Coleraine in 1988, 12 years before John's death in Dorset.

20   *Yorkshire Evening Post* (19 March 1927); *BNL* (5 April).

21   *Cheltenham Chronicle* (22 June 1929); *BNL* (11 July); *The Times* (10 July).

22   *The Times* (28 June 1934).

23   *Western Daily News Press*, Bristol (13 November 1935); *The Times* (15 November). News of the trial, replete with picturesque detail, even reached Wellington, New Zealand: *Evening Post* (16 December 1935).

24   *BPUD* (1948–67).

25   Annie's sponsor at the wedding on 12 December 1952 was her mother, though her father (described as an engineer) was still living.

26   Betty (Mrs Hezlett) to 'Dear Uncle Ernest', 12 December 1961 and undated: BP, P24/1680–1.

27   'In Memoriam: Mrs. Henrietta Blythe', in *Irish Christian Advocate* (4 July 1968): copy kindly supplied by Lizzie Shannon.

28   According to the register of deaths, she was widowed at the date of her death (26 May 1968), her husband 'John' Alexander having been a civil engineer. Yet the probate calendar returned her as a married woman (probate was granted on 4 July 1968 to her son-in-law, Benjamin William Hezlett, clerk to the Coleraine Rural District Council).

29   See following chapter.

30   Mary Helen Blythe married William Nassau Gibson (son of Francis William, an agent) in St James' parish church, Belfast, on 16 April 1930.

31   Four undated postcards from 'Cissie' (Malta) to 'Eileen' (probably her sister Helen), one with the placename inked over because 'we are not allowed to say where we are': BP, P24/2363–4.

32   Successive issues of *BPUD* (1932–54) indicate that 'Raneese', Marino, was occupied by Miss J. C. Blythe (1932–4), one 'William' Blythe, perhaps in error for James (1935–41), Miss (Nurse) Blythe once again (1942–53), and Alfred F. (E.) Blythe, her uncle (1954); father James was also living there at the time of his death (1941). The family's previous address (1922–31) was 4 Moffett's Terrace, Holywood (occupier James Blythe).

33   Ernest Blythe (journalist, 14 Hatch Street) married Annie McHugh (70 St Stephen's Green; daughter of Patrick McHugh, formerly district inspector) on 13 November 1919. Their sponsors were John E. Lester and Annie's co-founder of Scoil Bhríde, Louise Gavan Duffy.

34   'Baby Blythe' died on 13 September 1920 at 32 Leeson Street Lr (perhaps a maternity clinic), her address being 11a Casimir Ave, Harold's Cross, a house occupied by Mrs M. Fitzgerald in 1921. Blythe's residence in 'the last house at the blind end' of Casimir Ave in 1920–2 is mentioned in EB, WS 939, 120, 154. The 'company' directed by Blythe may also have been the Skibbereen *Southern Star*, briefly edited by Blythe in 1918 after its purchase by the West Cork Sinn Féin organisation: EB, WS 939, 79.

35   Earnán Pádraig de Blaghd, son of Earnán de Blaghd (Aire Airgid or minister for finance) was born at 11 Sandford Road, Ranelagh, on 19 March 1925. Ernest

had clearly insisted on accurate Irish, as 'Padraig' was crossed out by the registrar and replaced by its accented form.

36 After graduating from UCD with first-class honours for his MA in 1946, Earnán enrolled at the King's Inns, being called to the Bar in 1949. His versatility was displayed as Irish-language editor of the *Irish Independent* (also reviewing Irish-language plays in English), and editor of the *Irish Digest* of law reports for the period 1971–83. As ever, the *Irish Digest* transcended the border by incorporating Northern Ireland reports.

37 Blythe's papers for the Dublin Historical Society included 'The D.M.P.' and 'Cold War in the Dublin G.A.A. 1887', in *Dublin Historical Record*, xx, 3–4 (1965), 116–26, and xxii, 3 (1968), 252–62. This penetrating article explains that the IRB lost interest in directly controlling the GAA once Archbishop Croke's opposition had negated its attempt to inveigle the Catholic clergy into an informal alliance. Thereafter, 'right up to 1922, the I.R.B. strongly infiltrated the organisation' (262), in keeping with its customary preference for exercising indirect control through front organisations.

38 In the index to *Thom's Directory* for 1965, when Earnán turned 40, his address was given as 50 Kenilworth Square (his father being returned as the occupier).

39 Earnán Pádraig de Blaghd was buried at Glasnevin cemetery on 9 September 2014 after Requiem Mass at the Church of the Annunciation, Rathfarnham: *IT* (8 September 2014). His parents were likewise buried at Glasnevin after services at the Catholic Church of the Three Patrons, Rathgar, and St Patrick's Cathedral: *Irish Independent* (28 September 1957); *IT* (26 February, 1 March 1975); *Irish Independent* (26 February 1975).

40 Leon Ó Broin, *Just Like Yesterday: An Autobiography* (Dublin: Gill & Macmillan, [1986]), 96.

41 *Trasna*, 222–3.

42 *Slán*, 91.

43 *Slán*, 115.

44 Mrs Ina Heron, daughter of James Connolly, WS 919 (25 January 1954), 94–5; NAL, HO 144/1454/312169.

45 Postcards sent from Abingdon, Berkshire, to Helen and Josephine Blythe, 10 April 1916: BP, P24/2362–5. Blythe was placed in custody in Oxford gaol a few days later after failing to report to the police in Abingdon: HO 144/1454/312169. No correspondence with his parents or brother is listed in the comprehensive catalogue in UCDA.

46 On 4 January 1917, he undertook, as required by Major-General Fry (the 'competent military authority'), not to leave the specified district (which included Ballinderry and Magheramesk but not Lisburn) without the county inspector's permission: undertaking, with typed order and marked-up map, in BP, P24/1016.

47 *Gaeil*, 114.

48 Harry Shiels, F Co., 1st Battalion, was wounded at the Church Street barricade in 1916, resulting in amputation of an arm: Seumas Kavanagh, WS 1670 (9 September 1957), 27; Eilis Uí Chonnail (née Ryan), WS 568 (7 August 1951), 13.

49 *Gaeil*, 114–15.

50 On 16 February 1932, just short of a quota, Blythe was comfortably returned in County Monaghan, ahead of the second Fianna Fáil candidate and the sitting Independent, Alexander Haslett: *Parliamentary Election Results in Ireland, 1918–92*, ed. Brian M. Walker (Dublin: RIA, 1992), 136.

51 Helen [Gibson] to EB, 9 March 1932: BP, P24/1677.

52 On 24 January 1933, he was overtaken by Haslett, a leading member of the County Monaghan Grand Orange Lodge, who with the help of Fianna Fáil preferences regained his seat (of the Fianna Fáil surplus, 750 votes went to Haslett and only 312 to Blythe). In the final count, Haslett outpolled Blythe by 316 votes: Walker, *Parliamentary Election Results*, 143; Co. Monaghan GOL, Mss Minutes (esp. 2, 17 May 1932, 16 May 1933), in GOLI Archives; Peadar Livingstone, *The Monaghan Story* (Enniskillen: Clogher Historical Society, 1980), 411–12; *IT* (28 January 1933).

53 *IT* (16 January 1933), reporting a speech by Blythe at Clontibret.

54 Helen [Gibson] to EB, 11 June 1943: BP, P24/1678.

55 Jo [Josephine Blythe] to EB, 5 November 1958, 22 December 1960, 31 December 1967, and undated: BP, P24/1679.

56 Firearm certificate book in BP, P24/1743.

57 See Epilogue.

CHAPTER THREE: 'EARNÁN DE BLAGHD'

1 Though the Presbyterian Association did not run a hostel, two Presbyterian ironmongers were lodgers of the caretaker in 1901, and Blythe may have been lodging there with a maternal relative. Its occupier in 1911 was Robert James Thompson, a 'general secretary' aged 29 and married for 6 years, son of a retired farmer from County Down who had moved to Ranelagh: CIFS (1901, 1911). Blythe referred to his place of lodging in *Trasna*, 75, 88.

2 Excerpt from broadcast by EB, played on Myles Dungan's 'History Show' (RTÉ, 5 March 2017). I am grateful to Jane Leonard for reporting on this broadcast. George Irvine (1877–1954), the son of John Irvine, an Enniskillen evangelical bookseller, was educated at Portora Royal School, Armagh, became a teacher in Dublin, secretary of the Dublin Centres' Board, and an organiser of the Church of Ireland Gaelic Society. He manned an outpost of the South Dublin Union garrison in 1916 (B co., 4th battalion) but surrendered prematurely, underwent penal servitude, became director of service for the 1st battalion, Dublin Brigade, and was interned in Mountjoy as a republican in the civil war. In later life he taught at the Parnell Square branch of the Dublin Technical Schools, living with his brother William J. Irvine (also a teacher) at 6 Mount Pleasant Square, Ranelagh. Irvine taught both day and evening classes, using the English form of his name: George Irvine, WS 265 (20 June 1949); CIFS (1911); *IT* (1 July 1954); Valerie Jones, *Rebel Prods: The Forgotten Story of Protestant Radical Nationalists and the 1916 Rising* (Dublin: Ashfield Press, 2016), 147–57; *City of Dublin Technical Schools, Session 1937–38: Prospectus*,

Day Schools of Commerce and *Prospectus, Schools of Commerce, Evening Department* (Dublin, 1937).

3   EB, WS 939, 1–5.
4   John Olphart Gage Dougherty (1856–1939), ordained (1890), incumbent, St Mary's (1904–33); DGC, Dublin City from 1897, DGCI (1898–1939), DGM, Trinity College lodge (1920) and GM (1922): GOLI, *Report of the Proceedings . . . at the General Half-Yearly Meeting* (confidential print: full series in Schomberg House, Belfast) [hereafter, *Half-Yearly Reports*].
5   BP, P24/2181, 2222. Neither list included (O')Casey, perhaps because he was too close a friend to be forgotten.
6   Peter Murray, *Seán O'Casey: Writer at Work* (Dublin: Gill & Macmillan, 2004), 71–2; transcription of circular to Dublin branches of Gaelic League (22 April 1907), signed by Seoirse de h-Ireadhoin (Irvine), Earnan de Blaghd, Seaghan Ua Catasaigh (O'Casey), and Seamus [U]a Deacin, in possession of Padraig O Snodaigh: *IT* (25 February 1975). [Irish names are as reproduced in *IT*.]
7   *Trasna*, 65–6.
8   *Trasna*, 202. Though Blythe offered his resignation as a boy clerk in the Department of Agriculture and Technical Instruction as from 24 March, an official minute had already reminded the Department that he would be 'ineligible for further service' after his twentieth birthday on 13 April 1909: EB to Mr Butler, 19 March; J. L. Le B. Hammond, memorandum, 5 March 1909: NLI, MS 20654. The fact that he was in a position to resign before the contract's end was 'something that pleased me': *Trasna*, 153.
9   EB, WS 939, 5–6.
10 *Trasna*, 178. The college was founded by Seán Ó Catháin, one of Blythe's teachers.
11 EB, WS 939, 4A–6.
12 *Trasna*, 177.
13 Succinct biographies of Cotton, Heron, and Lester appear in Jones, *Rebel Prods*, 172–80, 180–4, and 186–91.
14 Lester, on holiday in Bangor, cycled with Blythe to the field at Cronstown outside Newtownards, where the novice showed precocious mastery of the required unionist clichés: 'The weather was exceedingly fine, and the demonstration proved to be one of the largest and most imposing that has ever been held in the district' (though several north Down lodges had joined the Belfast demonstration): *NDH* (16 July 1909); *Trasna*, 174.
15 Hugh Oram, *The Newspaper Book: A History of Newspapers in Ireland, 1649–1983* (Dublin: MO Books, 1983), 157; Douglas Gageby, *The Last Secretary General: Seán Lester and the League of Nations* (Dublin: Town House, 1999), 6. At the age of 17 in 1905, he too is stated to have worked for the *North Down Herald*: article by Michael Kennedy in *DIB*, vol. v, 469–70.
16 Darby, a teacher of navigation like his Liverpool-born father Peter, moved to Belfast in 1907 and later to Holywood, County Down, before his death in the Abbey sanatorium, Whiteabbey, County Antrim, on 5 October 1912. He played for Antrim in Ulster's first All-Ireland football final in January 1912 (won by Cork), also acting as a referee and as secretary to the South Antrim Board of

the GAA: Census of England (1901, 1911), family schedules (accessible online via ancestry.com); register of deaths, GRONI (accessible online); article on website of Pádraig Sáirséil CLG (Patrick Sarsfield GAA Club).

17   According to Blythe, Turley 'was shot as a spy by the I.R.A. about 1922 or 1923': WS 939, 4A. I am grateful to Jane Leonard for pointing out the correct date of his murder. He died shortly after an attack by three or four gunmen at Clonard Gardens, Belfast, on 4 December 1936, having been reportedly tarred and feathered, tortured with pliers and a poker, and forced into 'exile' in Dublin in 1933 and thence Southampton: *IT* (5, 12 December 1936, 17 February 1937); Brian Hanley, *The IRA, 1926–1936* (Dublin: Four Courts Press, 2002), 48–9. Turley's republican reputation has recently been rehabilitated by John O'Neill, 'Dan Turley, a 1916 Veteran Shot by the IRA?', in *The Treason Felony Blog* (web, 2 December 2015).

18   EB, WS 939, 4a; Alfred Cotton, WS 184 (24 January 1949), 1; EB, 'I.R.B. (Belfast)', in undated name lists, BP, P24/2222; EB, Address Book, *c.*1905–15, BP, P24/2181; CIFS (1911). Where necessary, information has been added from a previous census return: CIFS (1901).

19   The Census of England did not record Peter Darby's religion (assumed to be Catholic) or house description in Liverpool. Though David Boyd lived apart from his parents in both 1901 and 1911, statistics incorporate information on his father John, a carpenter from County Down.

20   Denis McCullough, WS 915 (11 December 1953), 10.

21   See ch. 9.

22   Tony Keating, 'D. C. Boyd and the *Waterford Standard*' (paper kindly supplied by Dr Patrick McCarthy) and CIFS (1901, 1911); for Irvine, see note 2, above.

23   Archie Heron and Frank Wilson are enumerated as Presbyterian and Brethren (1901) rather than as Catholic and under 'information refused' (1911); John Darby's father is enumerated as Catholic (see note 16, above).

24   Daniel McCullough (himself a former IRB man, a printer-compositor born in Belfast, father of Denis and Joseph) and James Robinson (a plate-moulder born in France).

25   Seagán Ó Diargasa (Darby), Ailfrid Ua hIaranora (Heron), Airt Ó Labhradha (Laverty), Donnchadh and Seosamh Mac Con Ulodh (MacCullough or McCullough), Seosaimh Mac Roibin (Robinson), and Enri and Micheál Ua Siaghail (Shiel). [Irish names are as given in household census forms.]

26   *Trasna*, 186. Robert Maxwell King, a 47-year-old Dubliner (1863–1923), was minister of the Unitarian (Non-Subscribing Presbyterian) church in Great Frances Street; George McKibbin, a 75-year-old widowed 'Prespterian' cotton weaver, lived in Ann St: CIFS (1911).

27   These stories came from the Doggarts, his hosts in Newtownards: *Trasna*, 186–7. The nearest equivalent that I have identified is the 'Green Flag' lodge 1059 in Newtownards, last returned in 1888, which came to the attention of the Grand Lodge of Ireland because of the display of a forbidden green flag in processions: cutting from *Belfast Telegraph* (14 June 1879) in Breaches Book, GOLI Archive; Co. Down GOL, *Annual Reports*.

28 *Trasna*, 187. For a similar account, see Earnán de Blaghd, *Briseadh na Teorann* [Breaching the Border] (Dublin: Sáirséal agus Dill, 1955), 101.

29 *Frank Roney, Irish Rebel and California Labor Leader: An Autobiography*, ed. Ira B. Cross (Berkeley: University of California Press, 1931), 59–62; Kerby A. Miller and Breandán Mac Suibhne, 'Frank Roney and the Fenians: A Reappraisal of Irish Republicanism in 1860s Belfast and Ulster', 34–5, in *Éire-Ireland*, li, nos 3–4 (2016), 23–54. I am indebted for both references to Dr Guy Beiner of the Ben Gurion University of the Negeev, Israel.

30 Elizabeth Bloxham (1877–1962), born Claremorris, County Mayo; Episcopalian, Irish-speaker by 1911; contributor to *Sinn Féin* (1906–12) and other nationalist journals; a founder of Cumann na mBan (1914); instructress in domestic economy at Newtownards technical school (January 1911–June 1916); died unmarried, leaving most of her small estate (£1,365) to an unmarried niece in County Galway: Elizabeth Bloxham, WS 632 (29 December 1951); CIFS (1901, 1911); will (29 June 1955) and grant of probate (13 December 1962) in NAI; see also Jones, *Rebel Prods*, 281–8.

31 *Trasna*, 216; see also EB, *Briseadh*, 42. Blythe's brief report as 'The Old Town Clock' did not name Bloxham or the second interviewee, merely noting discontent over losing the incumbent, Mrs Walker: 'The students have taken up the cudgels, and apparently intend to appeal to the Department from the committee': *NDH* (18 November 1910).

32 Elizabeth Lewis (aged 35, domestic economy instructress, boarding in a private hotel in Denny Street, Tralee): CIFS (1911). Bloxham defeated 'Miss Lewis, of Tralee' by 5 votes to 3, and took up the appointment on 1 January 1911: *NC* (19 November 1910, 7 January 1911).

33 *Trasna*, 216–17.

34 *NC* (3 February 1912); letter accurately transcribed in Bloxham, WS 632, app. A. Bloxham's second letter of protest has not been located in WS 632 or *NC*.

35 'Sea-Cob' of Ballywalter, sharing the irritation of 'Anon' at the anti-Bloxham effusions of 'Will Waterproof': *NC* (24 February 1912).

36 *NS* (16 February 1912); the verse by 'Puritan' first appeared in *NC* (10 February).

37 *NDH* (23 February 1912).

38 Bloxham, WS 632, 12–20, 24–6.

39 Her pious friend may have been John Martin, bread-server of Court Street, aged 56 in 1901, admitted to lodge 1501 in 1886: CIFS (1901); Minutes, district lodge no. 4, Newtownards [hereafter, District Minutes].

40 Bloxham, WS 632, 15–16, 26–7.

41 Bloxham, WS 632, 1. The value for probate of her father's estate was only £249: NAI, Calendar of Probate.

42 RIC Registers, NAL, HO 184/4, 8, 25, 28, 30 (microfilm, Gilbert Library, Dublin); digital copies of RIC Pension Ledgers (1873–1925), via ancestry.com. Records relate to John Bloxham, alias Blacksim, Blaxim, and Blacksom (1824–1906), appointed 1844, pensioned 1875; George Henry Bloxham (b. 1864), appointed 1881; John Edward Bloxham (b. 1870), appointed and discharged 1888; and Henry Joseph Bloxham (1880–1921), appointed 1898, pension

granted to widow and children 1921. Richard Blaxsim, appointed 1851, was probably Elizabeth's uncle, Richard being her paternal grandfather's name: genealogical details via ancestry.com. Richard Blaxsim resigned from the force in 1855 when he 'volunteered for Guards'.

43 Elizabeth Malcolm, *The Irish Policeman, 1822–1922: A Life* (Dublin: Four Courts Press, 2006), 56–61.

44 Richard Abbott, *Police Casualties in Ireland, 1919–1921* (Cork: Mercier Press, 2000), 187; Tim Herlihy and seven other witnesses from 3rd (Ovens) battalion, 1st Cork brigade, WS 810 (7 March 1953), 12–13, 33, 37.

45 Henry's widow received £39 annually, along with £2 13s. for each child: RIC Pension Ledgers.

46 Bloxham, WS 632, 10.

47 None of the unsigned or pseudonymous contributions reproduced in *The Voice of Freedom: A Selection from 'Irish Freedom' 1910–1913* (Dublin: *Freedom* Office, 1913) has been firmly identified as Blythe's work. Attributions in ink, most presumably by Hobson, appear in three of the four copies in NLI, Hobson having been asked by the library's director to commit this useful act of literary vandalism: Bulmer Hobson, *Ireland Yesterday and Tomorrow* (Tralee: Anvil Books, 1968), 39. In his autobiography, Blythe hinted that he also contributed anonymous pieces: 'And from time to time I would put my own name, in Irish, under an article in *Irish Freedom*': *Trasna*, 180.

48 *Gaeil*, 114.

49 *IF*, no. 2 (Dec. 1910). The author may, however, have been Hobson, who later claimed that all editorials were written by himself or P. S. O'Hegarty: Hobson, *Ireland Yesterday and Tomorrow*, 39.

50 *IF*, no. 9 (July 1911).

51 *IF*, nos 19, 20 (May, June 1912).

52 *IF*, nos 27, 28, 42; 32, 36, 40, 41 (February, March 1913, April 1914, June, October 1913, February, March 1914).

53 *IF*, no. 32 (June 1913).

54 'The Old-Time Farm', in *IF*, no. 42 (April 1914).

55 'Ireland's To-Morrow', in *IF*, no. 36 (October 1913).

56 'Men and Arms', in *IF*, no. 21 (July 1912), reproduced in *The Voice of Freedom*, 13–15.

57 *IF*, no. 21 (July 1912).

58 'Arms and Drill', in *IF*, no. 38 (December 1913).

59 'Young Men of the Volunteers', in *IF*, no. 39 (January 1914).

60 'Young Men of the Volunteers', in *IF*, no. 39 (January 1914).

61 EB, WS 939, 8–9.

62 'Belfast and Partition', in *Irish Independent* (14 May 1914). The terms 'partition' and 'exclusion' were used interchangeably, whereas 'partition' was subsequently applied to the creation of two Irish states rather than to the retention of part of Ulster in the United Kingdom, without devolution ('exclusion').

63   300 young men were enrolled at Castlewellan, where the chairman was a nationalist magistrate: *Irish Independent* (26 May 1914).

64   Handwritten draft speech marked '1914', stating that the celebrated 'compact' of 11 June 1795 had occurred 121 years earlier (presumably a slip): BP, P24/2193. Commemorative gatherings at Mac Art's fort were regularly held on Tone's birthday (20 June). According to James Connolly's daughter Nora, with whose family Blythe regularly stayed when in Belfast (in Glenalina Terrace), the speech was delivered in June 1915; but this date cannot be reconciled with accounts of his movements in WS 939 and in police reports: interview with Nora Connolly-O'Brien in *Survivors: The Story of Ireland's Struggle as told through some of her Outstanding Living People*, comp. Unseann MacEoin (Dublin: Argenta Press, 1987; 1st edn 1980), 204.

65   'And he shall judge among the nations, and shall rebuke many people: and they shall beat their swords into plowshares, and their spears into pruninghooks: nation shall not lift up sword against nation, neither shall they learn war any more': Isaiah 2:4 (AV).

66   'The Lowest Depth' (leading article), in *IF*, no. 42 (April 1914).

67   'Rocks Ahead', in *IF*, no. 43 (May 1914). Four decades later, Blythe recalled believing as a young nationalist that, if Protestants were placed under an all-Ireland parliament and fairly treated, they would be reasonably happy with their new situation, and would choose not to start a military or illegal campaign: EB, *Briseadh*, 77.

68   EB (Magheragall, Lisburn), letter to *Kilkenny People* (16 May 1914).

69   EB (115 Station Road, Sydenham, Belfast), letter to *Irish Independent* (21 May 1914). Blythe's hostess was the widowed grandmother of one Archibald Heron, perhaps a relation of his IRB namesake: CIFS (1901, 1911).

CHAPTER FOUR: 'PURPLE STAR'

1   *Trasna*, 206; *Slán*, 13.

2   See ch. 9, n. 40.

3   Though not an official emblem of any of the 'loyal orders', a five-pointed purple star appears on the current flag of the Orange Order and the name was commonly used in lodge titles from at least the 1860s (the Grand Orange Lodge of Ireland approved 13 such titles between 1869 and 1922, including 6 in Belfast and 4 in Antrim): GOLI, *Half-Yearly Reports*.

4   *Trasna*, 206.

5   Testimonial by W. H. Davey, MA, BL, 4 April 1913: BP, P24/1212.

6   *Trasna*, 221.

7   *UG* (27 May 1911). Blythe was fond of Isaiah 2:4, as shown by his address at Mac Art's Fort in 1914 discussed in the preceding chapter.

8   'Letters to Young Liberals', I, in *UG* (19 August 1911).

9   'Letters', II, in *UG* (26 August 1911).

10   'Letters', III, in *UG* (2 September 1911).

11   'Letters', IV, in *UG* (9 September 1911).

12   'Letters', IV, in *UG* (9 September 1911).

13   'Letters', V, in *UG* (16 September 1911).

14   'Letters', VI, in *UG* (23 September 1911).

15   'Letters', VII, in *UG* (30 September 1911).

16   'Letters', VIII, in *UG* (7 October 1911).

17   'Letters', IX, in *UG* (14 October 1911).

18   'Letters', X, in *UG* (21 October 1911).

19   Blythe recalled that Davey had such respect for his letters that he vainly urged Blythe to submit an article to a London literary review, the *Nineteenth Century* ('I had decided in my mind that I would never write about Irish politics in any English newspaper or periodical': *Trasna*, 206).

20   *UG* (30 September 1911).

21   Letter signed by James Cummings, 1 Laurel Cottages, Whitehouse: *UG* (21 October 1911). The only James Cummings returned in Whitehouse in April 1911 was a Congregationalist retired fireman (a widower aged 72 from Armagh), whose son James Cummings (a 33-year-old clerk born in Antrim and recently married) had moved from Whitehouse to Whiteabbey over the preceding decade: CIFS (1901, 1911). It is possible that the correspondent was James the younger, using his father's address.

22   *UG* (28 October 1911).

23   *UG* (4 November 1911).

24   *UG* (11 November 1911).

25   *UG* (18 November 1911). 'Young Radical' and 'Third Bangor' came to the defence of 'Purple Star' in the same issue.

26   *UG* (2, 9 December 1911).

27   The appeal by 'Young Liberal' was supported by J. Aubrey Rees, secretary of the League, which incorporated 500 branches in England and Wales and one in Dublin: *UG* (20 July, 3 August 1912).

28   *Trasna*, 206–7.

29   'The Irish Language Movement', V, in *UG* (11 May 1912).

30   'Movement', I, in *UG* (6 April 1912).

31   'Movement', II, in *UG* (13 April 1912).

32   'Movement', III, in *UG* (27 April 1912).

33   'Movement', IV, in *UG* (4 May 1912).

34   'Movement', VI, in *UG* (25 May 1912).

35   *UG* (13 April 1912). Peter Toner McGinley or Mac Fhionnlaoich (1856–1942) from Donegal, founder of the Belfast branch of the Gaelic League (1895) and the League's president (1925–40), wrote in Irish as 'Cú Uladh' (Hound of Ulster): article by Vincent Morley in *DIB*, vol. v, 1007.

36   'The Gaelic League', in *UG* (18 May 1912).

37   *Trasna*, 207.

38   BP, P24/1740.

39   *UG* (10 February 1912).

40 *NDH* (9 February 1912).
41 *Trasna*, 207.
42 *UG* (2 February 1913).
43 *Trasna*, 218–20.

CHAPTER FIVE: 'REPORTER, JUNIOR (PROTESTANT)'

1   In 1911, the population of Newtownards Urban District comprised Presbyterians (56.1%), 'Protestant Episcopalians' (24.3%), Catholics (9.2%), Methodists (6.5%), and miscellaneous categories (3.8%). The corresponding proportions for Bangor Urban District were 48.8%, 30.8%, 8.7%, 6.9%, and 4.7%: Census of Ireland (1911), printed report for Co. Down, 129–30.

2   The *North Down Herald* was published in Bangor; the *Newtownards Spectator* was a slightly modified local version of the *County Down Spectator* (Bangor).

3   Robert Delmege Montgomery, died 1956 (Presbyterian born in Tyrone, aged 36 in 1911, married); Henry Gaw, died 1958 (Presbyterian, Down, 21, single); George Craig (Episcopalian, Scotland, 22 in 1901, single); Robert Singleton Henry, died 1932 (Presbyterian, Belfast, 41, single); Stewart Spencer Churchill Henry, died 1922 (Presbyterian, Down, 33, single); James Singleton Henry, died 1943 (Presbyterian, Belfast, 49, married); David Edward Alexander, died 1943 (Presbyterian, Scotland, 38, married): CIFS (1911, 1901); PRONI, Calendar of Probate (accessible online).

4   Robert S., James Singleton, and Stewart S. C. Henry joined lodge 447 in 1893, 1894, and 1902 respectively; Robert D. Montgomery transferred to 746 in 1909; Harry Gaw joined 746 in 1919; David Alexander joined 447 in 1899, transferring to 746 in 1904; George Craig has not been reliably matched: Grand Lodge Registers.

5   Speech at Ballyrea demonstration by 'Bro. Captain James S. Henry': *NDH* (14 July 1911). Blythe also named Bob Henry as an Orangeman: *Trasna*, 170.

6   EB to Johnson, 1 November 1949: NLI, Johnson Papers, MS 17,200/2; see a similar account of Montgomery's 'crookery' in *Trasna*, 176.

7   The microfilmed version may be the Belfast edition: one issue carried several reports of Independent meetings under 'Among the Lodges', immediately following a verbatim account of T. H. Sloan's presidential address to the Protestant Alliance in Belfast: *NDH* (28 May 1909).

8   *IT* (10 March 1909).

9   *Trasna*, 152–3, 161.

10 Blythe's address, according to a postcard sent by his uncle Alfred on 21 December 1909, was 58 Abbey Street, Bangor: BP, P24/1676. The householder at that address in 1911 was Martha Bell, a 48-year-old Presbyterian widow who 'keeps boarding house'. The family comprised her two sons and two boarders including David Boyd (16), a Presbyterian reporter born in County Down. In 1901, as Culbert Boyd (7, born in Belfast), he was living in Omagh, County Tyrone, with the family of his grandfather David Boyd, a Presbyterian

colporteur. His parents John and Mary Charlotte (both Church of Ireland from Tyrone in 1901, yet Presbyterian from Down in 1911) and all of his siblings were 'visitors' in a relative's pub in Holywood in 1901, subsequently moving to Dundonald: CIFS (1901, 1911). For Boyd's career, see ch. 8, note 52 below.

11   *Trasna*, 199.

12   *Trasna*, 166–7.

13   Hugh Oram, *The Newspaper Book: A History of Newspapers in Ireland, 1649–1983* (Dublin: MO Books, 1983), 112.

14   *Trasna*, 161–5.

15   *Trasna*, 162, 164; *NDH* (26 March 1909).

16   *Trasna*, 165.

17   *Trasna*, 169, 170.

18   *Trasna*, 168–9. The auctioneer was clearly Henry Montgomery of Main Street, Bangor (with a branch office in High Street, Newtownards), a member of the Bangor Urban District Council who eventually became a magistrate: *BPUD* (1910, 1944).

19   Membership of the club had risen to 48, but damage over the winter to the bathing box, iron shelter, and high diving board had restricted actual swimming: *NDH* (24 May 1912). Blythe had been elected to the committee at the previous (fifth) annual meeting, where (already a stickler for discipline) he seconded a resolution to print membership cards displaying the club rules: *NC* (3 June 1911).

20   *Trasna*, 181.

21   *Trasna*, 187–8.

22   Jacques Jellen (journalist aged 22, born in Belgium), boarder in the household of Ellen Jane Baillie, Frederick Street (unmarried Unitarian dressmaker aged 47), along with a Presbyterian teacher from Armagh: CIFS (1911). The Belgian was not named in *Trasna na Bóinne*, but the entry 'Jacque Jeller' appears in a list of names probably compiled for the autobiography: BP, P24/2222.

23   *Trasna*, 167.

24   *Trasna*, 161–2.

25   *Trasna*, 181.

26   CIFS (1911).

27   *NDH* (20 January 2011).

28   *Trasna*, 184–6; CIFS (1911).

29   See ch. 7, note 15 below. William Laird Doggart's name was not listed in the roll of honour for district no. 4, or among the admissions confirmed by the district lodge; the William Doggart of Little Frances Street admitted to lodge 872 in May 1917 was William Lamont Doggart, an undertaker's clerk who also joined Masonic lodge 447 (Newtownards) in November 1918.

30   These included William Baird and 6 celebrated Roberts (Baird, Lynn, Sibbett, Sayers, and two Smyllies): Grand Lodge Registers.

31   For Jamieson's Scottish background, see ch. 6, note 32. He was returned as a slater in the Census of Scotland (1901) and in the certificate of his marriage to Esther McLeod Anderson in the town's Reformed Presbyterian church

(2 January 1903); his bride had been living with her widowed grandmother, a sewing agent, in Frances Street: CIFS (1901).

32 CIFS (1911); *BPUD* (1913). 'J. Jamison' was no longer listed as librarian in the issue for 1923. His dual occupation and Scottish birth are confirmed in *Trasna*, 195. The 'librarian' was therefore not James Jamison, Jr., son of the Orange deputy master, returned in 1911 as an 'Apprentice to Hem Stitching' aged 18 (who would in any case have been too young for initiation in 1909).

33 *Trasna*, 195.

34 *Trasna*, 183. Frederick William O'Connell (1876–1929), ministered in Longford and Connaught (1902–10), lecturer in Celtic Studies, Queen's University Belfast (1909–25), curate, St George's, Belfast (1911), contributor in Irish and English to many journals including *IN*, assistant director, station 2RN (1927), killed by bus (1929): article by Lesa Ní Mhunghaile in *DIB*, vol. vii, 205–6; extract from *IN* (20 March 1927) in *IN* (20 March 1999). His father William Morgan O'Connell (1853–1942) and uncle Redmond O'Connell (1852–1928) were ordained in 1891 and 1882 respectively, after serving as schoolmasters for Alexander Dallas' Irish Church Missions (ICM) to the Roman Catholics in Omey parish (Clifden). His grandfather Redmond O'Connell was the ICM's schoolmaster in Claddaghduff, Sellerna district, by 1856: *Clergy of Tuam, Killala and Achonry: Biographical Succession Lists*, comp. Canon J. B. Leslie, ed. Canon D. W. T. Crooks (Belfast: Ulster Historical Foundation, 2008); Agency Books, in ICM Archive, Dublin; Miriam Moffitt, *Soupers and Jumpers: The Protestant Missions in Connemara, 1848–1937* (Dublin: Nonesuch Publishing, 2008), 29, 40, 43, 165–6.

35 Muriel Lilah Matters (1877–1969), musician and actress from Adelaide; chained herself to a grille in the Ladies' Gallery of the House of Commons (28 October 1908), hired an airship emblazoned 'Votes for Women' (17 February 1909), Welsh organiser for Women's Freedom League (1910): article by David Doughan in *ODNB*. See also Robert Wainright's recent tribute, *Miss Muriel Matters: The Fearless Suffragist Who Fought for Equality* (Sydney: Allen & Unwin, 2017).

36 Charlotte Despard (1844–1939), born in England but of Irish lineage through her father (Captain John French, RN); moved from London to Dublin in 1921 and on to Belfast in 1934 and Whitehead, County Antrim, in 1935. While president of the Women's Freedom League that she helped found in London in 1907, she was a frequent visitor to Ireland: article by Frances Clarke in *DIB*, vol. iii, 188–9.

37 *The Times* (4 January 1909).

38 *Trasna*, 171–2.

39 The Bill had been introduced on 14 June 1910 by D. J. Shackleton, MP: 'Women and the Suffrage' (letter from officers of the National Union of Women's Suffrage Associations), in *The Times* (6 June 1910).

40 David Orr, principal of the Castle Gardens national school and an urban councillor, was one of four residents of Newtownards listed in Blythe's address book: BP, P24/2181. A Presbyterian aged 38 in 1911, he lived with his

wife and 4 children in a first-class house in Victoria Avenue with 9 rooms and 6 front windows: CIFS (1911). His histories of Masonic lodges 447 and 1000, cited in David Cargo, *Brotherhoods in Newtownards in the 20th Century* (Newtownards: Ards Borough Council, unpaginated [2003]), have not been located.

41 *NDH* (3 February 1911).

42 *NDH* (14 July 1911).

43 *NDH* (14 October 1910).

44 *NDH* (4 November 1910).

45 'Letter to Young Liberals', X, in *UG* (21 Oct. 1911), discussed in the previous chapter.

46 'In the "Congested Districts"' (12 parts), in *Manchester Guardian* (10 June–26 July 1905), reproduced with Jack Yeats' drawings in J.M. Synge, *Travelling Ireland: Essays 1898–1908*, ed. Nicholas Grene (Dublin: Lilliput Press, 2009), 40–99.

47 Synge, *Travelling Ireland*, 98–9.

48 *NDH* (11 November 1910).

49 An early example of 'these islands', that would-be neutral euphemism favoured by so many Irish politicians today.

50 *NDH* (11 November 1910).

CHAPTER SIX: 'HUMBLE ORANGE BROTHER'

1 *NDH* (23 September 1910); minutes of district lodge no. 4 (26 September 1910): see note 3 below.

2 Though the decision to divide town and country lodges into separate districts (nos 4 and 11) was taken in November 1879, it was inoperative until 1885 because of failure to organise Ards district no. 11: County Down GOL, *Annual Reports* (1879, 1885).

3 These statistics are derived from Co. Down GOL, *Annual Reports*, supplemented where necessary from the manuscript minutes of district lodge no. 4, Newtownards (8 vols, 1884–1972): GOLI Archives. I am grateful to the late David Cargo (senior archivist, DGMI, and a member of lodge 240, Newtownards) for collecting and allowing me to consult these and other manuscript records, and for showing me over the Newtownards Orange hall in July 2016.

4 The upper curve shows the membership returned for lodges in Newtownards district no. 4 in each year from 1884 to 1927. The lower curve gives the corresponding figures for lodge 1501. Logarithmic scale is used to allow comparison of the proportionate change from year to year in the two series.

5 Warrant registers and published reports record warrant renewals (following dormant periods) in 1867, 1874, and 1882, the number 1501 having previously belonged to military lodges in the 81st and 83rd regiments of foot. It is unclear

whether the lodge working in County Down in 1849 was originally a military lodge, or whether the number was duplicated. Records for district no. 4 and County Down (available from 1858 apart from 1860, 1867, and 1868) include no annual returns of membership for lodge 1501 in 1861, 1865, 1872–3, 1876, or 1880.

6 Suspensions for periods exceeding two years were published biannually in the Grand Lodge reports for both County Down and Ireland.

7 See David Cargo, *Brotherhoods in Newtownards in the 20th Century* (Newtownards: Ards Borough Council, unpaginated [2003]). This valuable booklet is apparently unique in having identified Blythe as a member of lodge 1501, on the basis of information given to the author by myself.

8 *Belfast Weekly News* (26 August 1937), identifying Senator Lavery (in Roamer's column 'Out and About') as the 'G.O.M. of Newtownards'. Lavery (1854–1940) was elected for Down to Northern Ireland's House of Commons in 1921 and (unopposed) in 1925, co-opted to the Senate in 1930, and re-elected in 1933 and 1938. Elected as a vice-president of the IGOC at its triennial meetings in 1923, 1926, and 1929, he missed out on the expected presidency in 1932: Imperial Grand Orange Council of the World, *Reports of the [18th–21st] Triennial Meetings* (1923–32), in GOLI Archives.

9 The wives of both district chaplains (Wright and Twist-Whatham) were appointed as branch vice-presidents under the Marchioness of Londonderry, and Wright chaired the male-dominated initial meeting: *NDH* (2 February 1912).

10 'The Old Town Clock': *NDH* (31 May 1912).

11 William Wright (1856–1919), son of Donegal estate agent, ordained 1879, minister, Second Newtownards (1879–1919); DGC, Down (1901–19), DGCI (1906–19).

12 *Trasna*, 188.

13 Wright became master of Masonic lodge 447, GC of the Masonic Province of Down, and a DGC of the Blacks: obituary in *Witness* (15 August 1919); Grand Black Chapter of Ireland, *Report of Half-Yearly Council* (1914: consulted in Brownlow House, Lurgan).

14 William Laurence Twist-Whatham (1867–1938), ordained 1889, rector of Newtownards (1896–1919) and Greyabbey (1919–38); confirmed for lodge 1501 (October 1898) but sometimes returned as a member of lodge 872.

15 'The Old Town Clock': *NDH* (31 May 1912).

16 The names and addresses of admitted brethren are taken from monthly returns of confirmation in the district minute books, which also give annual returns of elected district officers with their lodge affiliations. Members of lodge 1501 elected to higher office have been identified from the published reports of the Grand Lodges of County Down and Ireland held in Schomberg House, Belfast. Statistics exclude a few other brethren named only in press reports.

17 For detailed analysis of their reception in North Down, documenting the tensions arising from their Scottish origins, see Kyle Hughes, *The Scots in*

Victorian and Edwardian Belfast: A Study in Elite Migration (Edinburgh: University Press, 2013), 191–4.

18 Thomas Lorimer Corbett (1854–1910); MP for North Down (1900–10), unsuccessful candidate for East Tyrone (1892, 1895) and North Down (1898); member of GOLI Committee (1905–10).

19 On 12 October 1900, Corbett defeated Crawford by 4,493 votes to 3,230, having lost on 7 September 1898 to John Blakiston-Houston by 3,381 votes to 3,107: *Parliamentary Election Results in Ireland, 1801–1922*, ed. Brian M. Walker (Dublin: RIA, 1978), 157–9; B. M. Walker, 'Landowners and Parliamentary Elections in County Down, 1801–1921', 319–20, in *Down: History and Society. Interdisciplinary Essays on the History of an Irish County*, ed. Lindsay J. Proudfoot and William Nolan (Dublin: Geography Publications, 1997), 297–325.

20 *BNL* (28 September 1900), quoted by Walker, 'Landowners', 320. The resolution supporting Corbett was a source of sharp division within the district lodge, John Stuart (district master) having told the brethren 'that no such resolution was ever put before a Private, District, or County lodge': District Minutes (24 September, 29 October 1900).

21 William Mitchell-Thomson (1877–1946), 2nd Baronet (succ. 1918), 1st Baron Selsdon of Croydon (1932); MP for North-West Lanark (1906–10), North Down (1910–18), Maryhill, Glasgow (1918–23), South Croydon (1923–32); director, Restriction of Enemy Supplies Department (1916–18); British representative, Supreme Economic Council, Paris (1919); parliamentary secretary, Ministry of Food (1920–1) and Board of Trade (1921–2); postmaster-general (1924–9).

22 *NDH* (20 January 1911).

23 An interminable jingle addressed to 'The Old Town Clock' (mounted over the market house erected in about 1776) was composed by 'a local poet' and published by Wesley Guard Lyttle (1844–96), editor of the *NDH*, in *The Bangor Season* (Bangor, 1887), 54–7 (abridged, undated facsimile edn, Belfast: Appletree Press).

24 The table excludes six confirmed admissions unmatched with census returns (see following note). Census returns give the denominations of Bloor, Mitchell-Thomson, and Stevenson respectively as Church of England, Church of Scotland, and Wesleyan Methodist.

25 In 50 cases, both name and address have been firmly matched; in 17 cases, a single candidate of the same name has been located at a different address; in 6 cases, the candidate's family has been confidently matched in the absence of the candidate himself. In the remaining 17 cases, I have either failed to locate a credible name match or identified several equally credible candidates. The statistical analysis is restricted to 67 members in the first 2 categories, supplemented by household details for those in the third category and occasionally by information in *BPUD* or biographical compendia. Otherwise, information on age, occupation, address, and other personal details is drawn from CIFS (1901, 1911).

26 Of 31 identified fathers, 7 were farmers and 2 were agricultural labourers. Households containing 2 or more brethren are enumerated separately for each

member, leading to duplication of details of father's occupation and housing categories.

27 The median number of front windows was 5, the upper quartile figure being 7 and the range 1–27.

28 The first enrolment of Boy Scouts in Newtownards occurred on 30 January 1912, at a meeting in the Guild Hall chaired by William Wright: *NDH* (9 February). Its leaders included other members of lodge 1501 such as William Twist-Whatham, Thomas Maddock, W.J. Ferguson, Thomas Lavery (district chairman, 1922–34) and Hugh D. Maddock (district commissioner, 1923–46); another chairman (1946–9) was Blythe's friend William Laird Doggart: *'Be Prepared': 100 Years of Scouting in Ards District, 1911 to 2011*, comp. Hill Wilson, George Mawhinney, and Sam Moore (Newtownards: District Scout Council, 2012), 6–7, 126–7.

29 By late 1914, the Newtownards company was buying briars and knitting wristlets for local servicemen, making flags, and taking lessons in signalling: *Girl Guides' Gazette* (January 1915).

30 Cargo, *Brotherhoods in Newtownards*.

31 Two series of registers and relevant officer lists for all Craft lodges and Royal Arch chapters in Newtownards were consulted at Freemasons' Hall in Molesworth Street, Dublin (kindly provided by the acting archivist, Bro. Morgan McCready). Each series of lodge registers was arranged numerically, listing existing members (in about 1860 and 1900 respectively) followed by those initiated over subsequent decades, giving occupations for those initiated after 1900. All surviving Craft registers from the 1730s to the 1920s have recently become accessible in digital and searchable form through ancestry.com, greatly easing the task of identifying and matching elusive brethren. The lodges in Newtownards (with warrant dates) were Friendship 447 (1766), Union Star 198 (1810), Farmers 1000 (reissued for Newtownards, 1895), Wright Memorial 448 (1918), Unity 443 (1918), and Eklektikos 542 (1922). Royal Arch chapters with the same numbers were associated with the first 3 lodges.

32 Of the 37 matches of brethren with the same names, 22 are firm (usually because of similar occupational descriptions in census returns and Masonic registers) and 15 are probable. Seven other matches by name have been discarded as improbable because of anomalies in age or occupation; 1 Orangeman had multiple Masonic homonyms of equal plausibility; and 45 could not be matched.

33 Thirteen of the 37 in both bodies joined the Freemasons before the Orange, 3 joined both in the same year, and 18 joined the Freemasons in later years.

34 The register for lodge 198 records the transfer of a 'James Jamison' on the basis of a Scottish certificate from lodge 290 meeting at Dalry Blair in Ayrshire. In the register for Union Lodge 35 (Saintfield), he was listed as James Jamieson, merchant, also a member of RAC 183 (Greyabbey). The Freemason is clearly the James Jamieson returned with his parental family in Dalry in 1881, 1891, and 1901 (index to Census of Scotland, accessible through ancestry.com).

35   When admitted to Apollo lodge 357 (Oxford) in May 1900, Mitchell-Thomson
      was returned as an undergraduate from Edinburgh. He was admitted to Union
      lodge 346 (Bangor) on 10 August 1910 and resigned in 1919. The registers (up
      to 1929) of the United Grand Lodge of England are accessible and digitally
      searchable through ancestry.com.

36   *NDH* (22 December 1911).

37   In addition to 67 individuals matched with census returns, 1 birthplace was
      ascertained otherwise. In 6 cases, details of housing were taken from schedules
      for probable families of origin with whom members were not resident in 1901
      or 1911.

38   The median year of Orange initiation (available for 31 Freemasons and 45
      others, excluding brethren admitted before 1886) was 1904 for Freemasons
      and 1905 for others.

39   The occupational categories in which non-Freemasons were over-represented
      were clerks and agents (15% against 9%), officials (6% against 3%), shopkeepers
      and merchants (18% against 12%), and unskilled workers (15% against 9%).
      There was negligible disparity in the proportions in farming and managerial
      posts.

40   These proportions include 'multiple matches', in which several Covenant
      signatories bore the same name as Orangemen without any precise match by
      address. The proportion of Covenanters *(excluding* multiple matches) was 57%
      for Orange Freemasons and 42% for non-Freemasons.

41   *UG* (16 December 1911).

42   The grand lodge, meeting in Dublin on 6 December 1911, agreed 'that the
      Ulster area be formed into a Temporary Provincial Grand Lodge, in view of
      the Home Rule Crisis', and also 'that a Provincial Grand Lodge be appointed
      for Dublin and the South of Ireland, as in Belfast': GOLI, *Half-Yearly Report*
      (December 1911), 26–7. No discussion of these resolutions appeared in the
      confidential official report.

43   The Limavady cannon was mounted in front of the Orange hall, but that
      from Boveva (smuggled from Falkirk in 1870 and still held by 'Boveva Purple
      Star' lodge 260 in 2004) was intercepted by the RIC. The threat of a replay
      of the fabled 'Battle of Garvagh' of 1813, in which Orangemen killed several
      Ribbonmen from outside the town, had been increasing since Hibernians
      marching to the railway station were attacked on St Patrick's Day, 1907: *Weekly
      IT* (13 August, 20 August 1910); *Strabane Chronicle* (20 August); 'Irish News' in
      UG (17 September); David Brewster, *'The Sash Our Fathers Wore': The History
      of Orangeism in Limavady and District, 1798–2004* (Limavady: Printing Co.,
      2004), 13, 46, 75.

44   See 'The Orange Order and the Border', in David Fitzpatrick, *Descendancy:
      Irish Protestant Histories since 1795* (Oxford: University Press, 2014), 41–58.

45   No such report has been found in the available microfilm of the *Telegraph*'s
      second edition. The *News-Letter*'s correspondent was 'reliably informed that
      the subject was deliberated upon in that spirit of solemn earnestness which

the occasion required', the formation of two temporary grand lodges being approved 'with hearty unanimity': 'Home Rule Peril', in *BNL* (7 December 1911).

46 *UG* (16 December 1911).

47 *UG* (9 December 1911).

48 'The Lodge', stanzas 3–7, 10, in *UG* (9 December 1911).

49 For a ballad of the same form and overlapping themes, see 'David Brown's Farewell to Kilmood Lodge 541', in *The Crimson Banner Song Book: A Collection of Popular Songs and Poems for All True Orangemen* (Omagh: printed by S. D. Montgomery, undated), 17–18. Many early balladists were less scrupulous than Blythe in preserving secrets, especially of the higher Masonic and quasi-Masonic degrees, as in 'The Royal Robe', 'The Knight Templar's Dream', 'The Marksman's Journey', and 'Brilliant Light' (10–17).

CHAPTER SEVEN: 'THE OLD TOWN CLOCK'

1 'The Old Town Clock', in *NDH* (15 July 1910).

2 'Demonstration at Carrowdore', in *NDH* (15 July 1910). The platform party included Twist-Whatham, James Cherry, James Jamison, and Joseph Robinson from lodge 1501 as well as the speakers.

3 Minutes, district lodge no. 4, Newtownards [hereafter, District Minutes] (11, 18, 28 November 1910).

4 *NC* (26 November 1910).

5 *NC* (26 November 1910). Blythe's report was more cursory, ignoring the inflammatory speeches by Wright and Twist-Whatham: *NDH* (25 November 1910).

6 *NC* (26 November 1910).

7 District Minutes (27 February, 27 March 1911); *NDH* (17 March 1911).

8 *NDH* (29 March 1912).

9 *Trasna*, 190.

10 *NDH* (5 April 1912).

11 H. Gaw, editor, *NDH* (Imperial Buildings, 85 Main Street, Bangor), 2 April 1913: BP, P24/1211.

12 *NDH* (31 March 1911).

13 *NDH* (19 May 1911).

14 *Trasna*, 168.

15 *NC* (15 July 1911). The report did not indicate whether the platform party (including Messrs Ernest Blythe, W. L. Doggart, and Spencer C. Henry) were brethren; their names did not appear among those listed on the platform in the *Spectator* (which did specify brethren) or the *Herald*. Uninitiated sympathisers might occasionally have been invited to join the platform party. I am grateful to Jane Leonard for showing me the report in the *Chronicle*.

16 *NDH* and *NS* (14 July 1911).

17 *NDH* (21 July 1911).

18   District Minutes (25 August 1919).

19   District Minutes (29 June, 6 July 1885); B. M. Walker, *Ulster Politics: The Formative Years, 1868–1886* (Belfast: Ulster Historical Foundation and Institute of Irish Studies, Queen's University, 1989), 172–3, 199.

20   District Minutes (31 May, 8 June 1886).

21   District Minutes (9, 26 February, 29 April 1912).

22   *NDH* (12 April 1912).

23   The grocer's address is given in Orange registers as 53 or 54 Little Frances Street, whereas Blythe's Address Book, *c.*1905–15, lists Jas Jamieson of 48 Little Francis Street: BP, P24/2181. Confusingly, the corresponding numbers assigned by census enumerators in 1911 were 27 and 25, in two separate schedules covering sections of Little Frances Street (postal street numbers were not routinely applied in the census).

24   Earnán de Blaghd, *Briseadh na Teorann* (Dublin: Sáirséal agus Dill, 1955), 37.

25   *Trasna*, 172; Trevor McCavery, *Newtown: A History of Newtownards* (Belfast: White Row, 2013), 177; District Minutes (25 March 1912).

26   *NDH* (12 April 1912).

27   *NDH* (4 October 1912).

28   District Minutes (26 August 1912).

29   *NDH* (4 October 1912); see also McCavery, *Newtown*, 178–9.

30   Of 90 initiates and officers for the period 1884–1918, only 30 have been confidently matched and 11 tentatively matched through the names and addresses of Covenant signatories, identified through the admittedly defective digital index: PRONI, signature sheets (accessible online). Some brethren would of course have died or emigrated before 1912, or been too young in 1912 to qualify for inclusion.

31   District Minutes (30 September, 28 October 1912).

32   District Minutes (27 January, 31 March, 28 April, 26 May 1913).

33   Edward McCall, a retired draper and magistrate in High Street from Tyrone (aged 75) and his illiterate wife Margaret (67) were both returned as Catholics: CIFS (1911). Her mother, an illiterate widow from County Down (aged 80 in 1901, when she resided with them) belonged to the 'Church of England': CIFS (1901).

34   *NDH* (24 January 1913).

35   District Minutes (26 June, 25 August, 29 September, 27 October 1913); Co. Down GOL, *Annual Report* (1913).

36   Those listed under lodge 1501 included 3 riflemen in the Royal Irish Rifles, a private in the Royal Inniskilling Fusiliers, and 2 sappers in the 36th signals company, Royal Engineers (both sons of Thomas Maddock). An accurate transcription of the 7 panels displayed in the Orange Hall, which I inspected by courtesy of Br. David Cargo on 6 July 2016, is accessible through the website 'Newtownards Orangemen'.

37   The Roll of Honour lists 267 members of 13 lodges in the district, of whom 53 died (19.9%). The Roll evidently includes some ex-servicemen who joined the Orange Order subsequently, as well as former Orangemen who served.

The ratio of the number who served to district membership in 1919 (805) was 33.2%. The corresponding ratio for lodge 1501 was 21.6%, the third lowest ratio for the district's 13 lodges.

38 *Trasna*, 191–2.

39 *Trasna*, 193–4.

40 *Trasna*, 213–14.

41 *Trasna*, 220–2. These testimonials, and 2 others, are preserved in BP, P24/1210–1214.

42 *Trasna*, 222–3.

CHAPTER EIGHT: 'UNCLE DAN'

1 R. F. Foster, *Vivid Faces: The Revolutionary Generation in Ireland, 1890–1923* (London: Allen Lane, 2014), ch. 3 ('Playing'), 75–113.

2 His first visit occurred 'around Pentecost' or Whitsun (which in 1905 was celebrated on 11 June): *Trasna*, 81. *The Building Fund* was first performed at the Abbey on 25 April 1905: Robert Hogan and James Kilroy, *The Modern Irish Drama, A Documentary History III: The Abbey Theatre: The Years of Synge, 1905–1909* (Dublin: Dolmen Press, 1978), 26–9.

3 *Trasna*, 81–3. These one-act plays by Yeats, Synge (*bis*), and Lady Gregory were first performed on 2 April 1902, 25 February 1904, 8 October 1903, and 27 December 1904 respectively: Robert Hogan and James Kilroy, *The Modern Irish Drama, A Documentary History II: Laying the Foundations, 1902–1904* (Dublin: Dolmen Press, 1976), 134, 141, 139, 143.

4 At the end of 1905, Ryan had left Fleet Street to edit the *Irish Peasant*, founded in 1903 by James McCann, before becoming proprietor of the increasingly radical journals that replaced it after McCann abandoned the enterprise in face of clerical denunciation. Ryan's weekly survived until his return to London in December 1910, incorporating two papers founded by Blythe's Belfast associates, Bulmer Hobson's *Republic* (May 1907) and Cathal O'Shannon's *Irish Nation* (January 1909): Virginia Glandon, *Arthur Griffith and the Advanced-Nationalist Press in Ireland, 1900–1922* (New York: Peter Lang, 1985), 19–23.

5 *Trasna*, 136–8.

6 'K', review of George Fitzmaurice's *The Country Dressmaker*, in *The Peasant and Irish Ireland* (12 October 1907).

7 *The Drone* was first performed at the Abbey, with *Leader of the People* by 'Robert Harding' (James Winder Good), on 24 April 1908. It received favourable notices in *Sinn Féin* and the *Irish Independent*: Hogan and Kilroy, *The Abbey Theatre*, 256–7.

8 *Trasna*, 135–6.

9 Sam Hanna Bell, *The Theatre in Ulster* (Dublin: Gill & Macmillan, 1972), 36.

10 'Cnó Cúil', 'Ulster at the Abbey', in *Peasant* (2 May 1908). Uncle Dan was performed by 'Arthur Malcolm' (Sam Bullock): Hogan and Kilroy, *The Abbey Theatre*, 344.

11   Dáithí Ó hÓgáin, *The Lore of Ireland: An Encyclopaedia of Myth, Legend and Romance* (Cork: Collins Press, 2006), 62–3. Other fictitious Cairbres bore epithets signifying cat-headed, hard-headed, lover of the Liffey, and lover of games, but only Cairbre Mac Éadaoine had any obvious affinity with Blythe, then an aspirant poet-propagandist.

12   *Peasant* (10, 31 October 1908).

13   *INP* (30 January 1909).

14   *Trasna*, 140.

15   *INP* (29 May 1909). *The Gaol Gate* was first performed, at the Abbey, on 20 October 1906.

16   *INP* (19 March 1910). *The Captain of the Hosts* was first performed, at the Grand Opera House, Belfast, on 8 March 1910: Robert Hogan, Richard Burnham, and Daniel P. Poteet, *The Modern Irish Drama, A Documentary History IV: The Rise of the Realists, 1910–1915* (Dublin, Dolmen Press, 1979), 89–91.

17   *The Mist* was first performed, by the ULT at the Abbey, on 26 November 1909. Blythe's assessment (minus the jibe) was echoed by Sam Waddell, who deemed it 'an amusing parody on Synge's use of peasant speech in the *Playboy*': quoted in Bell, *Theatre in Ulster*, 41.

18   *Trasna*, 112–13.

19   The audience's response on first night is discussed at length in *Trasna*, 138–9.

20   *INP* (14 August 1909); also quoted in Murray, *Seán O'Casey*, 68 (citing a press cutting of the review in BP, P24/2528, and thence identifying 'Cairbre' as Blythe). In the same review, Blythe panned 'The Cross Roads' by Lennox Robinson, his future colleague on the board of the Abbey Theatre Co. (1935–58): 'Did S. L. Robinson ever hear the members of any Dublin political society talk like the young men of the Erin Debating Society?'

21   *Trasna*, 138. *The Witch* (a short Irish play, untraced) was directed by (Sir) John Martin Harvey (1863–1944), a celebrated English actor-manager whose touring Lyceum Theatre Company spent three weeks each summer in Dublin: article by Donald Roy in *ODNB*; *Irish Independent* (31 October 1905).

22   *Trasna*, 139–40. *The Piper*, by 'Norreys Connell' (Conal O'Riordan), was first performed at the Abbey on Thursday 13 February 1908. After the first night, 'some people walked away puzzled, some booed and hissed, others applauded'; on the second night, O'Riordan appeared before the footlights after vigorous booing from the pit; and, in response to calls for the play to be withdrawn, Yeats extended the run through the following week including a matinée (presumably that attended by Blythe), addressing the audience on several occasions: Hogan and Kilroy, *The Abbey Theatre*, 212–17.

23   *Trasna*, 134. Purcell's *The Enthusiast* and *The Pagan* were first performed in Belfast on 4 May 1905 and 4 December 1906 respectively: Bell, *Theatre in Ulster*, 18–26; Hogan and Kilroy, *The Abbey Theatre*, 50–4, 108–11. No Ernest Thompson is named as an actor in the ULT in either study, but Hogan and Kilroy identify a 'J. Thompson' as acting 'Congall, a Bard' in the first production of *The Pagan* (339).

24 *Suzanne and the Sovereigns*, first produced at the Exhibition Hall, Belfast, on 26 December 1907, was the ULT's 'first popular success': Bell, *Theatre in Ulster*, 29–32; Hogan and Kilroy, *The Abbey Theatre*, 183–5. Blythe wrongly attributed *Suzanne and the Sovereigns* to 'one of the Morrows': *Trasna*, 134–5.

25 *Trasna*, 135. Blythe may have written an anonymous review of a later performance in the Grand Opera House, pronouncing with Blythe-like condescension that, like the play's *femme fatale* 'Slippery Suzanne', 'woman's redeeming feature is that she never does the obvious': *UG* (26 Nov. 1910); also cited in Bell, *Theatre in Ulster*, 30. Yet this review seems more ornate and less concise than most authenticated pieces by Blythe.

26 Samuel Ernest Thompson, clerk, joined lodge 135 on 26 April 1905, evidently remaining a member until his death was noted in 1969. His father Samuel B. Thompson (1835/9–1917), contractor, had joined the lodge on 24 April 1895, being transferred to 'Prince of Wales Own' lodge 154 (Belfast) on 1 March 1911, and thence (as a founding member) to 'Claremont' lodge 423 (Belfast) on 2 June 1916.

27 Samuel Ernest Thompson (1881–1969), house, land, and estate clerk (1911). S. E. Thompson & Co. were listed as 'chartered auctioneers and estate agents, valuers' at 67 Donegall Street (1953), when he was a JP resident at Edenderry House (the family home since 1916): *BPUD* (1916–53).

28 Samuel Ernest Thompson, of '63' Donegall Street, Belfast, was awarded his full claim for compensation (£60) by the Property Losses (Ireland) Committee: NAI, PLIC/1/2328 (index accessible online).

29 BP, P24/2222.

30 William Robert Gordon (1872–1955); taught at Royal Belfast Academical Institution (1901–45); first secretary, Ulster Arts Club (1902), and its president (1914–15): CIFS (1901, 1911); article by Carmel Doyle in *DIB*, vol. iv, 150–1; John Jamieson, *The History of the Royal Belfast Academical Institution* (Belfast: William Mullan, 1959), 147, 189; Bell, *Theatre in Ulster*, 16.

31 Bell, *Theatre in Ulster*, 37. Cairbre missed Gordon's performance, being able to attend only once during the week: 'Irish Ideas. Ulster Literary Theatre', in *INP* (29 May 1909).

32 For example, in *INP* (10 October 1908).

33 *NDH* (15 July 1910). Lodge 1951 belonged not to Newtownards district no. 4, but to Upper Ards district no. 11. Captain James S. Henry was returned as secretary of the lodge and treasurer of the district for 1920: Co. Down GOL, *Annual Report* (1919), 34.

34 Theo Snoddy, *Dictionary of Irish Artists: Twentieth Century* (Dublin: Wolfhound Press, 1996), 146–7; information kindly provided by Jane Leonard.

35 James Peter Murnane (1890–1939), Catholic Irish-speaker from Dublin, returned as NUI undergraduate and RIC candidate (1911), appointed DI (25 March 1912), retired on pension of £260 when RIC dissolved (20 May 1922): CIFS (1901, 1911); Jim Herlihy, *Royal Irish Constabulary Officers: A Biographical Dictionary and Genealogical Guide, 1816–1922* (Dublin: Four Courts Press,

2005), 233; RIC Officer Service Records: NAL, HO 184/47 (microfilm in NAI); RIC Pension Ledgers via ancestry.com.

36   Murnane scored 80% and came first among over 40 candidates in 6 out of 12 subjects: *NC* (10 February 1912); *NS* (1 March 1912). Connell's Institute (Royal Avenue, Belfast) claimed credit for Murnane's success and that of one of the other two candidates accepted as cadets: advertisement in *UG* (10 February 1912).

37   CIFS (1901). This unusual gloss was inserted by David Murnane as head of the family, which resided in the Carrick-on-Suir barracks, though his own details as 'D. M.', head constable, appeared separately on the barracks return.

38   David Murnane (1857–1939), Catholic Irish-speaker from Caherconlish, County Limerick, son of Michael Murnane (1827–86), himself a (sub-) constable in the (R)IC (1847–78); joined RIC (1875), appointed DI while head constable in Carrick-on-Suir, County Tipperary (1901), retired on pension of £413 from Trim, County Meath (June 1919): CIFS (1901, 1911); Herlihy, *RIC Officers*, 233–4 (with photograph); RIC registers: NAL, HO 184/6, 22 (microfilm in Gilbert Library, Dublin); RIC Officer Service Records: HO 184/46; RIC Pension Ledgers; Catholic registers of marriages and baptisms for Caherconlish, Cashel & Emly (microfilm in NLI, accessible digitally via ancestry.com).

39   Regulation introduced in 1895: Elizabeth Malcolm, *The Irish Policeman, 1822–1922: A Life* (Dublin: Four Courts Press, 2006), 62.

40   *IT* (26 August 1901).

41   He received favourable records on five occasions between 1909 and 1918 and a 'good service' supplement from 1911, his sole reprimand dating from his term in Newtownards in November 1912: David Murnane, Officer Service Record: HO 184/46 (microfilm in NAI).

42   The five magistrates attending Brookeborough petty sessions on 5 September 1910 were all native to Fermanagh except the chairman and resident magistrate, Robert Sparrow (Episcopalian aged 48 from Clonmel, County Tipperary). Murnane's Catholic supporters were James Mulligan of Belle Isle (farmer and coroner aged 43) and Thomas Gavin of Lisnaskea (draper and farmer aged 51). His Episcopalian detractors were Samuel Coulter of Brookeborough (retired grocer aged 70) and John Lendrum of Corralongford (farmer aged 46): CIFS (1911).

43   *NDH* (9 September 1910).

44   *Trasna*, 196–7.

45   *NDH* (2 February 1912).

46   *Trasna*, 196–7.

47   *Trasna*, 199.

48   Ernest Blythe (144 East Street), membership card for Newtownards Amateur Dramatic Society (undated, *c*.1912): BP, P24/1739.

49   Review of 'Mr J. M. Harding' as Dan Fogarty in Miss M. F. Scott's *Family Rights* at the Grand Opera House, Belfast: *BNL* (10 December 1912), transcribed in

Hogan et al., *The Rise of the Realists*, 229–30. The actor, who had performed in Belfast and London productions of *The Drone*, was identified by Blythe as an embroidery agent for a linen business named Hodgins. He was in fact James Hodgen, a 33-year-old Church of Ireland textile designer born in County Down, living with his parents and 4 siblings in a first-class house with 7 rooms and 6 front windows in Albertville Drive, Clifton Ward: CIFS (1911); *Trasna*, 198–9; Bell, *Theatre in Ulster*, 16.

50   *NDH* (3, 17 January 1913).

51   *Trasna*, 199.

52   These cases occurred in 1928, 1929, and 1945: Tony Keating, paper on 'D. C. Boyd and the *Waterford Standard*', kindly supplied with additional information by Dr Patrick McCarthy. According to an obituary in the *Waterford News and Star* (29 October 1965), Boyd had already joined the *Waterford Standard* before the rebellion.

53   'Obituary: Mr. David Boyd', in *Irish Press* (29 October 1965).

54   Martha Blevings, a 20-year-old Presbyterian dressmaker from Belfast, lived with her widowed mother and family in a first-class house with 9 rooms and 6 front windows in Shore Rd: CIFS (1911).

55   *NC* (1 February 1913); *NDH* (7 February 1913), unchanged except for deletion of final section in *NC*.

56   The playwright himself had overseen the original production at the Abbey in the guise of Sam Brown, as Blythe and the audience discovered only when the 'servant man', in response to calls for the author, 'modestly bowed his acknowledgements': 'Cnó Cúil', 'Ulster at the Abbey', in *Peasant* (2 May 1908).

57   *Trasna*, 200–1.

58   *NC* (1 February 1913).

59   *Trasna*, 198.

60   Maggie McManus, a 22-year-old Catholic 'folder in factory', lived with her father (a general labourer in 1911 though a dealer in 1901) and family in a second-class house with 6 rooms and 3 front windows: CIFS (1911). She had performed in 'a melodrama called *Pike O'Callaghan*': *Trasna*, 198. Her brothers Patrick and James performed without Maggie in February 1912, when the St Patrick's Amateur Dramatic Club put on *Kathleen Mavourneen* in St Patrick's Hall, Ann St: *NDH* (16 February 1912).

61   EB, *Gaeil*, opp. 157.

62   *Trasna*, 202.

63   *Trasna*, 201.

64   A doffer, according to the *OED*, was 'a worker employed in removing the full bobbins or spindles', a task normally performed by young boys or girls.

65   Letter (postmarked 10 March(?) 1913) in BP, P24/1692.

66   *UG* (22 March 1913). Following an earlier revival of *The Drone* at the Opera House, the reviewer (probably again Blythe) had urged that the play be 'given in every country town in Ulster': *UG* (9 December 1911).

67   *Thompson in Tir-na-nOg* was first performed by the ULT at the Grand Opera House, Belfast, on 9 December 1912: Bell, *Theatre in Ulster*, 42–4.

68 *UG* (14 December 1912).

69 *UG* (22 March 1913).

70 Cluicheoirí Leasa Póil (Lispole Dramatic Company), ticket for entertainment in Christian Schools, Dingle, on Easter Sunday, 12 April [1914], in BP, P24/1699; Foster, *Vivid Faces*, 111; James Fitzgerald (Lispole, County Kerry), WS 999 (30 August 1954), 1. An earlier dramatic society in Lispole, formed by Thomas Ashe, had lapsed.

71 *Slán*, 51. Mayne's *The Turn of the Road* was first presented by the ULT at the Ulster Minor Hall on 4 December 1906, while MacManus' *The Lad from Largymore* was first performed at the Rotunda on 27 February 1905: Hogan and Kilroy, *The Abbey Theatre*, 339, 333.

72 'David Hogan' (Frank Gallagher), *The Four Glorious Years* (Dublin: *Irish Press*, 1953), 120.

73 W. B. Yeats to EB, 12 July [1925], in *Letters of W. B. Yeats* (Oxford: University Press, digital edition including unedited transcriptions), no. 4755.

74 Hugh Hunt, *The Abbey: Ireland's National Theatre, 1904–1979* (Dublin: Gill & Macmillan, 1979), 135–7, 150–3, 242–3; Anthony Roche, 'The Reclamation of Ernest Blythe', presentation at conference on 'Re-examining Irish Nationalism in Ulster', Queen's University Belfast (15 April 2016).

75 Undated typescripts of *Rachel Ryan* and *An Chuis da Pleithe* (*Trial by Jury*): BP, P24/2138–2142. Since the first act of *Rachel Ryan* is set on 'Saturday', 29 October 1934 (in fact a Monday), the script was presumably not written in 1934.

76 O'Casey to EB, 22 October 1928: BP, P24/1542.

77 EB to O'Casey, 29 October 1928: *The Letters of Sean O'Casey*, vol. i, 1910–41, ed. David Krause (London: Cassell, 1975), 316.

78 O'Casey to EB, 5 November 1928: BP, P24/1543; O'Casey to Lady Gregory, 1 November 1925, in Krause, *Letters*, vol. i, 154.

79 'An Old Supporter' introduced himself as 'a regular attendant at the Abbey Theatre almost since its foundation', and praised the government's introduction of an annual grant (instigated by Blythe) and its refusal to take the theatre into public ownership: 'The Abbey Theatre. Its Present Moribund Condition; A Crisis Requiring Action. New Board Suggested', in *United Ireland* (9 March 1935).

80 Yeats to O'Casey, 2 June 1935; Macnamara to *IT* (7 September 1935); 'Statement by Abbey Directors', 3 September: Krause, *Letters*, vol. i, 571, 582–4.

81 O'Casey to Guy Boas, 5 January 1950: *The Letters of Sean O'Casey*, vol. ii, 1942–54, ed. David Krause (New York: Macmillan, 1980), 669.

82 Leon Ó Broin, *Revolutionary Underground: The Story of the Irish Republican Brotherhood, 1858–1924* (Dublin: Gill & Macmillan, 1976), 146.

83 Entry for 'Ernest Blythe', widower aged 85 of 50 Kenilworth Square, Dublin 6, who died at Mount Carmel Hospital on 23 February 1975 as a result of broncho-pneumonia, congestive cardiac failure, and osteoarthritis. The informant was not his son Earnán, but the sister superior of the Little Company of Mary which ran the hospital.

CHAPTER NINE: SOME QUESTIONS

1   Jack Greenald, *The Life of Rev. Dr Richard Rutledge Kane* ([Belfast:] Boyne Cultural Association, 2008).

2   I am grateful to one of the publisher's readers for begetting this hypothesis, which had not occurred to me, by drawing attention to 'the holding of multiple (and ostensibly conflicting) cultural and political identities within other multi-national empires of this time (such as Austria–Hungary)'.

3   *Trasna*, 109–10; EB, WS 939, 3.

4   *Trasna*, 110–15.

5   EB, WS 939, 2–5, 22.

6   Interview with EB (50 Kenilworth Square), 19 June 1972.

7   EB, 'The Salvation of the Irish Language', MS returned with typed transcription from Gaelic League, Dublin, to Kinnard, Lispole, 21 August 1914: BP, P24/1899. This article was not published in the Gaelic League's journal, *An Claidheamh Soluis* (August–October 1914).

8   *Joseph Holloway's Abbey Theatre: A Selection from his Unpublished Journal, 'Impressions of a Dublin Playgoer'* (Carbondale and Edwardsville: Southern Illinois University Press, 1967), ed. Robert Hogan and Michael J. O'Neill, 217–18; Sean O'Casey, *Pictures in the Hallway* (1942), in *Autobiographies* (London: Macmillan, 1963 edn), 385–429; Christopher Murray, *Seán O'Casey: Writer at Work* (Dublin: Gill & Macmillan, 2004), 17, 453 (n. 19). The sole direct evidence that O'Casey was an Orangeman is Holloway's account of a conversation at the Abbey Theatre in April 1923, when O'Casey stated that he had belonged to 'the Purple Lodge, and getting on well till his love for processions and bands got him in disfavour with the members of his lodge, and he left the body and joined the Gaelic League class and became a Nationalist which he remains'. On other occasions, O'Casey denied that he had joined the Orange. There is no record of the alleged three-year suspension of a John Casey from the Dublin Orange Order from 1892 onwards, or of his initiation in any Dublin lodge from 1901, or in district no. 3 from 1898, or in district no. 2 from 1889 (the earliest returns in surviving minute books): PRONI, Minute Books of Dublin Orange Lodges, D 2947. It remains possible that Casey was initiated in district no. 1 before 1901.

9   *Trasna*, 81.

10 Leon Ó Broin, *Revolutionary Underground: The Story of the Irish Republican Brotherhood, 1858–1924* (Dublin: Gill & Macmillan, 1976), 146.

11 *Trasna*, 105–6.

12 *IN* (12 June 1909). In April 1909, President Matthew Cummings and the Revd Philip J. O'Donnell (state chaplain, Massachusetts) had visited Ireland as 'envoys' of the American AOH (controlled by Clan na Gael), subsequently forming an alliance with the 'Scottish section' and a small IRB-dominated minority of Irish Hibernians (most of whom remained under the 'Board of Erin'): Inspector-General, RIC, Monthly Confidential Reports (April, May 1909), in NAL, CO 904/77; John O'Dea, *History of the Ancient Order of Hibernians and Ladies' Auxiliary* (Philadelphia: National Board of the AOH,

4 vols, 1923), vol. iii, 1409–11. This 'Irish-American Alliance' contributed a contingent of Hibernian Rifles to the rebel forces in 1916. The official muster of Hibernian riflemen in 1908 was only 3,140, along with 655 'knights' (officers): O'Dea, *Hibernians*, vol. iii, 1391.

13 For a disparaging reference to Hibernian 'factionism' and hatred of Orangemen, see *Trasna*, 156.

14 EB, WS 989, 85–6.

15 EB, WS 989, 92–3.

16 EB, WS 989, 55.

17 *Gaeil*, opp. 27. The flat-topped headgear differs from the prescribed 'Cronje hat' with its central cleavage: G. White and B. O'Shea, *Irish Volunteer Soldier Uniforms, 1913–23* (Oxford: Osprey Publishing, 2003), 16–19. A similar but dogless close-up provides the frontispiece for *Slán*. This was taken 'by his sister [probably Helen] in a Belfast street': Michael McInerney, 'Ernest Blythe: A Political Profile', pt ii, in *IT* (31 December 1974).

18 *Trasna*, 40.

19 Mabel Doggart to Blythe, 12 October 1958: BP, P24/1449.

20 EB, WS 989, 5; *Trasna*, 178. Blythe remained friendly with James Connolly's wife and daughters up to 1922. As Nora Connolly O'Brien recalled: 'Anytime he was in Belfast, he came to our house in Glenalina Terrace and stayed as long as he could. . . . I was very fond of him and mother was, too. After the Treaty, he never came to see us again': interview in *Survivors: The Story of Ireland's Struggle as told through some of her Outstanding Living People*, comp. Unseann MacEoin (Dublin: Argenta Press, 1987; 1st edn 1980), 204. Connolly had rented 1 Glenalina Terrace, beside the Belfast General Cemetery off the Falls Road, after moving his family from Dublin on 27 May 1911; this remained the family home after his return to Dublin in 1913 and execution in 1916: Donal Nevin, *James Connolly: 'A Full Life'* (Dublin: Gill & Macmillan, 2005), 389.

21 EB, WS 989, 51.

22 EB, WS 989, 180–2.

23 Florence and Jessie MacCarthy, daughters of Dr Randal MacCarthy, were reputed to have been friendly with 'members of the British Crown Forces' before turning their attention to national army officers. On 22 June 1923, they were assaulted by Paddy Daly, the Kerry commandant, and two colleagues. Dr MacCarthy claimed that Daly had also 'stripped and painted several girls in Killarney'. Despite corroboration from military witnesses (who were arrested and threatened by Daly with being 'done in' if they persisted), Richard Mulcahy (minister for defence) and Hugh Kennedy (attorney-general) ensured that the assailants were neither court-martialled nor disciplined following an army enquiry: NAI, Executive Council Papers, S 3341; Michael Hopkinson, *Green against Green: The Irish Civil War* (Dublin: Gill & Macmillan, 1988), 264–5.

24 *Trasna*, 12.

25 A postcard depicting Tynan Village was sent by 'A. E. B.' to 'Mr E. Blythe' (58 Abbey Street, Bangor) on 21 December 1909: BP, P24/1676. Alfred Blythe's Masonic lodge met in nearby Caledon, County Tyrone: see ch. 2, note 43.

26   *Trasna*, 195–6.

27   EB, WS 989, 76. For Blythe's access to cash for 'small political subscriptions', see *Trasna*, 167.

28   EB to Revd Michael Hayes (Newcastle West), 26 January 1925: quoted in John M. Regan, *The Irish Counter-Revolution, 1921–1936* (Dublin: Gill & Macmillan, 1999), 236, citing BP, P24/416.

29   Commonplace Book (undated, mid 1960s): BP, P24/2191. The reference is presumably to the Knights of St Columbanus (based at Ely Place, Dublin), often confused with the Scottish Knights of St Columba or the American Knights of Columbus. In the 1920s, this fraternity included prominent Catholic politicians of all major parties, including Blythe's Cabinet colleagues Seán MacEoin and Richard Mulcahy (Cumann na nGaedheal), Seán T. O'Kelly, Gerald Boland, and Seán Lemass (Fianna Fáil), William Norton (Labour), and Frank MacDermott (Centre Party): Evelyn Bolster (Sr M. Angela), *The Knights of Saint Columbanus* (Dublin: Gill & Macmillan, 1979), 48.

30   Largely because of divisions and threats of suppression following the involvement of Masonic lodges in the United Irishmen and opposition to the Act of Union, the Grand Lodge of Ireland had effectively suppressed political resolutions and discussion at lodge meetings since the early nineteenth century: see John Heron Lepper and Philip Crosslé, *History of the Grand Lodge of Free and Accepted Masons of Ireland*, vol. i, and R. E. Parkinson, *idem*, vol. ii (Dublin: Lodge of Research, 1925, 1957); Petri Mirala, *Freemasonry in Ulster, 1733–1813* (Dublin: Four Courts Press, 2007).

31   EB, WS 989, 2–3.

32   'Young Men of the Volunteers', in *IF*, no. 39 (January 1914).

33   An election leaflet entitled 'Career of Ernest Blythe, Candidate for North Monaghan' (1918) calculated that he had spent 6 months in 'exile' and 21 in detention during the war years: BP, P24/1017 (1), also cited by Ben Novick, *Conceiving Revolution: Irish Nationalist Propaganda during the First World War* (Dublin: Four Courts Press, 2001), 232–3. Compiled while Blythe was in Belfast gaol, this remarkably misleading document claimed that he was 'born of an old Presbyterian stock' and a founding member of the Gaelic League and Sinn Féin: 'From his earliest years his mind was filled with Irish Republican principles.' Details of Blythe's spells of imprisonment, hunger-striking, and restriction to specified regions appear in the Chronology.

34   Recommendation for Action under Regulation 14B [Defence of the Realm Act]: NAL, HO 144/1454/312169; Desmond FitzGerald, *The Memoirs of Desmond FitzGerald* (London: Routledge & Kegan Paul, 1968), 111–12, 117.

35   EB, WS 989, 109, 184–7.

36   *An tÓglach*, i, no. 4 (14 October 1918), 1–2 (reprinted 30 November).

37   Collins, to whom Blythe had smuggled the article, passed it on to Piaras Béaslaí, editor of *An tÓglach*, which Blythe later edited while Béaslaí was in prison: EB, WS 989, 109; Seán McConville, *Irish Political Prisoners, 1848–1922: Theatres of War* (London: Routledge, 2003), 657 (n. 17).

38 As one of the publisher's readers rightly remarked, many terrorists today find indiscriminate attacks on civilians more cost-effective than targeted attacks on civilians accused of collaboration with adversaries or the state. 'Ruthless Warfare' is therefore relevant only to exponents of selective terrorism, until recently the dominant mode.

39 EB, WS 989, 181–2.

40 *DEPD*, vol. i (17 November 1922), cols 2273–5.

41 *DEPD*, vol. ii (8 December 1922), cols 86–9.

42 Crawford became editor of the recently founded *Ulster Guardian* in January 1907; but his advocacy of Home Rule and devolution, issues shelved in the interest of Liberal Party unity by Campbell-Bannerman's government, led to his forced resignation as editor (and expulsion from the Independent Orange Order) in May 1908: J. W. Boyle, 'The Belfast Protestant Association and the Independent Orange Order, 1901–10', 149–50, in *Irish Historical Studies*, xiii, no. 50 (1962), 117–52; article by Pauric J. Dempsey and Sean Boylan in *DIB*, vol. ii, 971–3.

43 *Trasna*, 176.

44 *UG* (16 December 1911, 22 March 1913).

45 Robert C. Haskin, WS 223 (13 October 1948), 1; see also Valerie Jones, *Rebel Prods: The Forgotten Story of Protestant Radical Nationalists and the 1916 Rising* (Dublin: Ashfield Press, 2016), 191–6. Blythe's statement confirms that his own circle included Frank Wilson, in whose house Seán McDermott lodged: EB, WS 989, 4a.

46 Frank Byron Wilson was already married (aged 20) and living apart from his parents in 1901. His father (William J. Wilson, shoemaker) was living with his wife, 2 daughters, and son-in-law in 1901, but died in 1903: CIFS (1901, 1911).

47 Haskin, WS 223, 1.

48 John Long, who joined lodge 1501 in 1904 and signed the Covenant in 1912, was returned in the 1901 census as a 32-year-old Colour sergeant in the 3rd Royal Irish Rifles.

49 Liam Gaynor, WS 183 (21 October 1948), 2.

50 Ancient Order of Hibernians, *Manual of Instruction to Officers and Ritual of Membership* (no provenance): copy issued 27 July 1916 in Cork Archives Institute, U389/29/7. Hibernian initiates were also required to declare that 'I do not, and will not, while a member of the A.O.H., belong to any Society condemned by the Holy Roman See', such as the IRB (whether McDermott remained a Hibernian after joining the IRB is unknown).

51 Seán Mac Diarmada (*Irish Freedom* office, 5 Findlater Place, Dublin) to Miss Helen Blythe (Magheragall), 6 January 1913, apologising for the non-arrival of the December issue, 'as I myself sent it', and recalling receipt of the subscription: BP, P24/2361.

52 *Irish Freedom* was not listed among his weekly orders: *Trasna*, 180.

53 Mabel Doggart to EB, 12 October 1958: BP, P24/1449.

54 Blythe 'discovered afterwards' that the delay was caused by O'Casey's failure to seek the usual authority before approaching him: EB, WS 989, 2–3; *Trasna*, 106–8; Murray, *Seán O'Casey*, 67–8.

55 EB, WS 989, 5.

56 EB, WS 989, 33.

57 *Kerry Advocate* (29 May 1915).

58 Alf Cotton, Blythe's close associate in the Belfast IRB, following dismissal from the civil service in March 1915, had been 'appointed full-time organiser and instructor to the Kerry Brigade': Alfred Cotton, WS 184 (24 January 1949), 6; see also Jones, *Rebel Prods*, 172–80. Albert Wesley Wellington Cotton (b. 1890), 'Brethern', was a farmer's son from 'Derry', living with his family in Hatfield Street, south Belfast (1901), Portstewart (1911), and later Rosemount Gardens, north Belfast: CIFS (1901, 1911); BP, P24/2181; Denis McCullough, WS 915 (11 December 1953), 10.

59 Nationalists of all shades commonly used 'Orangemen' as a pejorative term for all northern Protestant unionists.

60 See ch. 8.

61 His only unfavourable record arose from 'false statements regarding his official duties' when stationed at Woodford, County Galway, in summer 1913: RIC Officer Service Records, NAL, HO 184/47 (microfilm in NAI). See also preceding chapter, n. 40.

62 Blythe's name headed the list circulated by the RIC (identified in *Gaeil*, 138, as an entry in *Hue-and-Cry*), because (as he airily observed) the list was arranged alphabetically by county and by surname within county, thus favouring Blythe of Antrim. No copies of *The Police Gazette: Or, The Hue-and-Cry* (Dublin edn) for 1914 have been located. Along with Collins, Mulcahy, Béaslaí, and Denis Galvin of Cork, his portrait appeared under 'Apprehensions Sought' in the issue for 24 December 1920, revealing Blythe to be '5 ft. 8 in., grey eyes, broad face, broad nose, medium make, long dark hair, brown, clean shaven', with 'wart on right cheek': cutting in Michael Brennan, autograph book from Reading Gaol, kindly shown to me by Dr Maire Brennan.

63 EB, WS 989, 77–8; see also *Slán*, 92.

64 William Quinn, an unemployed commercial clerk (Presbyterian, aged 20 in 1911), living with his stepfather Samuel Heron in Victoria Avenue, was savagely attacked on 13 February 1915 at the gate of Heron's home (Flush Hall), dying two days later. Quinn worked for his stepfather, who managed the Ulster Print Works, and Heron was thrice charged with his murder, the jury being unable to agree on each occasion. Quinn was a popular amateur singer, a Freemason who entered Farmers' Lodge 1000 on 12 June 1914, and a member of Orange lodge 872: CIFS (1911); NC (20 February, 3 April, 11 December 1915; 13 March 1916); Grand Lodge Registers. Both 'Willie Quinn, murdered' and 'Sam Heron, murder' are listed in one of Blythe's notebooks: EB, P24/2222.

65 *Gaeil*, 138.

66 *Trasna*, 108–9.

67 See ch. 6.

68 Madan Lal Dhingra (1883–1909), an engineering student at University College, London, associated with the India House movement, assassinated Sir William Hutt Curzon Wyllie (1848–1909) on 1 July 1909 during an entertainment at

the Imperial Institute, South Kensington, also killing a Parsi physician from Shanghai who tried to save Wyllie's life. Wyllie's last assignment as a humane administrator in the native states was the successful organisation of famine relief in Rajputana (1899–1900); after his return he took particular interest in the welfare of Indian students: articles on Dhingra and Wyllie, *ODNB*.

69 *Trasna*, 179.

70 Annie (Amelia E.) McHugh (1889–1957), b. Dunlavin, County Wicklow, ed. Sisters of Mercy (Derry), Dominican College (Eccles Street, Dublin), UCD BA (1911) and Higher Diploma in Education (1916), certified Intermediate teacher (1918), served on Vice-Regal Committee on Intermediate Education (1918): CIFS (1901, 1911); BP, P24/2227, 2233, 2237 (calendar entries).

71 Article on Louise Gavan Duffy (1884–1969) by Mary Kotsonouris, in *DIB*, vol. iii, 514–15; *Thom's Official Directory* (1918–20). Louise, who witnessed Annie's marriage in 1919 but never herself married, remained close to the Blythes in both politics and location (also spending her later years in Kenilworth Square, Rathgar).

72 John McHugh (b. 1886), appointed DI (14 April 1908), resigned (15 February 1910) after service in Kilkenny, Wicklow, and Tyrone, having been warned on 4 November 1909 that he would be 'removed from the Force' if again found 'guilty of such conduct': RIC Officer Service Records, HO 184/47.

73 Patrick McHugh (b. 1854), Catholic labourer from Leitrim, joined RIC (11 March 1872), appointed DI (1 August 1896), retired on pension of £260 from Londonderry City (1 January 1915): Herlihy, *RIC Officers*, 217; RIC Officer Service Records, HO 184/46; RIC Pension Ledgers; RIC Registers, HO 184/20. No family members were returned as Irish speakers in either census, 21-year-old Annie being unusual in this respect when listed as a boarder at the Dominican convent, Eccles Street, in 1911. Annie and John were offspring of Patrick's first marriage; his second wife (Mary Agnes from Kerry) bore three more children between their marriage in 1899 and 1911: CIFS (1901, 1911).

74 Letter from James Kennedy (Nenagh, County Tipperary), discussed in EB, WS 939, 112.

75 Regan states that Mulcahy 'ascribed this sensitivity to family considerations', referring to Patrick McHugh's occupation, but I cannot locate this passage in the transcript: notes of conversation between Mulcahy and Peadar MacMahon, 15 May 1963, in Mulcahy Papers, UCDA, P7/D/3, also cited by Regan, *Counter-Revolution*, 92, 395 (n. 75).

76 *DEPD* (3 April 1930), vol. xxxiv, 488.

CHAPTER TEN: DOUBLE AGENT?

1 *Trasna*, 180–1.

2 *County Down Spectator* (6 August 1915), including extracts from *NC*. The *Newtownards Spectator* was an almost identical local edition of the *County Down Spectator* (Bangor). The address given by Blythe ('The Presbytery,

Rockcorry, Co. Monaghan') was designed to arouse nationalist outrage through his arrest at the home of a priest (Arthur Griffith's ingenious suggestion), but the stunt almost misfired as the RIC waited for a week before arriving to arrest him: William Murphy, *Political Imprisonment and the Irish, 1912–1921* (Oxford: University Press, 2014), 40, citing *Slán*, 167–73.

3   *Slán*, 185.

4   Willie to Belle Doggart, 9 January 1919, quoted by Mabel Doggart to EB, 12 October 1958: BP, P24/1449.

5   The Dr Douglas Hyde Literary Fund offered an annual award from 1935 for the best work in Irish published in the preceding year, as judged by the scholars and priests comprising the trustees: NAI, Department of Education, An Gúm Correspondence, GAEL/AN GUM/G 220.

6   *NC* (29 August 1958). 'Townsman', the anonymous author of 'Newtownards Viewpoint', was not one of Blythe's companions on the *Chronicle*, Doggart and the Henry brothers having since died. Only a brief snippet on Blythe's award appeared in *NS* (29 August 1958).

7   Mabel Doggart to EB, 12 October 1958.

8   *Slán*, 114.

9   BP, P24/1692.

10 *Southern Star*, 9 February, 2 March 1918.

11 EB, WS 989, 5.

12 Letter previously published in the *Nation* and *Athenaeum* (London), and extracted by many Irish newspapers, including *Southern Star* (25 June 1921).

13 *Trasna*, 156. A similar view is expressed in Earnán de Blaghd, *Briseadh na Teorann* (Dublin: Sáirséal agus Dill, 1955), 38–9.

14 Earnán de Blaghd to O'Higgins, 27 June 1923, and Éamon Ó Cugain (assistant commissioner, Civic Guard) to secretary, Ministry of Home Affairs, 20 July 1923, enclosing report from acting superintendent, Cavan–Monaghan division: NAI, H75/15.

15 In the absence of Eoin O'Duffy (who had topped the poll on 16 June 1922) following his appointment as chief commissioner of the Civic Guard, Blythe polled 11,290 votes on 27 August 1923, almost double the quota for election on the first count (6,402). His running-mate for Cumann na nGaedheal (Patrick Duffy) polled only 1,316 but was elected on Blythe's surplus, with the abstentionist Sinn Féiner Patrick McCarvill taking the second of 3 seats after winning 5,745 first preferences. The 4 independent and farmers' candidates together received 7,256 votes: Brian M. Walker, *Parliamentary Election Results in Ireland, 1918–92* (Dublin: RIA, 1992), 114.

16 See also Daithí Ó Corráin's valuable article, '"Ireland in his heart north and south": The Contribution of Ernest Blythe to the Partition Question', in *Irish Historical Studies*, xxxv, no. 137 (2006), 61–80.

17 EB, WS 989, 119–20.

18 Dáil Éireann, *Minutes of Proceedings of the First Parliament of the Republic of Ireland, 1919–1921: Official Record* (Dublin: Stationery Office, undated), 191–3 (6 August 1920). As secretary of trade and commerce, Blythe also argued

against a similar 'boycott of English goods': Dáil Éireann, *Minutes*, 255–6 (25 January 1921).

19   Dáil Éireann, *Minutes*, 193–4 (6 August 1920); EB, WS 989, 119–20.

20   As acting secretary for industries as well as director of trade and commerce, Blythe also sponsored bills to create a National Economic Council and provide for the protection of Irish industries: Dáil Éireann, *Minutes*, 228–32 (17 September 1920).

21   Craig considered that Home Rule would carry 'certain financial and other disadvantages' by comparison with dominion status, as envisaged for the Irish Free State, and suggested devolving the 'reserved powers' to two separate parliaments instead of an 'all-Ireland Parliament' as then proposed, in effect creating a dominion of Northern Ireland: Craig to Lloyd George, 11 November 1921, transcribed in St. John Ervine, *Craigavon: Ulsterman* (London: George Allen & Unwin, 1949), 449–51.

22   EB, WS 989, 134–5.

23   'Iris Dháil Éireann', *Official Report: Debate on the Treaty between Great Britain and Ireland signed in London on the 6th December, 1921* (Dublin: Stationery Office, undated), 194 (3 January 1922). Regan states without qualification that 'he advocated, almost alone, Sinn Féin's right to coerce the Northern majority into a unitary state': John M. Regan, *The Irish Counter-Revolution, 1921–1936* (Dublin: Gill & Macmillan, 1998), 92. Regan's reading is rejected in Ó Corráin, 'Partition Question', 63.

24   Ernest Blythe (acting minister for home affairs), memorandum on 'Policy in Regard to the North-East', 9 August 1922: *DIFP*, vol. i, 1919–1922 (Dublin: RIA, 1998), 489–93.

25   EB in Dáil Éireann, 9 December 1925, quoted and contextualised by Ronan Fanning, *The Irish Department of Finance, 1922–58* ((Dublin: Institute of Public Administration, 1978), 168.

26   *DIFP*, vol. ii, 1923–1926 (Dublin: RIA, 2000), 533–4, 561–3.

27   The terms were not published until 16 November 1926: Fanning, *Department of Finance*, 174, 648 (n. 128).

28   Blythe was responding, with marked courtesy, to points irrelevantly raised by Seán Lemass during a debate on the Central Funds Bill: *DEPD* (22 March 1928), vol. xxii, cols 1645–6.

29   *DEPD* (2 April 1930), vol. xxxiv, col. 399.

30   *IT* (26 February 1975).

31   *IT* (14 September 1927). Blythe later heard the same views expressed by Blueshirt novices, who 'do not want a Twenty-Six County republic which would set the seal of finality on Partition': Onlooker, in *United Irishman* (17 June 1933).

32   Michael Laffan, *Judging W. T. Cosgrave: The Foundation of the Irish State* (Dublin: RIA, 2014), 126.

33   *DEPD* (22 March 1928), vol. xxii, col. 1645.

34   *DEPD* (20 February 1929), vol. xxviii, col. 155; Tim Pat Coogan, *De Valera: Long Fellow, Long Shadow* (London: Hutchinson, 1993), 421.

35 'The Problem of Partition', in *United Ireland* (23 March 1935).

36 Report on annual congress of Irish Students' Association, TCD: *IT* (4 July 1936). This summary accords closely with reports in other newspapers, including the *Irish Press*, which added an Irish text. See also Eamon Phoenix, *Northern Nationalism: Nationalist Politics, Partition and the Catholic Minority in Northern Ireland, 1890–1940* (Belfast: Ulster Historical Foundation, 1994), 383.

37 *Ulster Herald, Strabane Chronicle* (11 July 1936).

38 *Irish Press* (6 July 1936). This significant gloss was omitted in the mid-Ulster reports just cited.

39 James Little (1868–1946), ordained (1900), ministered at Castlereagh (1915–46), retiring from 'active duty' in 1942; elected unopposed as unionist at by-election (1939), returned as independent unionist at general election (1945); DGC, Down (1931–46), DGCI (1933–8), and GCI (1939–46).

40 *BNL* (14 July 1936).

41 Enda Staunton, *The Nationalists of Northern Ireland, 1918–1973* (Dublin: Columba Press, 2001), 189, 216–17; Ó Corráin, 'Partition Question', 75–6.

42 EB, 'Towards a Six-County Dominion?', in NLI, Johnson Papers, MS 17200/3. In 1955, Blythe published a collection of his newspaper articles on partition in *Briseadh na Teorann*. For a comprehensive survey of Blythe's campaign against the anti-partition campaign, see Ó Corráin, 'Partition Question', esp. 62–5.

43 Conor Cruise O'Brien, *Memoir: My Life and Themes* (Dublin: Poolbeg Press, 1998), 141–9.

44 'Dominion?', 2.

45 'Dominion?', 5.

46 EB to Johnson, 1 November 1949: Johnson Papers, MS 17200/2.

47 'Dominion?', 6–7, 10–13, 16, 19.

48 'Dominion?', 27, 28, 31, 36, 40–9.

49 *Frontier Sentinel*, Newry (4 November 1950), also quoted and discussed in Christopher Norton, *The Politics of Constitutional Nationalism in Northern Ireland, 1932–70: Between Grievance and Reconciliation* (Manchester: University Press, 2014), 104. Exactly the same editorial and jibe, along with the same lengthy extracts from Blythe's article in the *Leader*, appeared in the other four newspapers published by the North-West of Ireland Printing and Publishing Co. Ltd. (accessible through Irish Newspaper Archives).

50 Anthony Mulvey (1873–1957) represented Fermanagh–Tyrone and latterly Mid Ulster at Westminster (1935–51), retiring from public life and editorship in 1951: article on Mulvey by Brendan Lynn in *DIB*, vol. vi, 778–9; Hugh Oram, *The Newspaper Book: A History of Newspapers in Ireland, 1649–1983* (Dublin: MO Books, 1983), 196–7.

51 Obituary of Louis' son Austin Lynch (1937–2014), in *IT* (1 November 2014). Louis Dominic Lynch (b. 1904), son of the company's founder Michael Lynch, was its secretary and one of 3 directors, his colleagues being 2 nationalist MPs at Stormont, Alexander Ernest Donnelly (1925–49) and Roderick Hugh O'Connor (1949–72): *BPUD* (1944, 1953). Lynch and Donnelly were former

anti-Devlinite Home Rulers who had joined the Irish Nation League in 1916 and thence Sinn Féin in 1917, supported the Treaty, denounced confirmation of partition in 1925, and vacillated on the issue of continued parliamentary 'abstention' in 1927: Phoenix, *Northern Nationalism*, 40, 333, 349, 362.

52 Staunton, *Nationalists*, 186. The 'Omagh Group' also included Cahir Healy (a director of the *Fermanagh Herald*), with whom Blythe frequently discussed his proposals in the later 1950s.

53 Despite Blythe's repeated later denials of involvement in the IRB after the Dáil's declaration of an Irish Republic in January 1919, a former member from Donegal told Ernie O'Malley that 'Ernest Blythe had been around during the Tan War reorganising IRB it was said, although I never met any people whom he had either sworn in or had meetings with': Notes of interview with Joe Sweeney, 43, in O'Malley Notebooks, UCDA, P17b/97, 38–44.

54 The constitution of the IRB was eventually amended to allow members to obey the Dáil and to abandon the pretence that the president of the Supreme Council was also president of the Irish Republic: Leon Ó Broin, *Revolutionary Underground: The Story of the Irish Republican Brotherhood, 1858–1924* (Dublin: Gill & Macmillan, 1976), 182–3.

55 Dáil Éireann, *Debate on the Treaty* (3 January 1922), 192.

56 Rutherford Mayne, *The Drone and Other Plays* (Dublin: Maunsell, 1912), 40, 42, 43, 3.

57 *NDH* (7 February 1913).

EPILOGUE: FASCIST ECHOES

1 The term 'Blueshirts' was applied successively in 1933 to the Army Comrades' Association (March), the National Guard (July), the Young Ireland Association (September), and the League of Youth (December), which was itself split into rival bodies of the same name after September 1934. All of these bodies are extensively documented in Blythe's papers: Mike Cronin, *The Blueshirts and Irish Politics* (Dublin: Four Courts Press, 1997), 28–37. O'Duffy's faction was reconstituted in June 1935 as the National Corporate Party ('Greenshirts').

2 Maurice Manning, *The Blueshirts* (Dublin: Gill & Macmillan, 2006; 1st edn 1971), 67, 158; Cronin, *Blueshirts*, 47, 93–4; John M. Regan, *The Irish Counter-Revolution, 1921–1936* (Dublin: Gill & Macmillan, 1999), 323, 332, 339, 369; Fearghal McGarry, *Eoin O'Duffy: A Self-Made Hero* (Oxford: University Press, 2005), 208, 265–7. Even when my assessment of Blythe's role in the Blueshirts differs from theirs, I remain indebted to these able scholars for pointing me towards many of the sources cited below.

3 Mark Phelan, 'Irish Responses to Fascist Italy, 1919–1932' (PhD thesis, NUI Galway, 2013), 137–8, 148–56.

4 Blythe intervened as a member of the Council of Defence in 1930 and as Desmond FitzGerald's acting minister for finance in 1931: Reagan, *Counter-*

Revolution, 297–8, 292, 294; notes of Richard Mulcahy's interview with Peadar McMahon, 18 August 1963, in Mulcahy Papers, UCDA, P7/D/3.

5   *An Reult / The Star* (22 March 1930); *Sunday Independent* (23 March 1930); *An Phoblacht* (5 April 1930, 9 April 1932).

6   As translated in *Sunday Independent* (23 March 1930). The translation, though ignoring passages relating to the army's importance in deterring foreign invaders, is generally accurate (analysis by Colm Mac Gearailt).

7   *IF*, no. 21 (July 1912).

8   As translated in *Sunday Independent* (23 March 1930).

9   *An Phoblacht* (5 April 1930).

10 This applies also to the brief discussion in McGarry, *O'Duffy*, 190.

11 *DEPD* (2, 3 April 1930), vol. xxxiv, cols 316–17 (Lemass), 412–14 (MacEntee), 480 (Rutledge).

12 *An Phoblacht / The Republic* (9 April 1932), quoting Blythe's 'signed article' (15 March 1932) published in the *Boston Transcript*.

13 *Irish Press* (22 March 1934), also cited in McGarry, *O'Duffy*, 257. Blythe's authorship is likewise asserted by Phelan, 'Irish Responses', 156–7.

14 The homely contrast between 'good boys' (*buachaillí maithe*) and 'bad boys' (*droch-buachaillí*) carries a whiff of Blythe. Two decades earlier, 'The Old Town Clock' remarked that 'this Hallowe'en proved a tame one for the bad boy': *NDH* (4 November 1910).

15 Blythe contradicted de Valera's summary, without denying authorship of such an article: *SEPD*, vol. xviii, cols 865–6 (21 March 1934).

16 During the period of bitter recrimination following O'Duffy's removal as leader of both the United Ireland party and the League of Youth, O'Duffy's organ identified several of Blythe's alleged pseudonyms: 'alias Onlooker, A Southern Priest, M. G. Quinn, Gerald Smith, Traveller, and all the rest of it': *Blueshirt* (26 January 1935); also cited in McGarry, *O'Duffy*, 388, n. 35. He used the additional pseudonym 'M' in *United Ireland* for a poem in Irish ('Spáinneach nó Gael'): BP, P 24/2148 (calendar entry); see also 'M', 'Oilean Chapraoi', in *United Ireland* (12 January 1935).

17 Blythe, described on his nomination paper as a 'journalist', was returned unopposed for one of two vacancies on 2 January 1934, having been nominated by Professor J. M. O'Sullivan, TD (another prominent Blueshirt). On 7 December 1934, he was re-elected, ostensibly for a 9-year term, to a chamber whose abolition had already been promised by de Valera. With 6 first preferences out of those cast by 209 members of the Oireachtais, Blythe was the last to be elected of 23 successful candidates, 6 others being eliminated: *IT* (3 January, 2 October, 8 December 1934); Donal O'Sullivan, *The Irish Free State and its Senate: A Study in Contemporary Politics* (London: Faber & Faber, 1940), 602–3.

18 *An Reult, The Star: A National Weekly Review* (1929–32); *The United Irishman* (1932–3), published by The Star Publishing Co.; and *United Ireland* (1933–6). Though not accredited organs of Cumann na nGaedheal and its successor Fine Gael, these newspapers were fiercely partisan and loyal to the party leadership.

19   *Star* (5 April 1930); also cited in Phelan, 'Irish Responses', 172–3, referring to 'an anonymous lead writer'; see also McGarry, *O'Duffy*, 190, citing *An Phoblacht* (12 April 1930).
20   Alexander Pope, *An Essay on Man* (1733–4). Minor slips have been corrected.
21   *Star* (5 April 1930).
22   *An Phoblacht* (12 April 1930). The journal interpreted this article and the editorial of 22 March 1930 as truly threatening dictatorship: 'We, in this paper, have written much of revolution – but we scarcely dared to hope that the Cosgrave junta themselves would make revolution inevitable within the near future.'
23   Speech at Broomfield, County Monaghan: *IT* (8 February 1932).
24   Speech at Clontibret, County Monaghan: *IT* (16 January 1933).
25   BP, P24/1745. The certificate issued in 1927 is absent from his archive, suggesting that Blythe eventually surrendered it; but he retained an undated permit issued during the civil war by 'Owen O'Duffy' (as Chief of Staff, Óglaigh na h-Éireann), informing officers that the bearer, Mr. E. Blythe, TD, 'has my authority to carry a revolver for the purpose of protection. You will facilitate him in every way possible': BP, P24/1744.
26   *IT* (31 July, 2 August, 1 December 1933). The decision to revoke all such certificates as from 31 July 1933 was in fact (as de Valera revealed during a heated debate in the Dáil) aimed at O'Duffy's National Guard: *DEPD*, vol. xlix, cols 1028–72 (1 August 1933), vol. 1, col. 710 (30 November 1933); O'Sullivan, *The Irish Free State and its Senate*, 330–1, 338; Manning, *Blueshirts*, 76–7.
27   *United Irishman* (1 April 1933).
28   *United Irishman* (15 April 1933). An extended, duplicated version of this article was issued in May 1933 as *The Diast (An Occasional Bulletin)*, no. 1, any future numbers being available from 'M. G. Quinn, Midland Hotel, Dublin', and 'issued by a group of Irishmen who feel that national progress is not possible unless a new type of organic or integrative state is created in the twenty six Counties': BP, P24/691; also cited and analysed in McGarry, *O'Duffy*, 205, and Phelan, 'Irish Responses', 158–60.
29   *The Diast*, no. 1 (May 1933).
30   *United Irishman* (15 April 1933).
31   For background, see John F. Harbinson, *The Ulster Unionist Party, 1882–1973: Its Development and Organisation* (Belfast: Blackstaff Press, 1973), esp. ch. 8; Graham Walker, *A History of the Ulster Unionist Party: Protest, Pragmatism and Pessimism* (Manchester: University Press, 2004).
32   Though sometimes attributed to Blythe because carbon copies appear in his papers, the undated 'Preliminary Notes on Planned Economics' and 'Memo. Vocational Corporations' were neither signed nor annotated by Blythe, and may have been drafted by other members of the party executive: BP, P24/678–9. Blythe's authorship is assumed in Cronin, *Blueshirts*, 94–6, and Eugene Broderick, *Intellectuals and the Ideological Hijacking of Fine Gael, 1932–1938* (Newcastle-upon-Tyne: Cambridge Scholars, 2010), 50.
33   Cronin, *Blueshirts*, 95–6, citing BP, P24/679.

34 BP, P24/680a, 680b, also cited in Cronin, *Blueshirts*, 96–7, and Regan, *Counter-Revolution*, 352; Broderick, *Intellectuals*, 51–3.

35 Earnán de Blaghd, 'The Old-Time Farm', in *IF* (April 1914).

36 BP, P24/680a.

37 BP, P24/680a, 680b. The proposal for an agricultural corporation was surely Blythe's, given his annotations to the preliminary draft, though Tom Gunning, an overt Fascist, has also been named as a possible author: Regan, *Counter-Revolution*, 352.

38 The rudiments of a 'corporate system' were introduced through the Palazzo Vidoni Pact (October 1925) and the 'Rocco Law' (April 1926), which banned strikes and lock-outs and created seven syndicates or corporations. A more elaborate system of 22 corporations, each 'a vertically structured alliance of employers and workers' under party oversight, was promulgated in February 1934: R. J. B. Bosworth, *Mussolini's Italy: Life under the Dictatorship, 1915–1945* (London: Allen Lane, 2005), 226–7, 308–9.

39 For an outline by 'E. C.' of the new system, followed by a detailed double-spread outline of the structure and composition of the new Italian corporations, see the *Blueshirt* (19, 26 January 1935). 'E. C.' may have been Edward Cahill or Edward Coyne, Jesuit intellectuals in sympathy with Michael Tierney, who later advised de Valera on vocational provisions in his new Constitution; but he was clearly not O'Duffy's rival Edmund Cronin.

40 *United Ireland* (28 October 1933), referring to articles in that newspaper by 'J. H.'

41 Report from Firenze by P. F. Gomez Homen (27 August 1934), cited in Dermot Keogh, *Ireland and Europe: A Diplomatic and Political History* (Cork and Dublin: Hibernian University Press, 1990; 1st edn 1989), 47–8.

42 M. G. Quinn, 'The Problem of Government', in *United Ireland* (27 January 1934).

43 *United Irishman* (25 March, 1 April 1933).

44 *United Irishman* (17 June 1933).

45 *SEPD*, vol. xviii (21 March 1934), cols 854–5, 860.

46 *SEPD*, vol. xviii (21 March 1934), cols 852–3; also cited in Broderick, *Intellectuals*, 92.

47 *Blueshirt* (5 August 1933), also cited in Broderick, *Intellectuals*, 94–5. It is not obvious that Onlooker's claims of affinity between the National Guard and the Volunteers were 'ridiculous', as asserted by Broderick.

48 *United Irishman* (8 April 1933).

49 *United Irishman* (25 April 1933).

50 'Young Men of the Volunteers', in *IF*, no. 39 (January 1914).

51 *United Irishman* (8 April, 13 May, 24 June 1933).

52 Cronin, *Blueshirts*, 47. W. B. Yeats, ever contemplating his own seminal influence, wrote that 'their organiser tells me that it was my suggestion – a suggestion I have entirely forgotten – that made them select for their flag a red St Patrick's cross on a blue ground': Yeats to Olivia Shakespear, 13 July [1933], in *The Letters of W. B. Yeats*, ed. Allan Wade (London: Rupert Hart-Davis, 1954), 812.

53 *United Irishman* (13 May 1933).

54 *United Irishman* (20 May 1933).

55 John Francis Larchet (1884–1967), appointed director of music at the Abbey (1907).

56 Yeats to EB, undated and 30 November 1933: BP, P24/1554; R. F. Foster, *W. B. Yeats, A Life: II. The Arch-Poet* (Oxford: University Press, 2003), 477–80, 744 (n. 31, 32); 'The Gardener and the Stable-Boy: Yeats, MacNeice, and the Problem of Orangeism', 67–9, in David Fitzpatrick, *Descendancy: Irish Protestant Histories since 1795* (Cambridge: University Press, 2014), 59–77.

57 *United Ireland* (3 March 1934), also quoted in Foster, *Arch-Poet*, 477.

58 *United Ireland* (10 February 1934), also cited in Foster, Arch-Poet, 479–80. The new title reflected the renaming of the Blueshirts as the League of Youth, following the suppression of the Army Comrades' Association. 'O'Duffy Abú' by 'Volunteer A. Lacey' was published beside Onlooker's column in *United Ireland* (28 October 1933). Printed and typed variants of 'The March of Youth' may be found in BP, P24/685a, 685b.

59 *IT* (25 January 1933).

60 *United Irishman* (20 May 1933).

61 *United Ireland* (23 September 1933). No longer 'News of the A.C.A.' or 'News of the Blueshirts', Onlooker's column in the renamed party paper was now entitled 'Blue Flag Notes'.

62 *United Ireland* (30 September 1933).

63 *United Irishman* (10 June 1933), partly quoted in McGarry, *O'Duffy*, 259.

64 *United Irishman* (24 June 1933).

65 *United Irishman* (22 July 1933).

66 *Blueshirt* (12 August 1933).

67 *United Ireland* (30 September, 28 October, 11 November 1933).

68 Manning, *Blueshirts*, 67, 158, 162–3; Maurice Manning, *James Dillon: A Biography* (Dublin: Wolfhound Press, 1999), 79, 105, 107 (stating that Blythe was 'compromised' and that his 'role in the Blueshirt adventure did him little credit'); McGarry, *O'Duffy*, 208, 249 (naming Blythe among O'Duffy's 'fickle allies'); Regan, *Counter-Revolution*, 369 (oddly suggesting that Blythe, like Ned Cronin, was motivated by 'personal advancement' in pushing O'Duffy out of the League of Youth).

69 *Blueshirt* (April 1935); O'Duffy to Capt. Patrick Quinn, 3 October 1934: quoted in McGarry, *O'Duffy*, 271.

70 McGarry, *O'Duffy*, 208, quoting statement by O'Duffy, 19 February 1935, in NAI, DJ 8/296.

71 *United Ireland* (18 October 1934).

72 *United Ireland* (19 January 1935); for blistering responses, see O'Duffy's *Blueshirt* (29 December 1934, 26 January 1935).

73 *Blueshirt* (26 January 1935).

74 *United Ireland* (25 July 1936). O'Duffy's branch adopted a green shirt and was succeeded by his National Corporative Party in 1935.

75 *United Ireland* (16 May 1936).

76 Onlooker in *United Ireland* (23 March 1935). For differing interpretations of the influence of *Quadragesimo Anno* on Blythe's corporatism, see McGarry, *O'Duffy*, 205; Cronin, *Blueshirts*, 94, 97.

77 *Blueshirt* (April 1935).

78 *United Ireland* (4 July 1936).

79 'Fine Gael and Agriculture', in *United Ireland* (12, 19 January 1935), also cited and summarised by Broderick, *Intellectuals*, 50–2.

80 BP, P24/1942, also cited in McGarry, *O'Duffy*, 221.

81 R.M. Douglas, *Architects of the Resurrection: Ailtirí na hAiséirghe and the Fascist 'New Order' in Ireland* (Manchester: University Press, 2009), 66–8, 71.

82 Douglas, *Architects*, 98 (citing BP, P24/970), 203, 234, 293; Clair Wills, *That Neutral Island: A Cultural History of Ireland during the Second World War* (London: Faber & Faber, 2007), 366–7 (citing BP, P24/969, 974).

83 *The Leader: A Review of Current Affairs, Politics, Literature, Art and Industry*, vol. lxxxiii, no. 3 (16 August 1941), 54–6. Though Douglas implies that Blythe edited this venerable weekly, established by D.P. Moran, its second and last proprietor and editor (identified as 'she' in a regular editorial note for correspondents) was in fact Moran's Irish-speaking daughter, Nuala Ní Mhoráin: Patrick Maume, 'Irish-Ireland and Catholic Whiggery: D.P. Moran and *The Leader*', 59, in *Periodicals and Journalism in Twentieth-Century Ireland*, ed. Mark O'Brien and Felix M. Larkin (Dublin: Four Courts Press, 2014), 47–60.

84 Eunan O'Halpin, *Spying on Ireland: British Intelligence and Irish Neutrality during the Second World War* (Oxford: University Press, 2008), 222, citing SIS ('MI6'), 'QRS' Political Reports (Ireland), 1 May 1943, in NAL, DO 121/85.

85 Translated extract from editorial on 'Current Affairs' in *Leader*, vol. lxxxvi, no. 20 (12 June 1943), 331: Douglas, *Architects*, 165.

86 These caveats, translated by Colm Mac Gearailt, significantly alter the thrust of the passage cited by Douglas. The context of this warning against the consequences of violence and illegality was Ó Cuinneagáin's arrest in Belfast, his intention to 'abstain' from the Dáil if elected, and his wish to attract 'a certain type of voter' sympathetic to the radical republican party Córas na Poblachta (whose few candidates polled no better than those of the Ailtirí on 23 June 1943).

87 *Leader* (12 June 1943), 330–1.

88 In all seven constituencies contested by Ailtirí na hAirséirghe on 30 May 1944, its candidates came last, an even worse performance than in June 1943, when only two of its four candidates came last though none was elected: *Parliamentary Election Results in Ireland, 1918–92*, ed. Brian M. Walker (Dublin: RIA, 1992), 154–66.

89 Douglas, *Architects*, 162, 203, 234.

90 McGarry, *O'Duffy*, 331, 339, citing NAI, G2/X/1091.

91 Paul McMahon, *British Spies and Irish Rebels: British Intelligence and Ireland, 1916–1945* (London, Boydell, 2008), 358, citing SIS report, 14 January 1941, in NAL, ADM 223/486.

92   According to McMahon's summary, Blythe and J. J. Walsh were named respectively as chairman and secretary of Clondalkin Paper Mills (in fact the reverse). Blythe was much praised and doubtless adequately paid for his work as the company's first secretary (1937–41) before he resigned to manage the Abbey Theatre. Unlike Walsh, undoubtedly a 'wealthy businessman', he was not listed as a director of any public limited company. His personal estate as valued for probate amounted to £10,689, of which half (£5,204) was in stocks or bonds, with household effects valued at £1,890: NAI, Schedule of Assets for Grant of Probate (1 August 1978).

93   O'Halpin, *Spying on Ireland*, 222, citing SIS, 'QRS' Political Reports (Ireland), 1 March 1943, in NAL, DO 121/85.

94   McMahon, *British Spies*, 358–9.

95   'Arms and Drill', in *IF* (December 1913).

96   *Cork Examiner* (18 June 1934); *Irish Press* (18 June), cited by Regan, *Counter-Revolution*, 358, and McGarry, *O'Duffy*, 235.

97   In Cronin's view, Blythe was 'a great advocate of the Italian system' who nevertheless 'recoiled from a commitment to total fascism' as advocated by O'Duffy, and devoted himself primarily to 'transferring intellectual ideas into policy': Cronin, *Blueshirts*, 59, 65, 93–4. McGarry, though deeming Blythe's position on fascism 'far more ambiguous' than O'Duffy's, convicts him of 'unhealthy political tendencies' and of hypocritically attributing 'the violence and anti-democratic rhetoric of this period to his [O'Duffy's] leadership': McGarry, *O'Duffy*, 267, 339. Laffan, smoothly exonerating Cosgrave of culpable Blueshirtery, maintains that 'only a small minority, most notably Blythe and O'Duffy, sympathised with the authoritarian patterns spreading across Continental Europe': Michael Laffan, *Judging W. T. Cosgrave: The Foundation of the Irish State* (Dublin: RIA, 2014), 306.

98   EB to Arthur Newman, 29 October 1934, quoted in Dermot Keogh, *Jews in Twentieth-Century Ireland: Refugees, Anti-Semitism and the Holocaust* (Cork: University Press, 1998), 96. The fact that Blythe had backed the overtly anti-semitic Berlin envoy Charles Bewley in an ugly dispute with Robert Briscoe (a Jew) in January 1922 does not demonstrate that Blythe's hostility to Briscoe was a matter of race: Keogh, *Jews*, 74–5.

99   McGarry, *O'Duffy*, 320, citing articles in the *Irish Independent* by O'Duffy vilifying 'International Jewry' and celebrating occupation of the Sudetenland in 1938. Apart from expressions of admiration for the preoccupation of German youth with athletics, mountaineering, and hiking (214–15), this is the first such statement by O'Duffy noted by McGarry.

100 For the young Blythe's dismissal of the prevalence of a Celtic Irish race, and denial of significant racial differences between the Irish and the British or between Ulster and the rest of Ireland, see 'Letters to Young Liberals', V, in *UG* (16 September 1911).

101 In 'Blue Flag Notes', Onlooker claimed that this proviso would limit the presidency to 'a man who was naturally and sanely Irish in his outlook, and neither cosmopolitan nor morbidly and artificially by-national' [*sic*]:

United Ireland (10 February 1934), amplified in the same issue by Onlooker, 'Definition of an Irish National'. The inference of a 'xenophobic mentality' appears in McGarry, *O'Duffy*, 253.

102 'Blue Flag Notes', in *United Ireland* (23 December 1933).

103 *SEPD* (13 November 1935), vol. xx, cols 1127–31. Italian propaganda about 'the great humanitarian work of the liberation of slaves' was 'reminiscent of the methods of Hamar Greenwood' (col. 1130).

104 John Ernest Lester (1888–1959), Methodist from Woodburn, Carrickfergus, Free State's permanent representative to League of Nations (1929), League secretariat (1933), high commissioner for Danzig (1934), deputy secretary-general (1937), acting secretary-general (1940–6): article by Michael Kennedy in *DIB*. Lester was Blythe's 'best man' in 1919 and the reverse in 1920. The Blythes also rented their Dublin home when the Lesters moved back to Geneva: Douglas Gageby, *The Last Secretary General: Seán Lester and the League of Nations* (Dublin: Town House, 1999), 213–14; correspondence (1936–7) on rental of Fairfield House, Highfield Rd, Rathgar, in BP, P24/2225 (calendar entry).

105 *Irish Press* (20 March 1935). The League of Nations having adopted the Lytton report on Manchuria in February 1933, Japan announced its withdrawal in the following month, though this was not effected until October 1938.

106 In summer 1933, Lester told the Geneva Institute of International Affairs that, despite their clear breach of the League Covenant, the Japanese might 'feel themselves unfortunate in being treated on a different basis because their action took place in 1931 rather than 1901': quoted in Gageby, *The Last Secretary General*, 34.

107 Paul McNamara, *Seán Lester, Poland and the Nazi Takeover of Danzig* (Dublin: Irish Academic Press, 2009).

108 For elaboration of this theme, see David Fitzpatrick, *The Two Irelands, 1912–1939* (Oxford: University Press, 1998).

109 For a penetrating critique of relevant studies, see Douglas, *Architects*, 5–42 ('Anti-Democratic Influences in Ireland, 1919–39').

110 Communism, though generating kindred paramilitary movements purporting to act as the 'vanguard of the proletariat', had little appeal for Irish republicans because of its espousal of atheism and working-class insurrection.

Chronology

July 14   Parents James Blythe and Agnes Thompson married, Lisburn

1889

Apr. 13   EB born, Magheraliskmisk, County Antrim
July 10   Uncle John Thompson married Sophia Hewitt, Moira

1890

Sept. 11   Brother James Alexander born

1891

Sept. 11   Sister Josephine Chelley born

1893

Feb. 13   *Second Home Rule Bill introduced (defeated in House of Lords, 9 Sept.)*
Apr. 14   Sister (Mary) Helen born

1895

July   *Salisbury's Unionists victorious in general election over Rosebery's Liberals*
Dec. 22   Grandfather Robert Blythe died (76), Magheraliskmisk

1899

May 25   Grandfather Thomas Thompson died (87), Deneight, County Down

1900

Jan. 30   *Nationalist factions reunited under Redmond (elected leader, Irish Parliamentary Party, 6 Feb.)*

Sept. 7   Grandmother Chelley Blythe died (71), Belfast

Oct.   *Unionists under Salisbury again victorious in general election (Redmondites dominant in Ireland)*

1901

Jan. 20   *Queen Victoria died, succeeded by Edward VII*

1902

July 12   *Salisbury replaced as prime minister by nephew Balfour*

1903

June 6   *National Council convened by Griffith from executive of Cumann na nGaedheal (formed 1900)*

June 11   *Independent Orange Order formed, Belfast*

1904

Dec. 27   *Abbey Theatre opened, Dublin*

1905

Mar.   Appointed boy clerk, Department of Agriculture, Dublin

Mar. 3   *Ulster Unionist Council constituted*

Mar. 8   *Dungannon clubs formed, Belfast*

June   First attended Abbey Theatre

July 13   *Independent Orange Order manifesto issued at Magheramorne, County Antrim*

summer   Joined Gaelic League, central branch

later   Converted to Sinn Féin on reading Griffith's *United Irishman*

Dec. 4   *Liberal Campbell-Bannerman replaced Balfour as prime minister*

1906

Jan.	*Liberals won large majority in general election*
early	Joined GAA, central branch hurling club

1907

spring	Admitted to IRB, Teeling circle, Dublin
Apr. 21	*Sinn Féin League formed at Dundalk convention of Dungannon clubs and Cumann na nGaedheal*
Apr. 22	Signed circular to promote Protestant involvement in Gaelic League

1908

Feb. 21	*Sinn Féin's only parliamentary candidate (until 1917) heavily defeated by Redmondite in North Leitrim by-election*
Apr. 6	*Asquith replaced Campbell-Bannerman as prime minister*
May 2	As 'Cnó Cúil' in Irish Peasant, reviewed ULT première of *The Drone* by 'Rutherford Mayne' at the Abbey Theatre
Nov. 11	*Irish Women's Franchise League formed*
Dec. 29	*Irish Transport (and General) Workers' Union formed*

1909

Feb. 15	*R. L. Crawford repudiated by Independent Orange Order after contemplating Home Rule*
Mar. 19	Resigned as boy clerk
Mar. 22	Moved to Bangor as junior reporter, *North Down Herald*
Aug. 16	*Fianna Éireann formed*
	Joined IRB, Dungannon club, and Fianna Éireann, Belfast

1910

Jan. 20	*Independent unionist T. H. Sloan defeated in South Belfast in general election (Liberals returned without working majority)*
Feb. 21	*Carson replaced Long as chairman of Irish Unionist MPs*
May 6	*King Edward VII died, succeeded by George V*

Sept.   Moved to Newtownards as *Herald*'s correspondent
Sept. 14   Joined lodge 1501, Newtownards Orange hall
Nov.   On editorial staff of IRB's *Irish Freedom*
Dec.   *Asquith remained prime minister after further general election,*
            again dependent on support from Labour and Home Rulers

1911

Jan. 26   Opposed women's suffrage at Presbyterian meeting, Newtownards
July 12   On platform at Orange demonstration, Ballyrea
Aug. 18   *Parliament Act curtailed power of House of Lords to veto major*
            legislation such as Home Rule
Aug. 19   As 'Purple Star', contributed first 'Letter to Young Liberals' in
            Ulster Guardian
Dec. 6   *Provincial Grand Lodge of Ulster constituted by Grand Orange*
            Lodge of Ireland
Dec. 9   His lampoon 'The Lodge' published in *Guardian*, followed by
            satirical account of Grand Lodge meeting (16 Dec.)

1912

Feb. 8   Attended Ulster Liberal Association's Celtic Park meeting for
            Winston Churchill, mocking liberals in report for *Herald*
Feb. 14   Resigned from Orange Order
Apr. 6   As 'Purple Star', began series on 'The Irish Language Movement'
            in *Guardian* (to 11 May)
Apr. 11   *Third Home Rule Bill introduced*
May   As 'Earnán', began contributing poems, then articles to *Irish*
            Freedom
June 7   Appointed secretary of new Freedom club, Belfast
July   Advocated 'military spirit' in 'Men and Arms', *Irish Freedom*
Sept. 28   Father James signed Ulster's Solemn League and Covenant,
            Donaghadee

1913

Jan. 30   *Home Rule defeated in House of Lords, after first of three passages*
            through Commons
Jan 30   First played Uncle Dan in *The Drone*, Newtownards

Jan. 31	*Ulster Volunteer Force formed, Belfast*
Apr.	Moved to Kerry to work as farm labourer for Ashe family, Lispole Gaeltacht
Sept. 24	*Ulster Provisional Government under Carson authorised by Ulster Unionist Council*
Oct.	Advocated martyrdom in 'Ireland's To-Morrow', *Irish Freedom*
Nov. 25	*Irish Volunteers formed, Dublin*
Dec.	Uncertain about Ulster Volunteer threat in 'Arms and Drill', *Irish Freedom*

1914

Jan.	Ruled out conflict with Ulster Volunteers in *Irish Freedom* (also Apr.)
Apr. 2	*Cumann na mBan formed*
Apr. 12	Produced entertainment by Lispole Dramatic Society, Dingle
Apr. 24	*Arms landed for UVF, Larne*
May	Sent to Belfast for IRB anti-partition campaign
May 25	*Home Rule passed Commons for third time*
June	Addressed Fianna on Wolfe Tone anniversary, Mac Art's Fort, Belfast
summer	Captain, Irish Volunteers, Lispole company
summer	Attended Irish College, Dingle
July 10	*Ulster Provisional Government convened, Belfast*
July 26	*Arms landed for Irish Volunteers, Howth*
Aug. 3	*Redmond pledged support for imperial war effort, offering Volunteers for coastal defence alongside Ulster Volunteers*
Aug. 8	*Defence of the Realm Act authorised regulations enabling easier detention and residence restrictions for persons accused of sedition*
Aug. late	Advocated monolingual Gaeltacht communes in 'The Salvation of the Irish Language', sent to Gaelic League
Sept. 15	*In House of Commons, Redmond supported enlistment for overseas service (appeal repeated to Volunteers at Woodenbridge, County Wicklow, 20 Sept.)*
Sept. 18	*Home Rule given royal assent but suspended*
Sept. 24	*Redmond's leadership of Volunteers repudiated by MacNeill's faction, supported by EB*
end	Sent to Ulster to organise IRB

1915

Feb.	IRB and Volunteer organiser, Munster (to July)
May 25	*Coalition government, including Carson, formed under Asquith*
May late	*Military committee formed by IRB to plan insurrection*
May 29	Denounced in *Kerry Advocate*, with fellow-Volunteer organiser Alf Cotton, as 'two Orangemen from Belfast'
May 30	Attended meeting of general council, Irish Volunteers, Dublin
July 23	Arrested Rockcorry, County Monaghan and imprisoned for about 2 months, Belfast gaol, after defying order to leave Ireland (17 July)
autumn	Resumed work as Volunteer organiser, Munster

1916

Jan. 27	*Ireland excluded from Military Service (Conscription) Act (again 25 May)*
Mar. 18	Arrested in County Limerick
Mar. 24	Detained Arbour Hill barracks, Dublin, and removed to Abingdon, Berks (9 Apr.), after continuing to defy order; imprisoned, Oxford and Abingdon
Apr. 16	Transferred to Brixton, missing Dublin rebellion, 24–29 Apr.
Apr. 25	*Martial law declared, Dublin (extended to Ireland, 29 Apr., terminated 4 Nov.)*
July	Transferred to Reading, writing first articles in Irish for Griffith's gaol journal, *The Outpost / An Foraire*
July 1	*Heavy losses by 36th (Ulster division) at the Somme*
Dec. 7	*Lloyd George replaced Asquith as Liberal prime minister in coalition government*
Dec. 22–23	*'Sinn Féin' internees released*
Dec. 26	Released from Reading, returned to Dublin, then Magheraliskmisk

1917

Jan. 4	Accepted restriction order to Mullaghcarton district, after arrest, Belfast, and detention, Arbour Hill, Dublin
early	Spent 6 months at home improving his Irish, sending articles in Irish to Gaelic League journal, *An Claidheamh Soluis*
June 17	Breached restriction order (allowed to lapse)

June 17   *Released convicts welcomed, Dublin*
July 10   *De Valera defeated nationalist candidate, East Clare by-election*
later   Organised Volunteers, Limerick, then appointed paid Gaelic
            League organiser for West Cork, also organising Volunteers
            and Cumann na mBan
Oct. 26   Elected to Sinn Féin executive

1918

Jan. 19   Editor, *Southern Star*, Skibbereen, County Cork
Feb. 2   *South Armagh by-election won by nationalist, EB having*
            campaigned for Patrick McCartan (Sinn Féin)
Feb. 6   *Representation of the People Act granted adult male and limited*
            female suffrage
Mar 2   Arrested Skibbereen, imprisoned Cork gaol (on hunger strike
            for a week), then sentenced to one year's imprisonment by
            court-martial, missing anti-conscription campaign
Apr.   Transferred to Dundalk gaol
Apr. 9   *Military Service Bill introduced (enacted 18 Apr.)*
Apr. 18   *anti-conscription conference, Mansion House, Dublin*
July   Transferred to Crumlin Road gaol, Belfast; edited gaol journal,
            Glór na Corcrach, elected prisoners' commandant
Oct. 14   Article on 'Ruthless Warfare' published in *An tÓglach*
Nov. 11   *Armistice between Allies and Germany*
Dec. 14   Elected MP (TD), North Monaghan, defeating unionist and
            nationalist, but lost to unionist, North Armagh, in 'coupon
            election' (Lloyd George confirmed as prime minister; Sinn Féin
            dominant in Ireland)

1919

Jan. 18   *Peace conference convened, Paris*
Jan. 21   *Dáil Éireann convened, Dublin*
Jan. 30   Brother James Alexander married Harriett Hill, Broomhedge,
            County Antrim
Mar.   Released after helping to organise riots and prison takeover,
            Crumlin Road
Apr. 4   Dáil director of trade and commerce, raised to ministry (17 June)

June 28	*Peace treaty signed by Allies and Germany, Versailles*
Sept. 12	*Dáil proclaimed as unlawful organisation*
late	Arrested, sentenced by court-martial to one year's imprisonment (on hunger strike for 4 days, Mountjoy, soon released)
later	Opened first departmental office, Fleet Street, as Irish and Overseas Shipping and Trading Co. Ltd
Nov. 13	Married Annie McHugh, Dublin
Nov. 25	*Republican organisations proclaimed as unlawful*

1920

Feb. 25	*(Better) Government of Ireland (Partition) Bill introduced, House of Commons*
Aug. 6	Opposed 'Belfast Boycott' in Dáil
Sept. 13	Daughter died, aged 5 hours, 11a Casimir Ave, Harold's Cross
Sept. 17	Appointed by Dáil to Commission on Organised Opposition to the Republic (proposed by Griffith, seconded by EB)
Dec. 10	*Martial law imposed in 4 counties (and 4 more, 4 Jan. 1921)*
Dec. 23	*Government of Ireland Act assented, establishing Home Rule parliaments for Northern and Southern Ireland*
end	Told de Valera, on return from USA, that there was no chance of getting a republic

1921

Jan. 25	Opposed 'British Boycott'
Feb. 5	*Craig succeeded Carson as Ulster Unionist leader*
May 24	Elected unopposed for Monaghan (House of Commons of Southern Ireland and Second Dáil)
June 7	*Craig elected prime minister, after unionist victory in first election for House of Commons of Northern Ireland (24 May)*
July 11	*Truce implemented between British forces in Ireland and IRA*
Aug. 16	Secretary for trade and commerce, Second Dáil, no longer in ministry (to 9 Jan. 1922)
Aug. 26	*De Valera elected 'president of the Irish Republic' by Dáil*
Oct. 11	*Peace conference opened, London*
Dec. 6	*Articles of Agreement for a Treaty between Britain and Ireland signed, London (repudiated by de Valera, 9 Dec.)*

1922

Jan. 3	Supported Anglo-Irish Treaty in Dáil, rejecting coercion against North
Jan. 7	*Treaty narrowly approved by Dáil*
Jan. 10	Secretary for trade, outside new Dáil ministry under Griffith (to 9 Sept.)
Jan. 14	*Provisional Government established under Collins*
May 20	*Electoral pact signed by Collins and de Valera*
June 16	Elected second of 3 TDs, Monaghan in general election (Provisional Parliament and Third Dáil)
June 28	*Civil war initiated by National Army attack on IRA garrison, Four Courts, Dublin*
June end	Camped in Government Buildings with other ministers, then (with wife) in Royal College of Science
July 17	Replaced O'Higgins as minister for economic affairs
Aug. 19	Advocated conciliation of 'north-east' in Cabinet memorandum
Sept. 9	Minister for local government, Provisional Government and Third Dáil Ministry, then Executive Council (6 Dec.)
Sept. 28	*Dáil approved creation of military courts to try civilians, with capital powers*
Oct. 23	*Conservative Bonar Law replaced Lloyd George as prime minister*
Oct. 25	*Free State constitution approved by Provisional Parliament (ratified by UK statute, 5 Dec.)*
Nov. 17	Defended first official executions of republican prisoners, also reprisal executions (8 Dec.)
Dec. 6	*Irish Free State created under Cosgrave*
Dec. 7	*Parliament of Northern Ireland opted out of Free State*

1923

Mar. 31	*Customs control introduced on border with Northern Ireland*
Apr. 27	*IRA offensive suspended; abandoned after instruction from de Valera as president of republican Provisional Government (24 May)*
Aug. 27	Topped poll with almost two quotas, Monaghan, in general election confirming Cosgrave as president
Sept. 10	*Free State admitted to League of Nations*

Sept. 19   Minister for finance (to 9 Mar. 1932, replaced by Cosgrave, 30
            June to 28 Aug. 1924)

Nov.   Announced budget cuts for 1924–5, including old-age pension

1924

July 11   *Anglo-Irish Treaty registered with League of Nations*

Dec. 13   Mother Agnes died (74), Holywood, County Down

1925

Mar. 19   Son Earnán Pádraig de Blaghd born, 11 Sandford Rd, Ranelagh,
          Dublin (died 6 Sept. 2014)

Dec. 3   Signed Anglo-Irish agreement, perpetuating partition
        Introduced annual grant for Abbey Theatre

1926

Mar. 19   With Churchill, signed Heads of Ultimate Financial Settlement,
          London
          Established An Gúm (the Scheme), Irish-language publishing
          agency for Department of Education

1927

June 9   Elected second, Monaghan, but topped poll in second general
         election (15 Sept.), confirming Cosgrave as president with hung
         Dáil

July 10   Replaced O'Higgins (murdered by IRA) as vice-president,
         Executive Council (to 9 Mar. 1932)

Oct. 11   Minister for posts and telegraphs, as well as finance (to 9 Mar.
         1932)

1928

Mar. 22   Rejected military and economic coercion of Northern Ireland
         during Dáil debate, stating dominion preferable to republic

1930

Mar. 22   In attributed Irish-language article in the *Star*, discussed circumstances under which army might overthrow government

Apr. 5   As 'P.A.P.' in *Star*, analysed defects of parliamentary democracy

Apr. 16   Sister Helen married William Nassau Gibson, Belfast

1931

May 15   Pius XI issued encyclical, Quadragesimo Anno, advocating vocational organisation of society

Oct. 17   Constitution (Amendment no. 17) Act established military tribunal to try cases of sedition, illegal drilling, and membership of unlawful bodies (suspended 18 Mar. 1932)

Oct. 20   IRA among twelve bodies proclaimed as unlawful associations

1932

Feb. 9   Army Comrades' Association formed

Feb. 16   Elected second of three, Monaghan, in general election leading to Fianna Fáil minority government under de Valera as president (9 Mar.)

1933

Jan. 24   Supplanted by independent (Orange) candidate on Fianna Fáil preferences, Monaghan, in general election confirming de Valera as president with Fianna Fáil majority

Jan. 30   Hitler elected German chancellor

Mar. 25   As 'Onlooker' in *United Ireland*, began series of Blueshirt notes (to 25 July 1936)

Apr. 15   As 'M. G. Quinn' in *United Ireland* first proposed adaptation of corporative state on 'Diast' principle

July 20   O'Duffy elected leader of Army Comrades' Association, renamed National Guard (proclaimed as unlawful, 22 Aug.)

July 30   Refused to surrender protective revolver (again, 1 Aug.)

Sept. 2   O'Duffy, again with EB's support, elected leader of new United Ireland Party (Fine Gael), with EB on executive

Sept. 13   *Young Ireland Association (formerly National Guard) became youth section of United Ireland Party (proclaimed, 8 Dec., replaced by League of Youth, 14 Dec.)*

1934

Jan. 2   Elected unopposed to fill Senate vacancy

Jan. 22   *Seán Lester, Free State representative at League of Nations, appointed high commissioner, Danzig*

Mar. 21   Helped defeat Wearing of Uniform (Restrictions) Bill in Senate

Sept. 21   Engineered O'Duffy's resignation as leader of Fine Gael and thence removal as director of League of Youth (replaced by Cronin)

Dec. 7   Last of 29 nominees elected to Senate (for 6-year term)

1935

Jan. 12   As 'Gerald Smith', proposed vocational organisation for agriculture in *United Ireland*

Mar. 9   As 'Old Supporter' in *United Ireland*, proposed 3 new directorships for Abbey Theatre

Mar. 9   Among 3 new directors for life, Abbey Theatre

Mar. 20   Advocated nationalist abstention from voting in Northern Ireland elections to placate unionist fears, infuriating all northern parties

Aug. 12   *O'Casey's* The Silver Tassie *belatedly opened, Abbey Theatre*

Nov. 13   In Senate, supported League of Nations sanctions against Italy over Abyssinian invasion

1936

May 29   *Senate abolished (last meeting 9 May)*

June 18   *IRA and surrogates proclaimed as unlawful organisations*

Oct.   *Cronin's League of Youth disbanded by Fine Gael*

Nov. 1   Appointed secretary to new company run by ex-Blueshirts, Clondalkin Paper Mills Ltd (resigned 1941)

Nov. 20   *O'Duffy led Irish Brigade to support nationalist forces in Spain*

1937

July 1   *Fianna Fáil victorious in general election and referendum on draft constitution*

Dec. 29   *New constitution of Ireland (Éire) operative (de Valera elected as first taoiseach)*

1938

June 17   *Fianna Fáil victorious in general election*

Sept. 2   *De Valera declared Éire's neutrality on eve of war with Germany*
          Slim volume of poems published (*Fraoch is Fothannáin*)

1941

Jan.   Appointed managing director, Abbey Theatre; resigned as secretary, Clondalkin Paper Mills

Feb. 15   Father James died (88), Marino, County Down

1943

June 12   Warned Ailtirí na hAirséirghe (Architects of the Resurrection) against violence and illegality

June 23   *Fianna Fáil victorious in general election (again, 30 May 1944)*

1945

Nov. 14   *Irish Anti-Partition League formed at Catholic convention, Dungannon*

1947

First president, de Valera's An Comhdháil Náisiúnta na Gaeilge

1948

Feb. 4   *General election resulted in first inter-party government under Costello (elected taoiseach, 18 Feb.)*

Dec. 21   *Republic of Ireland Act (operative 18 Apr. 1949) ended association of Éire with British Commonwealth*

1949

June 2   *Ireland Act guaranteed retention of Northern Ireland in British*
          Commonwealth unless consent given by its parliament
Oct.   Circulated memorandum, 'Towards a Six Counties Dominion',
          denouncing multi-partisan anti-partition campaign

1950

Oct.   Attacked anti-partition campaign in the *Leader*, provoking
          excoriation in Ulster nationalist press for his 'return to the
          Orange orchard'

1951

May 30   *Fianna Fáil victorious in general election*
July 18   *Abbey Theatre destroyed by fire*

1954

Apr. 18   Signed statement for Bureau of Military History
May 18   *General election resulted in second inter-party government under*
          Costello

1955

          Essays on partition published (*Briseadh na Teorann*)

1957

Mar. 5   *Fianna Fáil victorious in general election (retained power to 1973)*
Aug.   First autobiography (*Trasna na Bóinne*) won Hyde Literary
          Award for year's best publication in Irish
Sept. 25 Wife Annie died (67), Dublin

1958

          Appointed by de Valera to Commission for the Revival of the
          Irish Language

1959

June 23   *Lemass elected taoiseach following de Valera's election as president*
          (17 June)

1960

June   Appointed for five years to board of Radio Éireann Authority
          (established under act of 12 Apr.)

1966

July 18   *New Abbey Theatre opened to public*

1967

Aug. 30   Retired as managing director, Abbey Theatre

1969

Nov. 7   Sister Josephine died unmarried (78), Belfast

1970

          Second autobiography published (*Slán le hUltaibh*)

1972

Sept. 5   Resigned as director, Abbey Theatre, retaining life membership
          and shares

1973

Mar. 14   *Costello elected taoiseach of coalition government, following*
          general election (28 Feb.)
July 18   *Northern Ireland parliament abolished, with guarantee of Northern*
          Ireland's retention in UK unless consent given in referendum
          Third autobiography published (*Gaeil Á Múscailt*)

1975

Feb. 23   EB died (85), Mount Carmel hospital, Dublin

Index